AGING AND SOCIAL POLICY
IN THE UNITED STATES

AGING AND SOCIAL POLICY
IN THE UNITED STATES

Nancy Kusmaul

University of Maryland, Baltimore County

cognella®

SAN DIEGO

Bassim Hamadeh, CEO and Publisher
Amy Smith, Senior Project Editor
Alia Bales, Production Editor
Jess Estrella, Senior Graphic Designer
Kylie Bartolome, Licensing Associate
Sue Murray, Interior Designer
Natalie Piccotti, Director of Marketing
Kassie Graves, Senior Vice President of Editorial
Jamie Giganti, Director of Academic Publishing

Cover image copyright © 2015 iStockphoto LP/LUNAMARINA.

Printed in the United States of America.

3970 Sorrento Valley Blvd., Ste. 500, San Diego, CA 92121

BRIEF CONTENTS

DETAILED CONTENTS

Unit 2   Individual Health in Late Life

Unit 5   International Perspectives on Aging Policy

CHAPTER 13   Canada: A Federal/Provincial Model of Nursing Home Care   172

CHAPTER 14   Finland: Social Safety Net   183

CHAPTER 15   Japan: Importing Help—The Role of Caregiving Visas   197

ACTIVE LEARNING

This book has interactive activities available to complement your reading.

Your instructor may have customized the selection of activities available for your unique course. Please check with your professor to verify whether your class will access this content through the Cognella Active Learning portal (http://active.cognella.com) or through your home learning management system.

PREFACE

The proportion of older adults in the population is growing every year due to combinations of declining childhood death rates, longer age spans, and declining birth rates. In the United States, societal assumptions are that aging is a process of decline and thus that older adults are frail, poor, and in need of care. At the same time American values of rugged individualism portray dependency as a negative trait, and thus emphasize care of elders as an individual pursuit best accomplished within the family structure. Social policies that address the needs of older adults in the United States reflect a range of perspectives, with some programs covering all older adults regardless of need and other policies focusing on specific populations that fail to adequately address other unmet needs. In addition, many of these policies are deficit focused and may not recognize the autonomy of older adults.

I have always been interested in working with older adults. The time I spent with my grandparents and great-grandparents led me to a decade-long career as a nursing home social worker. Through that work I saw the places where aging and community policies failed to meet the needs of older adults and their families, and saw that many workers were unaware of the complexities of those policies. I believe all students who will work with older adults in any profession, as well as anyone who will be conducting research with communities, should be well versed in relevant policies.

This book focuses on all aspects of social policies and policymaking that address the needs of older adults and their families, even those that are not specific to aging. It also considers the different experiences that diverse populations encounter as they engage with these policies. This book will provide undergraduate and graduate students with a foundational education on the complexities of addressing the needs of an aging population. Aging is a common human experience embedded in the context of identity and environment. This book begins with an introductory unit, providing a foundation for the book, defining key terms, describing how to analyze the impacts of a policy on a population, and examining the ways policy is positioned within societal assumptions. Utilizing the life course perspective, the middle three units of this book situate individual biological and psychological changes of aging in the context of how they are addressed by individuals, families, and societies, identifying the strengths and challenges of existing and proposed social policies at each of these levels. The concluding unit provides comparative insights as to how aging issues are addressed in a sample of countries around the world. Upon completion of this book, students will be able to discuss all types of policies at all levels, such as local, state, and federal. They will be able to examine the implementation of those policies from a critical analytic lens that will consider what problem a policy is attempting to solve, which individuals the policy assumes are deserving of help, what unintended consequences the policy may have, and how the policy is implemented in direct practice.

When you are a not-quite-middle-aged person writing a book about aging policy, there is a strong temptation to "other" older adults, turning them into that group over there, different from yourself, and different from the students who will be reading the book. Some of that is because the students who read these books are often "youngers" (Applewhite, 2019). Most students, even "non-traditional" or "returning" students, tend to be below the age that has been assigned by society to older adults. But age is a funny thing. Whenever we "other" other people because of their age, whether older or younger, we are discriminating against our once or future selves. People in a college classroom have all been aging since they were born, but most, including myself, have never been what we typically consider to be an "older adult." While I attempt to avoid othering language in this book, I do use the term *older adult* to refer to, for the most part, those individuals over age 65.

This book situates the experiences of older adults in the context of their environment, examining social welfare policies that affect the rights and interests of older adults. It is intended for students of social work, gerontology, and other social sciences and human service fields. It takes a diversity perspective and strikes a balance between the challenges of aging and a strengths perspective.

This core text will be able to be used alone but will also be a solid foundation for instructors who wish to supplement with additional content such as relevant current policy activity at the local, state, and federal levels. The theoretical framework for this book is the life course perspective with an intersectional lens. Life course perspective is widely accepted in the field of gerontology and posits that life is a series of events that unfolds over the course of time (Hutchinson, 2005). It considers the interplay of chronological age, relationships, life transitions, and social structures in defining an individual's journey through that series of events.

Intersectionality was described by Crenshaw (1989) as the various ways in which race and gender interact to shape individuals' experiences with the broader world, as she illustrates with the case of a woman who experiences both race and gender discrimination in employment without experiencing each individually, and it has since been applied to the many ways our various identities create privilege and oppression. This book will use concepts of intersectionality to explore the experiences of aging and ageism at multiple levels that are informed by discrimination and advantage across the life course. The assumption of this book is that aging individuals may have physical, financial, and social challenges that arise as they age. How these challenges are experienced is shaped by the individual's intersectional identity and their social environment, as well as the individual's strengths and resilience. Societies/nations attempt to address those issues through social policies, which reflect the unspoken values of that society.

Thus, this book describes: the physical, mental, and social changes that people experience as they age; how those changes impact and are impacted by their families, communities, and societies; what policies we have to address them; and what kind of a job those policies do at addressing them. It also discusses the contributions older adults do make addressing social issues, as well as their potential contributions that are discounted in current policy practices. Finally, solutions to similar problems in other nations are described.

Each chapter of this book includes two or more illustrations for clarity and depth. Some are actual illustrations while some are case studies that illustrate the application of the concepts described in the chapter. This will provide students with the "so what?" of the policy concepts. This book is also accompanied by online active learning materials for students. Instructor resources are available for instructors who adopt the book for their courses.

This book would not have been possible without the support of Kassie Graves and Amy Smith at Cognella. I want to thank the reviewers and colleagues who read through various versions of this book as it was in the works, especially Doyle Pruitt, Leanne Clark-Shirley, Carolyn Tice, Corey Shdaimah, Joan Davitt, and Paul Sacco. I also want to thank the colleagues who contributed their knowledge in response to my calls for resources: Lisa O'Neill, Sandra Butler, Robyn Stone, Stephanie Wladkowski, and many more. I want to thank Ji Hyang

Cheon, Jennifer Greenfield, Marie Gualtieri, and Beth Prusaczyk, who made written contributions to some of the chapters. Networks get things done. Their expertise in these areas far exceeds mine, and the book is richer because of them. My friends, both academic and otherwise, supported me as I rode the roller coaster that is book writing. Special thanks to Joslyn, Mary, Leanne, Meg, Cara, Stephanie, and Allison. To my kids, who asked for a year, "Mom, are you done writing your book yet?"—Keira, Emily, and Nathan, yes, I'm finally done. Finally, to my ever-patient husband, Eric, who shakes his head and sighs every time I say I'm just going to do this one more thing—thank you for letting me drive you nuts as I wrote this in the midst of a global pandemic with all of us working and schooling from home. This book is dedicated to you.

REFERENCES

Applewhite, A. (2019). *This chair rocks: A manifesto against ageism.* Celadon Books.

Crenshaw, K. (1989). Demarginalizing the intersection of race and sex: A Black feminist critique of antidiscrimination doctrine, feminist theory and antiracist politics. *University of Chicago Legal Forum, 1989*(1), Article 8, 139–167. http://chicagounbound.uchicago.edu/uclf

Hutchinson, E. (2005). The life course perspective: A promising approach for bridging the micro and macro world for social workers. *Families in Society: The Journal of Contemporary Social Services, 86*(1), 143–152. https://doi.org/10.1606/1044-3894.1886

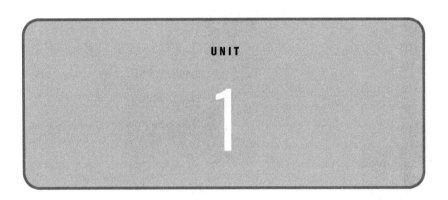

UNIT

1

INTRODUCTION TO THE POLICY LANDSCAPE

1

What Is Policy?

INTRODUCTION

In the 1930s the United States (U.S.) was deep in the Great Depression, and many people were homeless, hungry, and desperate. When Franklin Delano Roosevelt (FDR) became President in 1933, he enacted sweeping changes to improve the economy and to relieve human suffering. One of the most significant changes that impacted older adults, at the time and in the years since, was the 1935 **Social Security Act**. The **Social Security Act** is an example of a policy. **Policy** is the formal structure by which unmet human needs are addressed by society. In this case, the Social Security Act provided "for the general welfare by establishing a system of Federal old-age benefits ...," thereby addressing the income needs of older Americans.

By the end of this chapter, students will be able to

1. Define policy.

2. Describe how policy addresses human needs and how it influences the human services sector.

3. Explain what intersectionality is and describe its impact on the experiences of life, aging, and policy.

4. Discuss the different formal structures that influence the ways the United States, individual states, and social service agencies provide services to older adults and their families.

The Social Security Act is a type of policy called a law, put into place by a legislature. Policy, broadly speaking, includes all of the laws and regulations that shape the delivery of all types of services. The laws and regulations, in turn, are shaped by societal assumptions about problems and populations, such as what **the problem** is, how it is caused, and characteristics about people who have the problem. **The problem** is the challenge identified that needs to be addressed. Social problems are complex, with multiple causes and multiple potential solutions. The solutions that are chosen to be put into policy are based on the assumptions that are made about why something happens.

Not all groups have a voice in shaping policy. It is important to understand who has the power to define the problems policies are addressing. Some policymakers have never experienced the problems they are addressing and may have unrealistic views about how solutions should work. If a policy impacts everyone in a population, not all individuals are impacted in the same way. This book focuses on policies that addresses the needs of those in the final third of the natural lifespan in the United States. It will discuss how people experience those policies in their everyday life, how people differentially experience those policies, and how everyone can become involved in shaping policies. This book will explore both aging-specific policies and policies that impact older adults along with the rest of the population.

Since policies are shaped by societal assumptions, it is important to be aware of how people who are getting older are treated in the United States and what messages are portrayed about getting older. While getting older is an individual journey, the messages individuals receive from society can be conflicting and confusing. Many Americans prefer growing older to the alternative of dying young, yet they fear the limitations and changes that some people experience as they age. Fears about the limitations of aging are stoked by popular use of a **declinist lens**, a viewpoint which promotes the idea that getting older is a time of decline. Older adults are besieged by greeting cards that tell them "it's all downhill from here" and birthday party decorations with tombstones. Getting older is thus considered to be about losing memory, sanity, and senses, and gaining aches and pains. Eighty-year-old triathletes and 90-year-old marathoners make the news because they are considered exceptions to be marveled at.

On the other hand, there is a rich literature about "**successful aging**" and "productive aging," describing the ideal as being useful as long as possible. While successful aging may encourage some people to remain active, the concepts of successful aging and productive aging do not offer an alternative. Rather, they imply that people who are no longer able or who no longer want to actively contribute to society by doing or producing something no longer have social value. These lenses dismiss those who experience physical declines as "unsuccessful." They also put more emphasis on doing than on being, which is a particularly American idea. Overall, neither the declinist lens nor the successful aging paradigm tells the whole story, which is much more complicated.

The whole story has pieces of both perspectives. Many physical bodies do experience some declines in some areas. Yet most people are able to live independently and to participate in activities of their choosing. More on the physical body can be found in Chapter 5. Some people do develop dementia or Alzheimer's disease and need support and supervision. But loss of cognition is not a natural part of normal aging. More on cognitive changes can be found in Chapter 6. While there is a widespread perception that old people end up in nursing homes, less than 4% of those over the age of 65 live in one permanently, though some do enter one for short-term rehabilitation or recuperation. Policies for older adults need to provide for and protect everyone—those who are able to age in the home and community with little care, those who ultimately need a full range of care, and everyone in between. More on long-term services and supports can be found in Chapter 11.

INTERSECTIONALITY

While each person's journey through life is unique, their journey is influenced by the many facets and many roles that make up a person's identity. **Intersectionality** (Crenshaw, 1989) describes how various aspects of identity overlap or "intersect." Personal identity factors such as age, race, gender, sexual orientation, marital status, and many more may lead to privilege and disadvantage in different contexts and spaces, often at the same time. The **life course perspective** views each individual through their lifetime experiences. These lifetime experiences are shaped by an individual's intersectional identity factors, influenced by structural advantage or discrimination that occurs as a result of racism, sexism, homophobia, transphobia, xenophobia, ableism, and ageism. **Cumulative advantage/disadvantage** theory (Dannefer, 2003; Ferraro & Shippee, 2008) suggests that each advantage or disadvantage leads to another, such as those in health, education, or opportunity, resulting in the exponential growth of disparities over time.

Cumulative advantage and disadvantage are seen most clearly in older adults. Older adults have had a lifetime to accumulate advantages and disadvantages, thus disparities are high in many areas, such as health and wealth. For example, Blacks have higher rates of late-life disability than whites even when accounting for access to education, health care, and overall socioeconomic status (Taylor, 2008). Access to education, health care, and jobs in earlier life are shaped by policies which are generally outside the scope of this book. For our purposes, it is important to consider the impact of disparities, such as the disability disparity example, on care needs. Policies that address disparities in late life may have great gaps to fill, and policies that address disabilities may need to target some populations over others to meet the greatest needs.

The privileges and disadvantages of identity factors also intersect with geography and history. Where and when someone lives or lived are key in shaping the opportunities available to them, such as housing, education, and employment. A Black, gay man in the rural south in the 1950s would have probably dealt with both separate facilities for Blacks and whites in a legally segregated society and states where sodomy was a crime, making a "gay lifestyle" illegal. A white, gay man in San Francisco in the 1980s faced neither of these, yet the poorly understood, highly lethal, and highly stigmatized AIDS epidemic meant he was also likely isolated and in mortal danger. Experiences in younger life might have influenced job and housing choices but also things like self-esteem, self-worth, and acceptance. In the 2020s both of these men are older adults, shaped by their earlier experiences.

What happens when you get to late adulthood can vary because of physical and social changes that may occur in late life. Peter Laslett coined the terms third and fourth age (Aronsen, 2019; Laslett, 1991) to refer to distinct periods of older adulthood. These are the continuation of the first and second ages of childhood and adulthood. The third age is differentiated from the second age, or adulthood, by the onset of retirement. The members of the third and fourth ages are "primarily distinguished by their differences in health, activities, and consumer roles" (Aronsen, 2019, p. 243). These ages used to be described chronologically, as in "young-old" and "old-old," but the terms were refined to reflect difference in ability rather than numerical age. The third age encompasses the time in which the person experiences good health and high functional independence. The fourth age is marked by disability and decline. Individuals in the fourth age often require assistance with **Activities of Daily Living (ADLs)** and **Instrumental Activities of Daily Living (IADLs)**, explained further in Chapter 6 and Chapter 11.

WHY SHOULD WE FOCUS ON DIVERSITY AND AGING?

Policies provide benefits either to those in need of assistance who meet clear criteria, or to everyone in equal measure. Yet well-intentioned policies often fail to reach those in need. Those who truly need help may not receive it, and some groups are more likely to experience intentional or unintentional adverse effects of policies than others. One's social position and intersectional identity factors, including but not limited to gender, race, ethnicity, social class, and geographic location, influence how people interact with policies, and they also may influence assumptions about: getting older, family roles as they relate to aging and caregiving, and death and dying. These assumptions impact the types of services desired and how those services are experienced and accessed.

For example, some policies and programs seek to address the needs of family caregivers. A **family caregiver** is a family member or friend who provides mostly unpaid care. This is described in more detail in Chapter 8.

Yet the challenges of family caregiving may be experienced differently based on differences in expectations. Importantly, is family expected to provide care at all costs? Who within the family is expected to provide care? Is providing care viewed as a burden or as the fulfillment of family expectations in life? Cultural and ethnic identity can influence the answers to these questions, as can individual personality factors, trauma, and life circumstances. It is difficult to account for all these variabilities in one or even several policies.

Within Chinese and other Asian cultures, caring for parents and other aging relatives is both an obligation and a source of honor. These cultures are driven by the idea of **filial piety**, a concept that derives from Confucian teaching and includes a focus on intergenerational relationships and the good of the family over that of the individual (Lai, 2010). Thus, caring for one's parents both is culturally expected and may be considered a source of pride rather than a burden, despite its challenges.

In a completely different part of the world, among Native and Indigenous communities in the United States, elders report high rates of chronic health conditions but also high rates of social support (Conte et al., 2015). Elders are highly respected in many Native cultures, though it is important to recognize that Native cultures and Native communities are not homogenous. **Federally recognized tribes** are eligible for funding and support from the Bureau of Indian Affairs (Saenz, 2020), but systems like the **Indian Health Service** are chronically underfunded. Many Native communities experience barriers to formal supports, such as the challenges their tribes face in accessing federal and other financial resources and the extreme rurality of their living situations. As a result of these conditions and cultural norms, their families provide the majority of their services (Jervis et al., 2002). Cultural values such as those found in Chinese and Native American cultures may lead to different appraisal of the strains of caregiving, and differences in the use or non-use of formal services, than those that are experienced by other cultural subgroups within the United States (Lai, 2010). Policymakers might need to consider different types of services to address the needs of these groups.

POLICY FUNDAMENTALS

The specific needs of caregivers will be explored further in Chapter 8. Before we get there, we will talk about policymaking fundamentals in the United States. To understand the impacts and influences of policies on the

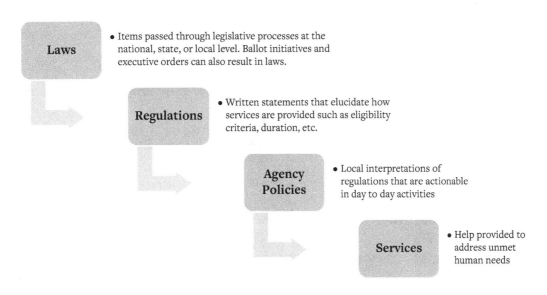

FIGURE 1.1 Policy Framework

human experience, we must first understand how policies that address social issues are created, regulated, enacted, and enforced.

Introduction to Key Terms

Laws. Laws are passed through legislative processes at the national, state, or local level. Once a law is approved by the legislative body, the executive, such as the president or governor, approves or **vetoes** the law. A **veto** is when the executive fails to sign or approve a law passed by the legislative body. There are mechanisms for legislatures to enact laws the executive has vetoed, which is called an **override**.

> **Override of a veto** – The process by which each chamber of Congress votes on a bill vetoed by the President. To pass a bill over the president's objections requires a two-thirds vote in each Chamber. Historically, Congress has overridden fewer than ten percent of all presidential vetoes. Ballot initiatives, in which voters express approval or disapproval of proposed approaches to addressing problems can also result in laws. (United States Senate, n.d.)

Regulations. Once a law is established, a governing body establishes the rules that surround that law's implementation. Regulations provide the specifics for putting the law into practice. Laws that are passed by the U.S. Federal Government are referred to the agency of jurisdiction (the agency responsible for implementing the law). Examples of these agencies are the Department of Health and Human Services (HHS), the Centers for Medicare and Medicaid Services (CMS), the Department of Housing and Urban Development (HUD), and many others. That agency develops rules and regulations for that law.

The regulatory process is governed by the **Administrative Procedure Act of 1946**. Rulemaking is open to the public through the **Federal Register**, published daily online. Once a law is referred to an agency, the agency may, but is not required to, notify the public of their intention to issue regulations through an "advance notice of proposed rulemaking." As the next step or a first step, an agency publishes a "notice of proposed rule making" (NPRM). The NPRM provides interested parties such as **consumers** and **provider agencies** with information about the proposed rule and the opportunity to submit comments. The agency must read every comment submitted. Once the comments are reviewed, the agency may issue a "final rule making." The preamble to the final rule in the Federal Register often includes a summary or analysis of the comments received (Lexis Nexis Congressional, 2007). **Consumers** are the recipients of services. **Provider agencies** are the health and human service organizations who deliver services paid for and regulated by the rules.

For posted and proposed rules at the e-Federal Register, visit: https://www.federalregister.gov/

Agency policies. In social and human services, agencies that are subject to laws and regulations for payments and licensure establish policies, which outline the procedures for the ways in which services are provided in their setting. These often include measures for determining eligibility, and expectations for service delivery such as duration and frequency.

Services. Services are the things that are done or given to individuals to address social problems.

The Three Branches of Government in Policy

The United States is governed by three branches: **legislative**, **executive**, and **judicial**. As you saw in the Introduction to Key Terms section, both the legislative and executive branches are involved in the creation of policies through laws and regulations. The U.S. government structure deliberately provides some powers to the states and some powers to the federal government. The structure of government is similar in states and at the federal level, and both consist of these same branches. While the states and the federal government have authority over different things, some issues, like those impacting older adults, become the responsibility of both.

The legislative branch at the federal level is the U.S. Congress, which has the power to make laws. Each state has some type of legislature too. The U.S. Congress consists of two chambers, the Senate and the House of Representatives. Each state has two senators, and a number of representatives proportional to its population. There are 100 senators and 435 representatives in the House of Representatives. Territories such as Guam, Puerto Rico, and Washington DC have non-voting representatives and no representation in the Senate. At the time of this writing in 2021, there are bills before Congress to make Washington DC the nation's 51st state. Anyone impacted by policy (all of us) should know who their representatives are and how to contact them. This information can be found through any internet search engine. You can get involved with policymaking with the legislative branch through your representatives by writing letters and emails, meeting with their staff at their local or Washington DC offices, and by following which bills they do and do not support.

> To look up bills in Congress, including sponsors and actions, visit: https://congress.gov.
> To find your elected officials, visit: https://www.usa.gov/elected-officials.

The executive branch consists of the head of state and the head of government. In the United States, the head of the executive branch is the president. The president appoints the heads of the federal agencies and the members of the Cabinet. The agencies that write regulations are part of the executive branch. Since the president appoints the heads of the agencies, they may change when an administration changes. The workers in the agencies are civil servants who do not change as a result of executive branch changes. The best way for citizens to get involved in policymaking in the executive branch is through the regulatory comment process described in the definitions section above.

The judicial branch consists of the courts, and the highest court in the land is the Supreme Court. The judicial branch gets involved with lawmaking when laws are challenged through class action lawsuits, which allow groups of individuals negatively affected by a policy or company to take action collectively. Federal cases that are appealed may rise to the Supreme Court, who collectively decide which cases to consider. Implementation of the law may be shaped by court decisions, or the law may be overturned entirely.

> For current information on Supreme Court members and decisions, visit: https://supremecourt.gov.

An example of a court case that shaped policy came with the **Patient Protection and Affordable Care Act of 2010 (ACA)**. This law, considered by some to be the most sweeping healthcare reform law since Medicare was created in 1965, held several provisions that some states thought were an overreach by the federal government. The controversial provisions were the "individual mandate" requiring people to buy insurance or face a tax penalty, and a provision that required states to expand their Medicaid health insurance program for low-income individuals or risk losing federal payments (Liptak, 2012). In *National Federation of Independent Business v. Sebelius* (2012), the Supreme Court of the United States determined that the federal government was within their rights to tax individuals who chose not to purchase health insurance but had exceeded their jurisdiction by requiring states to expand Medicaid, thereby overturning the Medicaid expansion part of the law. In Chapter 11, we'll discuss the role of Medicaid in care provision for older adults and the impacts of Medicaid expansion.

MEDICAID EXPANSION

By Ji Hyang Cheon

Federal Legislation:

The Patient Protection and Affordable Care Act (ACA) enacted on March 23, 2010 required states to expand Medicaid (The Kaiser Family Foundation, 2012a). The Medicaid expansion provision simplified Medicaid eligibility requirements to income alone and extended eligibility to people at 138% of the poverty line, allowing more people to receive Medicaid benefits (Healthcare. gov, n.d.).

Judicial Intervention:

On the same day as the ACA was enacted, 25 states and the National Federation of Independent Business filed a lawsuit against the constitutionality of the ACA in federal court. In 2012, the Supreme Court found that the federal government exceeded their jurisdiction by requiring states to expand Medicaid, thereby overturning the Medicaid expansion part of the law (The Kaiser Family Foundation, 2012a).

State Actions:

States can now autonomously decide whether or not to implement the Medicaid expansion. For example, Maine residents voted to expand Medicaid in their state in 2017 as part of a ballot initiative. The "yes" vote required the state to provide Medicaid through MaineCare for persons under the age of 65 and with incomes equal to or below 138% of the federal poverty line. By April 2021, 38 states, and Washington DC, had adopted the Medicaid expansion.

Flexibility Within the Law

The ACA provides Section 1115 Medicaid demonstration waivers to give states discretion in Medicaid expansion. Forty-six states have used at least one Section 1115 Medicaid waiver or have pending waivers (The Kaiser Family Foundation, 2021b). Waiver provisions include eligibility and enrollment restrictions; work requirements; benefit restrictions, copays, and healthy behaviors; behavioral health; delivery system reform; and Medicaid long-term services and supports (MLTSS) (The Kaiser Family Foundation, 2021b). Of these, work requirements were endorsed by the Trump administration in 12 states and are pending permits in 7 states (The Kaiser Family Foundation, 2021b). However, the Biden administration allowed the repeal of work requirements requested by Michigan and Wisconsin, as they did not meet Medicaid's goal of providing medical services to vulnerable and low-income populations (Ollove, 2021).

Examples of court cases that overturned laws entirely were ***Brown v. Board of Education*** (1954) and ***Loving v. Virginia*** (1967). In ***Brown v. Board of Education*** (1954), racial segregation in public schools was ruled unconstitutional, opening up access to schooling for children of all races. In ***Loving v. Virginia*** (1967), the Lovings were an interracial couple who were arrested in their home because their marriage violated Virginia's anti-miscegenation law. The court unanimously decided that Virginia's law violated the equal protection clause of the 14th Amendment of the U.S. Constitution. These cases are also significant for older adults because they impacted access to and experience of education and marriage, respectively.

OUTLINE OF THE REMAINDER OF THE BOOK

Policy classes in the social sciences, particularly in social work, often equate policy with advocacy, as the primary means by which policy can be influenced. Advocacy has been a practice strategy for human service nonprofits to respond to factors that impact the services they provide; it is also used by professionals to speak about issues affecting the populations they serve (Austin, 2000). Lipsky (2010) first described "**street-level bureaucracy**" in 1980 as the way that frontline workers, including teachers, police officers, social workers, and caregivers, function as policy makers in their everyday work through the ways in which they provide services. He argues that laws and regulations are supposed to be administered as they are written, with some uniformity, but that the realities of caseloads, workplace demands, and agency policies result in adaptations that lead to uneven delivery of services. Lipsky (2010) argues that no matter how clear policies are intended to be, they are always open to some interpretation as they are implemented in practice in concrete situations. This is a concern because the need to triage and ration implicates discretion and raises moral and ethical concerns.

This book will discuss both how policies are operationalized in the care of older adults and how older adults, their families, and workers can influence policymaking in an attempt to improve quality of life and quality of care for all. Some social work texts consider direct practice, or street-level bureaucracy, as separate from macro-level advocacy. This text argues for a both/and approach that uses individual experiences and the empowerment of policy recipients to shape policy for the betterment of all. Through concrete case examples you will learn how to evaluate the assumptions inherent in policy and the ways in which those assumptions shape the effect of policies on aging individuals and their caregivers.

This book is divided into five units. Unit 1, in which this chapter is contained, provides an overview of policymaking, policy analysis, and the assumptions that underlie aging policy in the United States. Here in Chapter 1, you learned how practitioners and clients could influence policy in the legislative, executive, and judicial branches. Subsequent chapters provide examples of how practitioners and clients can impact different policy topic areas. In Chapter 2, I present the policy analysis framework that will be used in Units 2–5. Broadly, this framework involves understanding existing laws, the assumptions they incorporate, and the effects they have on individuals in need of services. This chapter also includes a definition of advocacy and discusses the opportunities that exist for policy advocacy at all levels, including the agency, family, and individual levels, and many more. In Chapter 3, I delve more deeply into U.S. societal assumptions about growing older, caregiving, and the role of the family, which influence the ways in which we address aging issues.

The remaining units delve into specific problems and the policies through which we address them, including gaps in those policies that lead to unmet needs. The units are organized to move from the micro- to the macro-level: individuals, families, communities, and society in the United States. Unit 2 covers the individual.

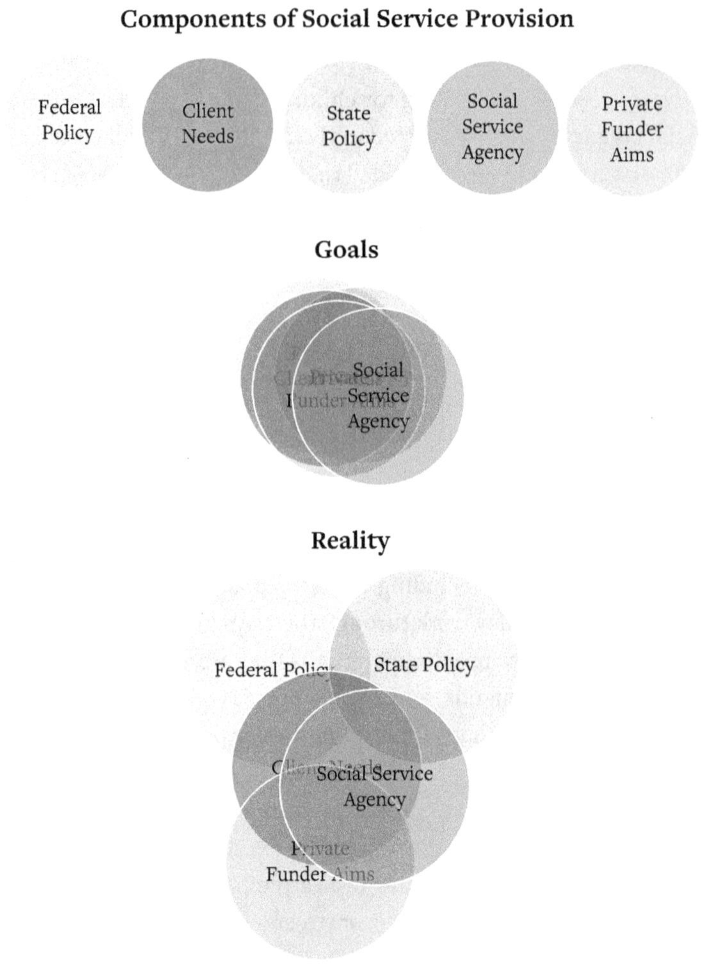

Components of Social Service Provision

Federal Policy · Client Needs · State Policy · Social Service Agency · Private Funder Aims

Goals

Client · Private Funder · Social Service Agency

Reality

Federal Policy · State Policy

Client · Social Service Agency

Private Funder Aims

FIGURE 1.2   The Interaction of Laws With Clients and Agencies—Goals Versus Reality

Chapter 4 discusses the meaning of being healthy, chronic conditions, and health in the social environment. Chapter 5 reviews physical changes that normally occur in late life and those changes that sometimes occur but are not normal. Chapter 6 covers mental and cognitive challenges that are normal and not normal.

Unit 3 goes from the individual to the family and community levels. Chapter 7 looks at all the ways that older adults fit into the family structure, and the intergenerational dynamics that exist. Chapter 8 looks at who is caring for whom—from older adults who need care from others, to older adults who provide care. Chapter 9 describes how local policies shape the day-to-day experiences of older adults in community.

Unit 4 covers societal responses to aging-related problems including federal laws that address income (Chapter 10), health (Chapter 11), and daily living (Chapter 12). The final unit, Unit 5, includes three chapters on the global perspective, comparing U.S. policies with approaches from other countries that address similar issues in very different ways: the Canadian approach to nursing home care; the Finnish approach to a social safety net; and Japan's approach to addressing labor shortages through immigrant visas.

SUMMARY

Policy is the formal ways in which societies address social problems. Societal assumptions about those social problems shape how laws and regulations define and address problems, including what causes and prevents them and who experiences them. Not everyone has a seat at the policymaking table, which is reflected in how different groups experience the outcomes of policies. While this chapter gave an overview of the creation and implementation of policies in the United States, this book specifically discusses policies that impact people who are growing older and their families.

Intersectionality, or the many identities that each person holds and the way those identities come together, impacts how each person experiences advantages and disadvantages in the world and from policies. Factors of identity, such as culture, may also impact how people experience aging-related issues and thus the policies that address those issues.

Broadly, policies consist of laws passed by the legislature, which are implemented through regulations handed down by executive branch agencies. The judicial branch may get involved if a law is challenged through the courts. Agencies create their own policies to provide services under the auspices of the laws and regulations.

Practitioners and clients can get involved in policymaking at each of these levels. Everyone residing in the United States should know their representatives and senators, and know how to contact them. Residents can contact these officials with policy ideas, concerns, and feedback on specific bills or issues before Congress. Executive branch agencies provide opportunities for public comment during the rulemaking process. Finally, people can participate in class action lawsuits challenging the jurisdiction or constitutionality of laws.

KEY TERMS

Activities of Daily Living (ADLs)

Administrative Procedure Act (1946)

Agency policies

Brown v. Board of Education (1954)

Consumer

Cumulative advantage/disadvantage

Declinist lens

Executive

Family Caregiver

Federal Register

Federally recognized tribes

Filial piety

Indian Health Service

Instrumental Activities of Daily Living (IADLs)

Intersectionality

Judicial

Laws

Legislative

Life course perspective

Loving v. Virginia (1967)

National Federation of Independent Business v. Sebelius (2012)

Override

Patient Protection and Affordable Care Act (ACA)

Policy

Problem/The problem

Provider agencies

Regulations

Services

Social Security Act

Street-level bureaucracy

Successful aging (productive aging)

Veto

DISCUSSION QUESTIONS

1. Discuss the broad definition of policy and how policy is used to address social problems.

2. Define the three branches of government and the roles they play in federal policymaking.

3. Describe how people can get involved in policymaking in each of the three branches of government.

4. Provide examples of how expectations can impact the ways policy is received. Compare and contrast with classmates' examples.

Ancillary materials for student practice can be found within Active Learning

REFERENCES

Aronsen, L. (2019). *Elderhood.* Bloomsbury Publishing.

Austin, D. (2000). Greeting the second century: A forward look from a historical perspective. In J. G. Hopps & R. Morris (Eds.), *Social work at the millennium* (pp. 18–41). The Free Press.

Brown v. Board of Education, 347 U.S. 483 (1954). https://www.oyez.org/cases/1940-1955/347us483

Conte, K., Schure, M., & Goins, R. T. (2015). Correlates of social support in older American Indians: The Native Elder Care Study. *Aging & Mental Health, 19*(9), 835–843. http://doi.org/10.1080/13607863.2014.967171

Crenshaw, K. (1989). Demarginalizing the intersection of race and sex: A Black feminist critique of antidiscrimination doctrine, feminist theory and antiracist politics. *University of Chicago Legal Forum, 1989*(1), Article 8, 139–167. http://chicagounbound.uchicago.edu/uclf

Dannefer, D. (2003). Cumulative advantage/disadvantage and the life course: Cross-fertilizing age and social science theory. *The Journals of Gerontology: Series B, 58*(6), S327–S337. https://doi.org/10.1093/geronb/58.6.S327

Ferraro, K., & Shippee, T. (2009). Aging and cumulative advantage: How does inequality get under the skin? *The Gerontologist, 49*(3), 333–343. https://doi.org10.1093/geront/gnp034

Healthcare.gov. (n.d.). *Medicaid expansion & what it means for you.* Retrieved May 3, 2021 from https://www.healthcare.gov/medicaid-chip/medicaid-expansion-and-you/

Jervis, L., Jackson, M. Y., & Manson, S. (2002). Need for, availability of, and barriers to the provision of long-term care services for older American Indians. *Journal of Cross-Cultural Gerontology, 17*(4), 295–311.

The Kaiser Family Foundation. (2012a). *A guide to the Supreme Court's Affordable Care Act decision.* Focus on Health Reform. https://www.kff.org/wp-content/uploads/2013/01/8332.pdf

The Kaiser Family Foundation. (2021b). *Medicaid waiver tracker: Approved and pending Section 1115 waivers by state.* Medicaid. https://www.kff.org/medicaid/issue-brief/medicaid-waiver-tracker-approved-and-pending-section-1115-waivers-by-state/

Lai, D. (2010). Filial piety, caregiving appraisal, and caregiving burden. *Research on Aging, 32*(2), 200–223. http://doi.org/10.1177/0164027509351475

Laslett, P. (1991). *A fresh map of life: The emergence of the third age.* Harvard University Press.

Lexis Nexis Congressional. (2007). *Stage 9: The law is implemented and enforced. Regulatory activity.* https://www.lexisnexis.com/help/cu/CU.htm#The_Legislative_Process/Stage_9.htm

Lipsky, M. (2010). *Street-level bureaucracy: Dilemmas of the individual in public service* (30th ann. ed.). The Russell Sage Foundation.

Liptak, A. (2012, June 28). Supreme Court upholds health care law, 5-4, in victory for Obama. *The New York Times*. https://www.nytimes.com/2012/06/29/us/supreme-court-lets-health-law-largely-stand.html

Loving v. Virginia, 388 U.S. 1 (1967). https://www.oyez.org/cases/1966/395

National Federation of Independent Businesses v. Sebelius, 567 U.S. 519 (2012). https://www.supremecourt.gov/opinions/11pdf/11-393c3a2.pdf

Ollove, M. (2021, April 7). *Biden revokes Medicaid work requirements in 2 more states.* The Pew Charitable Trusts. https://www.pewtrusts.org/en/research-and-analysis/blogs/stateline/2021/04/07/biden-revokes-medicaid-work-requirements-in-2-more-states

Saenz, M. (2020). *Federal and state recognized tribes.* National Conference of State Legislatures. Retrieved May 4, 2021 from https://www.ncsl.org/research/state-tribal-institute/list-of-federal-and-state-recognized-tribes.aspx

Taylor, M. (2008). Timing, accumulation, and the Black/White disability gap in later life: A test of weathering. *Research on Aging, 30*(2), 226–250. http://doi.org/10.1177/0164027507311838

United States Senate. (n.d.). *Override of a veto.* Retrieved June 4, 2020 from https://www.senate.gov/reference/glossary_term/override_of_a_veto.htm

How Do I Conduct a Policy Analysis?

INTRODUCTION

As we learned in Chapter 1, **policy** is the formal structure by which unmet human needs are addressed by society. Policies can be laws, rules, or regulations, at the federal, state, local, or agency level. Any type of policy at any level can be examined using the steps outlined in this chapter. In the next section we will consider how to choose what you will analyze. But first, a brief note to the student who is reading this. If you consider yourself a policy person, you are probably looking forward to this, and that is great. Policy makers need the expertise of social scientists like yourself. If you are not look-

CHAPTER-LEVEL LEARNING OBJECTIVES

By the end of this chapter, students will be able to

1. Describe how to isolate a policy for analysis.

2. Explain an individual policy's primary goals and the expected benefits to the target population.

3. Discuss the steps involved in searching for the unintended consequences of policy interventions.

4. Present the findings of your policy analysis in a way that is understandable to policy makers, researchers, and recipients of the policy.

ing forward to this, perhaps because you consider yourself to be clinically or individually focused, stop here and consider this. Whether you want to engage in it or not, policy will shape every interaction you have with someone in need, whether you are a social worker, a researcher, a gerontologist, a teacher, or a person working in any other related human services field. Policies define when, where, and how you can interact with potential individual and group clients. How many times can you meet with a client? Does an individual or family qualify for a program? Does your agency meet the criteria to apply for that grant? Questions like these all depend on policy. Policy is like the air we breathe. It is invisible, but we know it is there, and like a stiff wind, it directs and shapes the flow of events and activities. Policy analysis allows you to see that wind. Seeing it allows you to work towards redirecting it for the benefit of vulnerable groups such as older adults.

WHY WOULD A SOCIAL SCIENTIST WANT TO ANALYZE POLICY?

This book is written for social science students in fields such as gerontology, social work, sociology, and psychology. The specific reasons why one would want to analyze a policy may differ depending on which of those fields you are in. But the overarching reason is the same—to understand how people and populations are impacted by existing or proposed policies. If you are in an action-oriented field such as social work, you may use this information to advocate for better policies and advocate against unintended consequences that policies create. In other fields you may want to conduct research on a population, do a **cost analysis** (a specific type of policy analysis that examines the true costs of the intervention or proposed intervention), compare alternative policies, and analyze policy for many more reasons. A policy analysis can answer many questions, as well as inform future interventions.

The purpose of this book is for you to understand all the ways policy shapes the experiences of older adults. **Policy analysis** allows you to do a deep dive into one policy to understand its impact. There are volumes written about how to conduct different types of policy analyses that are beyond the scope of this book. Government agencies such as the Centers for Disease Control and Prevention (2021) offer models and tools for conducting policy analysis. This book will help you understand the policy landscape in which older adults and their families are situated. This chapter will give you basic tools for a deeper dive into one policy, using five basic steps: (1) defining a distinct policy to measure; (2) determining the stated goal of the policy; (3) defining the target population; (4) evaluating the impact of the policy; and (5) examining the landscape for unintended consequences. This basic model will serve your purposes in most human service settings. Refer to books such as Bardach and Patashnik (2020) if you need a more detailed process for publication.

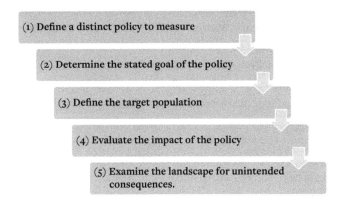

FIGURE 2.1   Flow Chart: Steps of a Policy Analysis

As a social scientist, you will conduct a policy analysis because you are concerned about a problem or policy issue that influences life for a particular subset of the aging population. Policy issues could be related to: how Medicare and Medicaid are applied; challenges with advance directives in your state, or the fact that advance directives are not transferrable between states; access and barriers to home- and community-based services; and other factors (more on these policy examples can be found in Chapter 8 and Chapter 10). Whatever issue you choose, you should be able to state the issue clearly in one to two sentences. In brief, how, why, and to whom is this issue problematic?

A **problem** is the gap between what could be and what is, such as a group experiencing a systematic unmet need. Usually you would conduct a policy analysis because there is a difference of opinion between or among major stakeholders about how to solve the problem. Your one- to two-sentence **problem statement** should specify what the conflict you are addressing is about. What is the extent of the problem? Provide quantitative estimates, if possible, of the problem's magnitude and intensity: for example, how many lives are affected, how many dollars are spent or lost. If you are conducting the policy analysis to advocate for change, you also need to provide estimates of losses or gains if no action is taken to change the status quo. This will help you later, in your policy analysis, to explain the impact of the policy you are evaluating. Finally, consider what makes this a public policy issue. Who believes this is a problem? Who is in a position to define what a problem is? Often, those experiencing the problem are not the same people who have the power to define or change it. In order to advocate for change, you need to be able to explain why the time and resources of a particular branch of government (legislative, judicial or executive), or government monies, should or should not be spent to help resolve the problem.

DEFINING A DISTINCT POLICY TO MEASURE

Once you have stated your problem, you need to find a policy. Policies encompass a vast range of different entities. A policy analyst must clearly state which policy they intend to analyze. The larger the policy, the broader your analysis will need to be. For example, if you choose the **Social Security Act** as your policy, you may need to further decide if you are looking at the whole thing—a nearly impossible task for one policy analysis, as the Social Security Act includes disability, retirement, and survivors' benefits, **Supplemental Security Income** (**SSI**) (Chapter 10), **Medicare**, **Medicaid** (Chapter 11), and much more—or one particular program. On the other end of the spectrum, you can choose one specific piece of a law to analyze. You may see the parsing of laws into smaller parts when laws are being challenged in court. There is an example of how this was applied to the Social Security Act in Chapter 8. Also, remember the story from Chapter 1 about how the individual mandate part of the **Patient Protection and Affordable Care Act** (**ACA**) was challenged in the Supreme Court.

The policies you analyze do not have to be federal. They do not even have to be laws. Policies are everywhere, and you need to determine which one best addresses your problem. Taking the example outside of older adults for a moment, your workplace likely has policies—when and how to request vacation time, how to complete an intake or transaction, or where to go to receive your employee benefits. Each of these policies can be analyzed. The main point of a policy analysis is to figure out if the policy accomplishes what its creators set out for it to do, and sometimes, if there is another policy that would do it better. Many times, policies may do what they were created to do but have unintended consequences for different groups. For example, a workplace policy on vacation time that requires everyone to make their requests by a certain day at a certain time may accomplish the goal of making sure everyone has an equal chance to use their time off. It may give the supervisors adequate time to plan for backup to ensure that the schedule is filled. But it may also disadvantage workers whose lives are less predictable or who have emergencies come up. Those workers may have life circumstances that keep them from being able to plan as far in advance as others. The hassles caused by the policy may lead them to decide not to take vacation time at all.

In sum, the first thing you need to do is decide which policy to analyze. In the next step, you will determine what that policy was created to do. Then you can determine what questions you want to ask about the policy and how to find the answers.

WHAT ARE THE GOALS OF YOUR CHOSEN POLICY?

Once you have figured out which policy you want to examine, you need to determine the aims of that policy. If the policy is a law that was introduced in the U.S. Congress or a state legislature, the aims are often found in the three- to four-sentence summary at the beginning of the bill. The aim or purpose of the **Social Security Act** was:

> To provide for the general welfare by *establishing a system of Federal old-age benefits*, and by *enabling the several States* to make more *adequate provision for aged persons, blind persons, dependent and crippled children, maternal and child welfare, public health, and the administration of their unemployment compensation laws;* to establish a Social Security Board; to raise revenue; and for other purposes. (Social Security, n.d.) [Emphasis added]

Legal language can be intimidating, so let's break down what that means. What does the Social Security Act do? In the first two lines we can see that it gives authority to the Federal government and the States. Many bills do this. This means that the legislature is instructing the agencies of the federal government, such as the **Department of Health and Human Services** (**HHS**), **the Centers for Disease Control and Prevention** (**CDC**), **and the Centers for Medicare and Medicaid Services** (**CMS**), to do something. In this case, federal agencies are instructed to establish a system of old-age benefits. The Act wants to tell the states that they should enhance their provisions to care for the groups listed in the bill, but it cannot instruct the states directly. The federal government has limited jurisdiction in what it can tell the states to do, but it can provide monetary incentives to encourage the states to do what it wants them to do. In this case, the Social Security Act provides states with the financial means to address the needs of particular populations that are the target of the policy.

This leads us to the next question. Who is it that the policy wants to reach? The Social Security Act has a broad scope, mentioning several populations including aged persons, blind persons, dependent and crippled children, mothers and children, and the unemployed. It also mentions the health of the population. Note that policy terms such as "aged persons" and "crippled children" reflect the vernacular of the time and may not be the terminology used today. If you were to conduct an analysis of a policy like the Social Security Act, you would need to either decide which of the targeted groups you wanted to examine more closely, or ensure that your analysis evaluated the impacts on all of them. Fortunately, many policies are much narrower.

DEFINING THE TARGET POPULATION

The **target population** is the group that is intended to be impacted by the policy. Some policies target "everyone" while others target specific groups. Policies like highway, transportation, or public education policies, for example, target all people who traverse a particular route or live in a particular area. Human service policies tend to target more specific groups, such as people below a certain income, people above a certain age, or people who have certain medical conditions such as blindness or limitations on their ability to work due to disability.

Once you discover (from the goals of the policy) the population that the policy targets, you need to define that population clearly. You should always check to see how the policy defines the population, as this will give you specific clues about who might be excluded. Federal policies of the scope of the Social Security Act define the population for you. Section 6 of the Social Security Act defines **old age** as encompassing "individuals who are 65 years of age or older" (Social Security Act, 1935).

Regional, local, or company policies may be less specific. The population defined in the policy may be different from the population you described earlier as having the problem, which is probably why you are conducting the policy analysis in the first place. Perhaps the group that the policy defines—seniors in poverty, or seniors in need of food—are not those most in need in your community. Your analysis would demonstrate the gap between the policy and the people in need. For the purposes of your analysis, your target population should be the population affected by the **problem**. Your analysis looks at how that population is affected by the policy.

EVALUATING THE IMPACT OF THE POLICY

We have now spent several pages talking about defining problems, policies, and populations. We have finally reached the analysis part of the chapter. Using the information you acquired above, your analysis will examine **outcomes**. **Outcomes** are what happens as a result of the policy. For example, if the system of old-age benefits established by the Social Security Act was intended to reduce poverty in older adults, you need to examine poverty rates with and without income from Social Security. If you were conducting the policy analysis because you wanted to suggest changes to Social Security after learning that Social Security was not meeting its goals, you would want to demonstrate which people are still in poverty under the current policies.

Going back to the goals of the policy will give you the best clue as to what outcomes to consider. The outcomes should be directly related to the goals. Time frame is important too. Using the Social Security example, the Social Security Act was passed in 1935 to reduce poverty in older adults. However, reporting in the 2020s that the bill was effective at reducing poverty in 1935 is not useful to current policy debates. It would be more useful to report current poverty rates among older adults or Social Security recipients and demonstrate how those rates would change, depending on which changes were made to Social Security and how they were implemented.

A policy may have impacts beyond its stated goal, and it is also important for a policy analysis to consider those. Realize, however, that those outcomes may be harder to prove beyond correlation. **Correlation** is a relationship or interconnection between two or more things. Suppose you want to say that a senior nutrition program that reduced food insecurity in older adults also improved their health outcomes and decreased their doctor visits. You may be able to find data to support your claim. The reduction in doctor visits may, in fact, be related to the nutrition program, because people were better able to control their weight or their diabetes or their consumption of sodium. But just because two things are correlated, it doesn't mean that one caused the other. For example, the *Harvard Business Review* (2015) reported that there is a correlation between how much margarine each person in the United States consumes, on average, and the divorce rate in Maine. If you are making claims about a bill or law that are beyond the scope of that policy, be sure that you have evidence to support the relationship.

EXAMINING THE LANDSCAPE FOR UNINTENDED CONSEQUENCES

Unintended consequences are events or impacts that are not part of the policy's goal but occur as a result of the policy. Unintended consequences do not have to be bad, though negative consequences often receive the greatest scrutiny. This section will discuss two types of negative unintended consequences and conclude with potential positive unintended consequences.

The first type of unintended consequence is around eligibility. Often, a policy will establish criteria for receiving a good or service. Policies include eligibility criteria for programs and services for a variety of reasons. It is often too expensive (or thought to be) to provide the service to a larger population. Eligibility criteria are used to ensure that the resources go to people who are perceived by policy makers as needing them the most; conversely, they may be used to ensure that people who are perceived by policy makers as undeserving of the service do not receive it. Eligibility criteria almost always exclude some individual or group who would benefit from the service and include some individual or group who arguably does not need the service. Sometimes, these criteria are based on evidence regarding who is most in need. Other times, they reflect the biases of lawmakers that determine which groups they particularly do or do not want to include, though explicit biases are often difficult to prove. See figure 2.2 for information about who was excluded from the Social Security Act. Understanding who was excluded and why is important. DeWitt (2010) argues in his policy analysis that the exclusions from Social Security were not racially motivated because 75% of those excluded were whites. He fails to consider that 65% of all non-white workers were excluded. This is why, in a policy analysis, you should consider both those that are included and those that are excluded. What you decide to include in a formal write-up will depend on your particular audience.

These groups were excluded from the Social Security Act in 1935

☐ Self-employed
☐ Farmers
☐ People working for non-profits
☐ Professionals such as doctors, lawyers, and ministers (often self-employed)
☐ Merchant marines
☐ Members of Congress
☐ Federal, state, and local government employees

Adapted from DeWitt (2010)

FIGURE 2.2   Who Was Excluded From the Social Security Act?

Medicare can be used to demonstrate exclusion and inclusion eligibility criteria. **Medicare** is medical insurance for all people over age 65 who met work requirements and people under age 65 *with certain medical conditions.* The phrase *with certain medical conditions* is italicized because this is an eligibility requirement that includes some and excludes others. According to the Center for Medicare Advocacy (2021), people under age 65 who have **End Stage Renal Disease** (**ESRD**) or who have **Amyotrophic Lateral Sclerosis** (**ALS**), also called **Lou Gehrig's disease**, are eligible for Medicare. People with ESRD have little to no functioning in their kidneys and receive dialysis treatments several times per week to rid their bodies of toxic waste products. ALS is a progressive, neurodegenerative disease, meaning that it affects the brain and spinal cord (neuro), causing it to break down (degenerative), and that it gets worse over time (progressive). In people with ALS, the brain eventually loses connection with the muscles. This results in an inability to walk, talk, eat, and breathe. People generally die from ALS in 2–5 years (ALS Association, 2021). In addition to these groups, people who have received Social Security disability for at least 24 months are also eligible for Medicare before age 65. If you were to analyze Medicare policy, you could clearly make an argument for why these groups would need early Medicare.

Every other kind of diagnosis is excluded from Medicare before the age of 65. Can you think of other chronic diseases, not limited to people over the age of 65, for which medical expenses are high? What about something like type 2 diabetes? Type 2 diabetes is widespread. It is possible to prevent or reduce the occurrence of many complications of type 2 diabetes, such as ESRD, with regular medical follow-up and proper medications. Providing Medicare to this population would provide consistent access to medical care and medications. This would help this population control and maintain their blood sugar levels and be screened promptly for signs and symptoms of complications. Of course, there are also reasons for excluding this group, such as costs. Additionally, many people in this population continue to work and have health insurance through their employers. U.S. healthcare policies are structured such that insurance through employers is preferred over anything sponsored or paid for by the government. A policy analysis of Medicare coverage for people under age 65 should consider which conditions are excluded, why they are excluded, and the benefits and drawbacks of expanding coverage to include them.

A second type of unintended consequence is around safety. Now, you may be thinking that safety is always a good thing. But safety laws often have the unintended consequences of infringing on personal freedoms or restricting movement. Different people tolerate different levels of infringement on personal freedoms, related to their beliefs about the role of government. Analyzing these types of laws requires being aware of your own beliefs about the role of government, and the beliefs that supporters and opponents may hold. When seat belt regulations first went into effect, many people opposed them because they believed the government should not tell them what to do in the privacy of their own cars. Despite these protests, seat belt laws have been effective at reducing highway deaths. Other laws that have faced similar protests have included no-smoking laws and, during COVID-19, masking and vaccination laws and policies. Therefore, a policy analysis around a safety law should include considerations of personal freedoms and the risks/benefits of the proposed or existing laws to individuals and public health.

There are some cases where safety laws and policies can actually cause harm to some people. On a very small level, you sometimes see this in nursing homes, where residents are told not to walk around by themselves. The policy is there to prevent falls and to keep residents safe from injuries. However, an unintended consequence is that some residents walk less frequently because they need to wait for staff, lose muscle tone, and become weaker and more prone to falls. A larger example is in social work licensure. Licensing laws were created to protect citizens from the work of unprepared social workers. However, the costs of licensure, such as fees for the required exam, application, and background check, create barriers to entering the social work profession for individuals from lower-income groups. Perhaps the licensure laws were well intended, but their unintended consequences are not neutral. Policy analysis should consider all aspects of impact.

Positive unintended consequences can occur as a result of a policy. When that happens, it can be grounds for expanding the policy, or it can demonstrate that something is working. So what is a positive unintended consequence? Let's say that some children in a school are eligible for free or reduced-price lunch. Many members of the community will likely qualify. The forms are sent out to family members, and as it turns out, nearly half the children qualify. Administrators know that there are likely families in need who did not fill out the form but are still in need of the lunches. Despite frequent reminders to parents the forms go unreturned, and without the forms, the eligible children may go without lunch. Administrators, not wanting this to happen, secure a grant from a community foundation to provide free lunches to everyone in the school. As a result of that grant, did some children who did not need the free lunches get food? Probably. But it also guaranteed that all of the children who needed lunches got them too. The school's policy became that no one was turned away from lunch because of an inability to pay, which resulted in all children getting fed, regardless of need. Children did better in school because they were not hungry. In addition to the academic benefit, another unintended consequence was that school spirit was better. No one felt worse or different because they got free meals, and bullying was reduced. An analysis of this school's lunch policy might recommend that all schools adopt this approach, despite the increased food costs, because the social benefits are worth the expense. There are many other policies that have this kind of secondary benefit beyond the stated intent. This is a real example from a real school. The following section will provide additional examples on how policy analysis has been applied to advocacy and shaping policy.

Policy Analysis Examples

Hebert et al. (2019) used policy analysis to inform the development of a dementia home safety kit for the Department of Veterans Affairs (VA). Before they developed their toolkit, they wanted to understand how useful it would be to the end users. Their analysis focused on policies that helped or hindered providers—doctors, nurses, therapy staff, and so on—in implementing new and innovative treatment models, in general. They hoped their findings would allow them to identify barriers they would need to overcome for people to use and benefit from the toolkit. One barrier they identified, for example, was a VA policy that requires providers to justify interventions based on the patient's current condition. This requirement would make it difficult to justify the toolkit, which is a preventive measure. Their extensive policy analysis identified several other barriers, as well as conditions that would facilitate the use of their toolkit. They concluded with recommendations to the VA about aligning policies across disciplines and departments at the local, state, and federal levels to address barriers and inconsistencies. Their recommended changes would facilitate the use of their toolkit and would also create policies more conducive to preventive interventions.

In a completely different type of policy analysis, Foster et al. (2019) examined existing social policies in England that relate to death, identified gaps, and proposed a comprehensive societal policy response to death that provides people with the services they need. In England many services related to death and survivorship are subsidized by the government. Foster et al.'s (2019) analysis identifies the reasons why more comprehensive policy is necessary to better meet needs and to be more efficient at providing these services. They also identify ways that their policy recommendations would increase equity by addressing unequal distributions of resources that occur across the life course.

LeBihan (2012) analyzed the evolution of home care policies in France over time, with particular emphasis on the introduction of a regulated cash payment. The cash payment policy was introduced to recognize the value of informal care work, allowing family caregivers to receive payments for the care they provide to relatives. Similar policies have been attempted in parts of the United States, particularly in Medicaid waiver programs that allow payments to family caregivers. LeBihan's (2012) analysis explores the benefits and drawbacks of such a program, both to the individuals who give and receive care and to the care system as a whole. For us, reading and reviewing international policy analyses reveals important lessons about underlying policy assumptions in other countries as compared to underlying assumptions in the United States. Such analyses also provide information about policies that have worked—and, importantly, those that have not worked—which U.S. policymakers should take into consideration. State-level policy experiments and analyses can also provide insight for policy makers who wish to implement policies on the national level.

The policy analysis techniques described in this chapter can be used to identify the underlying assumptions of policy, such as beliefs about who is deserving and undeserving of help. An important indicator of these assumptions is the language that is used in policy. Dizon and colleagues (2020) conducted a policy analysis of aging policies, specifically focusing on rooting out the assumptions of language. For example, individual aging is usually discussed in the public discourse as a problem, framed in the context of physical, social, and cognitive decline. Population aging is also discussed as a problem, caused by the many and growing numbers of people who experience physical, social, and cognitive decline, causing a drain on the system. Dizon et al.'s (2020) study found that policies often stated that their goal to "meet the challenges" (p. 400)" was to encourage active participation in life, work, etc. They found that the policies implied that aging well was synonymous with participation. On the other hand, their study uncovered a significant lack of opportunities for older adults to participate in the policy process. This is not uncommon, as often those with the ability to define problems are not those who experience them. Ironically, while older adults as a whole have limited ability to participate in the policy process, in the 117th Congress of the United States installed January 3, 2021, the average age in the Senate is 63 years and the average age in the House of Representatives is 58 years. The two oldest senators, Dianne Feinstein (D-CA) and Chuck Grassley (R-IA), are both 87 at the time of this writing, as is the oldest representative, Don Young (R-AK) (Magan, 2021). But given that members of Congress are disproportionately white and have substantially higher average incomes than the U.S. population, it is likely that they do not experience age-related social issues in the way most Americans do either; they may not represent the interests of older people as a whole.

SUMMARY

This chapter has described a basic process for analyzing policy, both to help you understand its impacts and to allow you to advocate for better policy. The five basic steps are: (1) defining a distinct policy to measure; (2) determining the stated goal of the policy; (3) defining the target population; (4) evaluating the impact of the policy; and (5) examining the landscape for unintended consequences. This process can be used on policies at any level and of any size. This chapter also provided examples of how policy analysis was used to improve services, including: identifying the barriers to adoption of innovative care models (Hebert et al., 2019); arguing for the need to coordinate systems of care related to end of life (Foster et al., 2019); and illustrating the benefits and drawbacks of cash payments to family caregivers (LeBihan, 2012). Finally, Dizon et al.'s (2020) analysis reported on how the use of language in policy reflects society's beliefs about aging. Policy analysis is an important tool in any social scientist's toolkit for influencing and changing ineffective social structures.

KEY TERMS

Amyotrophic Lateral Sclerosis (ALS)

Centers for Disease Control and Prevention (CDC)

Centers for Medicare and Medicaid Services (CMS)

Correlation

Cost analysis

Department of Health and Human Services (HHS)

End Stage Renal Disease (ESRD)

Lou Gehrig's disease

Medicaid

Medicare

Old age

Outcomes

Patient Protection and Affordable Care Act (ACA)

Policy

Policy analysis

Problem

Problem statement

Social Security Act

Supplemental Security Income (SSI)

Target population

Unintended consequences

DISCUSSION QUESTIONS

1. What population are you interested in studying and/or working with? Clearly define a specific subpopulation whose issues would allow you to conduct a compelling policy analysis. Compare the population you've chosen with those your classmates have chosen. Help each other refine your chosen population to be more specific.

2. What problem are you hoping to examine? What situation is your chosen population facing that you want to see policy address? Why did you choose that issue?

3. Suppose you consider yourself a clinically oriented person. After reading this chapter, discuss why you would want to analyze a policy. How could it help you help your clients?

4. If you consider yourself a policy person, how you would explain the importance of policy analysis to a more clinically oriented classmate? What impacts can policy analysis have on individuals?

5. Choose a policy at your school. Any policy will do. Describe the target population, the desired effect, the actual effect (if you know it), and any unintended consequences you can think of. Recommend ways to strengthen the policy to address gaps.

Ancillary materials for student practice can be found within Active Learning

REFERENCES

ALS Association. (2021). *What is ALS?* Retrieved February 22, 2021 from https://www.als.org/understanding-als/what-is-als

Bardach, E., & Patashnik, E. (2020). *A practical guide for policy analysis: The eightfold path to more effective problem solving* (6ᵗʰ ed.). CQ Press.

Center for Medicare Advocacy. (2021). *Medicare for people under 65.* Retrieved February 22, 2021 from https://medicareadvocacy.org/under-65-project/

Centers for Disease Control and Prevention. (2021). *Policy analysis.* Office of the Associate Director for Policy and Strategy. Retrieved February 17, 2021 from https://www.cdc.gov/policy/polaris/policyprocess/policy_analysis.html

DeWitt, L. (2010). The decision to exclude agricultural and domestic workers from the 1935 Social Security Act. *Social Security Bulletin, 70*(4). Social Security Office of Retirement and Disability Policy. https://www.ssa.gov/policy/docs/ssb/v70n4/v70n4p49.html

Dizon, L., Wiles, J., & Peiris-John, R. (2020). What is meaningful participation for older people? An analysis of aging policies. *The Gerontologist, 60*(3), 396–405. https://doi.org/10.1093/geront/gnz060

Foster, L., Woodthorpe, K., & Walker, A. (2019). From cradle to grave?: Policy responses to death in the UK. *Mortality, 24*(1), 1–16. https://doi.org/10.1080/13576275.2017.1414776

Harvard Business Review. (2015, June). *Beware spurious correlations.* https://hbr.org/2015/06/beware-spurious-correlations

Hebert, C., Trudeau, S., Sprinkle, W., Moo, L., & McConnell, E. (2020). Directed content analysis of Veterans Affairs policy documents: A strategy to guide implementation of a dementia home safety toolkit for veterans to promote ageing in place. *Health and Social Care in the Community, 28*(1), 182–194. https://doi.org/10.1111/hsc.12852

LeBihan, B. (2012). The redefinition of the familialist home care model in France: The complex formalization of care through cash payment. *Health and Social Care in the Community, 20*(3), 238–246. https://doi.org/10.1111/j.1365-2524.2011.01051.x

Magan, V. (2021, February 2). *How old is the 117th Congress?* Fiscal Note. https://fiscalnote.com/blog/how-old-is-the-117th-congress

Social Security. (n.d.). *Social Security Act (as amended through December 20, 2019).* Compilation of the Social Security Laws. https://www.ssa.gov/OP_Home/ssact/title00/0000.htm

Social Security Act, 42 U.S.C. § 306 (1935). https://www.ssa.gov/OP_Home/ssact/title00/0006.htm

Credit

Fig. 2.2: Adapted from Larry DeWitt, "The Decision to Exclude Agricultural and Domestic Workers from the 1935 Social Security Act," Social Security Bulletin, vol. 70, no. 4, 2010.

CHAPTER 3

What Does Policy Say About Societal Assumptions?

INTRODUCTION

This chapter discusses **societal assumptions** and how they become embedded in policy. As we talked about in Chapter 2, not everyone has a seat at decision-making tables, and those who frame problems are often not those experiencing them. In addition, it is difficult to discuss what a **societal assumption** is without getting into the diversity of the United States and the varied viewpoints nestled or hidden within what "we" believe. If recent elections, protests in the streets by people on all sides of political ideologies, and stalemates in Congress have taught us anything, it is that there seems to be very little that "we" believe in the United States.

By the end of this chapter, students will be able to

1. Describe how policies reflect what "we" believe, even when they do not reflect what every individual person believes.

2. Using the skills gained in Chapter 2, explain how a policy's stated goals could be based on race, gender, or role expectations.

3. Describe commonly held assumptions about aging that are embedded in U.S. policies.

4. Identify how policies can be detrimental to those who do not fall within the stereotypes perpetuated by the policies.

Despite ideological divisions, patterns exist in policies that have been developed over generations. That is, in spite of decades of political divides—and, yes, some fundamental differences in beliefs—there are consistent approaches to addressing social problems that are present across time. For example, U.S. policy has always sought to divide those in need of help into categories of "worthy" and "unworthy;" that is different from the universal approaches sought by some other countries that the United States considers to be peers. Sometimes these divisions between worthy and unworthy are covert, meaning that the policy seems to be equal on its face, yet the application of the policy creates difference and inequality. Sometimes they are overt, meaning that the policy and/or the messaging around who should be included or excluded explicitly describes those who are worthy or unworthy. Nowhere was a narrative of unworthiness more obvious than in the welfare queen stereotype promulgated in the 1970s and 1980s.

The myth of the **welfare queen** was based on a real woman from Chicago who, in difficult circumstances, used fake names, children who were not hers, and fake stories to receive welfare benefits to which she should have not been entitled from the **Aid for Families with Dependent Children** (**AFDC**) program (Covert, 2019). Conservative politicians, including governors and senators and extending all the way up to President Ronald Reagan, used her story to promote stereotypes about the poor, about Blacks (this woman happened to be Black), and about those in poverty. Their narratives depicted these groups as lazy and unwilling to work and then used those stereotypes to justify significant cuts in welfare payments at the state and federal levels, including the reduction of cash benefits and the creation of more difficult stipulations to prove need. The stereotypes were used to justify the work requirements and the lifetime limits incorporated into the 1996 **Temporary Assistance for Needy Families** (**TANF**) laws, passed under the watch of Democratic President Bill Clinton. These and other exaggerated stereotypes, sometimes based on actual cases, are used to defend decreases in spending and policies that require stringent adherence to specific criteria to access benefits. This example suggests a societal belief that people should be willing to work for what they need, and that those who are not willing to work are not worthy of our help.

You might be wondering what welfare policy and societal assumptions have to do with aging policy because you think Social Security and Medicare cover all older adults. Well, first, Social Security and Medicare do have eligibility criteria; even though they are broader than those of many other federal policies, they are not universal. (See more on Social Security in Chapter 10 and Medicare in Chapter 11.) More importantly, Social Security and Medicare are by far not the only policies to address the needs of older adults, and how we address the needs of older adults is far from universal.

Societal beliefs and their influence on policies are complex because of differences in social norms within and between groups, and because of how policy is made in the United States. In Congress the majority party has decision-making power, particularly in the House of Representatives. In the Senate, the majority party has the power to set the agenda, but cooperation from the minority party is generally needed to advance legislation. Similar dynamics play out in policymaking bodies at the state and local levels. As a result, the most successful policies incorporate perspectives from both sides of the political spectrum and thus include an array of societal beliefs.

HOW IS AGING VIEWED IN THE UNITED STATES?

Since societies are made up of different people with different perspectives, how can you tell what societal beliefs are? All types of media are an excellent place to start. News media has become more partisan; it is possible to find a news source that caters to your particular policy platform, and people may choose to watch only that with which they agree. But other types of media, such as advertising, movies, and television shows, offer a broader view of societal beliefs through the products that are advertised, who is in the shows and ads, and who is not. A line from a 1990s movie called *The First Wives Club* sums it up well—"There are only three ages for women in Hollywood: Babe, District Attorney, and Driving Miss Daisy." The latter refers to a 1989 movie about an older woman. Nearly all advertising for beauty products promises to stop aging, remove wrinkles, and get rid of the grays. Older adults are either absent from television and movies or depicted as grumpy or senile. Research shows that these depictions influence how society views older adults and how people see themselves as they grow older (Prieler, 2020).

Other clues can be found in greeting cards and common expressions. Greeting cards advise people at milestone birthdays that they are now "over the hill." Nothing says that younger means better more clearly than when we tout that "50 is the new 30," or "60 is the new 40." What is wrong with 50 or 60 being 50 or 60? Finally, and most importantly, beliefs can be seen in the way a group is treated. Older adults are disparaged in nearly all of the aforementioned categories.

This **ageism**, or discrimination on the basis of age, can go both ways (towards older people or towards younger people) and is equally dangerous in both directions. As much as older adults are stereotyped or prejudged based on age, so too are younger people, who are assumed to be inexperienced or to either have or lack certain competencies because of their age. One example can be seen when it comes to technology. It is equally harmful to assume that younger people, sometimes called **digital natives**, know all there is to know about technology, or to assume that **digital immigrants** know nothing or are universally inept. The use of the word **natives** in this regard refers to the fact that younger people have always had access to certain types of **digital** technology, like computers and smartphones. Digital immigrants came into these technologies later in life. Like many stereotypes, this view only tells part of the story. Stereotypes are true for some people who are part of a group, and the tendency is to try to apply that framework to everyone in that group. Yet it was the digital immigrants who invented many existing technologies. It took a lot more knowledge and skill to know about computer programming before Microsoft and Windows came along, and the people who invented that technology are often assumed to be digital immigrants! In the workplace, older people are often considered obsolete or untrainable, while younger people are sometimes considered unreliable. Long story short, not only do these assumptions do a disservice to individuals in these age groups, but when we create policies based on these false narratives, we do a disservice to all.

Telehealth is health care provided via technology, including telephones and video conferencing platforms. Telehealth visits proliferated during the COVID-19 pandemic, when patients were afraid to go into health care centers in person, and health care providers were seeking to reduce the numbers of people in their offices. In the context of COVID-19 and beyond, there were benefits. Telehealth provided increased access to many groups, such as those with physical disabilities, for whom getting to a doctor's office can be challenging. They also protected patients from potential COVID-19 exposure and prevented medical staff from being exposed to more people.

As a result of the proliferation of telehealth, telehealth policies also proliferated. Unfortunately ageism was present in many of them, as was discrimination against those in poverty and those in rural areas. For example, some **telehealth** policies provided visits through inaccessible platforms, failing to address the variety of access and skill levels older people have in relation to technology. Other policies excluded coverage for "voice only" telehealth, meaning visits in the form of phone calls. Excluding voice only telehealth assumed everyone had access to a device with video capability, the ability to use it, and broadband internet access, which is a challenge in many rural and inner city areas in the United States. Some of these policies were temporary and are scheduled to end when the public health emergency passes. It will be important to watch, over the years following the pandemic, whether policy keeps up with available telehealth technology.

Social structures that promote the gathering of individuals within the same age groups and not the intermixing of people of different ages promote ageism. When older and younger people have opportunities to interact with each other, they get to know each other as people. Without those personal connections, their opinions are more likely to be formed based on **stereotypes** or first impressions. Stereotypes are fixed generalizations, or pictures in our head, about a group or class of people (Kurylo, 2012)—in this case, people who are "older" or "aging." Those words are in quotes because despite stereotypes about getting older, there is no fixed definition of who is an older person, nor is there a point when someone begins aging. Scholars disagree about whether stereotypes are always negative, and whether stereotypes are individually held beliefs or beliefs held by groups (Kurylo, 2012). In the United States, stereotypes about aging are generally negative, and they are commonly held. This is not to say that everyone holds them, but enough people do that they are part of the societal fabric. What is most ironic about stereotypes about aging is that every one of us is getting older every minute, every day of our lives. Aging stereotypes create bias towards our future selves. Negative stereotypes about aging are so embedded in U.S. culture that they impact how people view themselves as they age, not just how they view those around them, and this can impact well-being, behavior, and health outcomes (Hausknecht et al., 2020).

Reducing ageism would promote better policies, and it would also reduce social isolation and loneliness, both of which are associated with significant health problems (World Health Organization, 2021). When it comes to health care and health care policy, ageism can be implicit or explicit. Implicit ageism occurs when medical students do not receive specialized training on the health needs of older adults. They are then less prepared when older adults present with different symptom profiles for common ailments than younger people do. This lack of recognition may lead them to delay diagnosis or misdiagnose someone, resulting in negative outcomes or death. Medical students also receive insufficient training on the appropriate use of certain medications in older people, who are more sensitive to the effects of medications and have different prescribing criteria (Inouye, 2021).

Explicit ageism occurs when policies exclude older people from medical trials, and/or create decision-making algorithms that ration care based on age. Many of the conditions for which clinical trials are conducted are more likely to be experienced by older adults. So why would they be excluded from these trials? Some clinical trials have explicit age cutoffs that exclude older people. It is easier for manufacturers and researchers to show positive effects in younger, healthier populations. Other times, the exclusion criteria appear age-neutral but result in the exclusion of older people. For example, criteria that exclude people with **co-morbidities,** other medical conditions which may or may not have anything to do with the problem being investigated but which older adults are more likely to have, may overwhelmingly exclude older people. Other criteria, such as a need for video conferencing, may exclude older adults, as well as other marginalized groups as above. Finally, exclusion criteria may be designed to exclude older people because of **paternalistic protectionism,** a specific form of ageism. Paternalistic protectionism occurs when well-meaning researchers exclude older people because they believe that medical trials are too dangerous or too inconvenient for them (Inouye, 2021).

Age-based care rationing was discussed during COVID-19, when some hospitals faced ventilator shortages and medical teams needed to decide who had priority for limited vaccines. These types of policies can also be seen in decisions regarding organ transplants, when younger recipients are favored over older patients. Some organ transplant programs, for example, will not enroll people over age 80 on their transplant lists, though official U.S. government policy is that there is no upper age limit for donation or receipt of organs.

DESERVING AND UNDESERVING GROUPS

So what stories do we tell through our policies about older adults? Paternalistic protectionism and **benevolent ageism** suggest that all older adults are in need of help and protection simply because they are older. These attitudes create policies that cover people on the basis of age, yet do not address those with specific needs. Another story is that older adults are **greedy geezers. Greedy geezers**, according to the narrative, have plenty of their own resources and do not need help, yet they seek more than their fair share of the policy pie. This narrative is used to pit older adults against younger generations, when it comes to things like Medicare spending as a percentage of the total U.S. budget.

As is often the case when stereotypes are applied, the truth lies somewhere in between. For older adults who function at the financial margins or have more unmet needs, these falsehoods create policies that do not work for them. According to the United Nations Global Report on Ageism (World Health Organization, 2021), "institutional ageism refers to the laws, rules, social norms, policies and practices of institutions that unfairly restrict opportunities and systematically disadvantage people because of their age" (p. 2). Policies that are based on one stereotype or the other provide useful benefits to people who may not need them while not providing sufficient support to those who do need help.

As we discussed above, one of the societal assumptions about deserving recipients is they should not be lazy and should have to work for their benefits. This is one of the reasons that **Social Security** and **Medicare** are widely accepted policies for older adults—they are tied to work. In order to qualify for Social Security benefits, someone has to have worked for 40 quarters, or the equivalent of 10 years. For someone who retires at full retirement age, 67, this is actually a fairly low hurdle. Many people, even those who stayed at home for many years or who had cycles of unemployment, are able to come up with 10 years of paid employment. Additionally, rules that allow spouses and dependent adult children to access benefits through a worker's record can boost the eligibility and benefit amounts of individuals whose family situations kept one or more people out of the workforce. Because of this near universal coverage, many people believe that Social Security benefits cover everyone to an adequate degree, which is not true, as is discussed more fully in Chapter 10. The amount of someone's monthly benefit is based on their previous income and does not replace all of that income, leaving some older adults who have worked low-wage jobs throughout their lives without sufficient income to meet basic needs.

Some Calculations Based on Current Policy

A few calculations will demonstrate this point. The Social Security online calculator, https://www.ssa.gov/OACT/quickcalc/, shows that someone with an annual work income at the federal poverty line ($12,670/year in 2020) would receive a Social Security payment of $729/month if they retired in 2022 (Social Security, 2014). Someone working full time and earning minimum wage ($7.25 an hour in 2021, or $15,080/year) would receive a Social Security payment of $862/month. A Social Security payment of $862/month comes to a total of $10,344 per year, and it is too high to qualify for **Supplemental Security Income** (**SSI**) payments. SSI is a federal policy that provides a minimal level of income to low-income individuals who are "aged, blind, or disabled." (See Chapter 10 for a more complete discussion of SSI and Social Security.)

For now, it is important to understand that our societal assumptions have resulted in policies that allow some older adults to receive around $10,000 per year in income. There are no areas of the country where $10,344 per year allows someone to rent a place to live and covers even basic food, utility, and medical expenses. The National Low Income Housing Coalition (2021) reports that the national average rent for a one-bedroom dwelling is $1,017/month, well above the Social Security payment for someone in this situation. This does not include food, heat, medical care, medications, or any of the other essentials for life. There are other programs that address many needs that go unmet when someone's income is inadequate to meet their living needs, such as **Supplemental Nutrition Assistance Program** (**SNAP**) (Benefits.gov, n.d.-a), the **Low Income Home Energy Assistance**

Program (**LIHEAP**) (Benefits.gov, n.d.-b), the **Housing Choice Voucher Program** (**Section 8**) (Benefits.gov, 2020), and **Medicaid** (Medicaid, 2021). However, the disjointed nature of these policies, including the mix of federal and state funding and the division of programs by category, makes it difficult for individual older adults to access the services they need most.

HOW IS POLICY INFLUENCED BY SOCIETAL ASSUMPTIONS?

The influence of societal norms and assumptions on policies can be seen by looking at the ways policies have changed over time as societal norms have changed. It can be seen in the progression of laws that took the United States from slavery, in which Black people were owned by White people, to the ***Dred Scott v. Sanford*** (1857) decision, in which the Supreme Court ruled that both free and slave African Americans were not American citizens and could not sue in federal court, to the **Thirteenth Amendment** of the U.S. Constitution, in which slaves were freed, to the **Civil Rights Act**. Despite these advances, there are still many instances of **systemic racism**, in which seemingly race-neutral policies actually create differences between groups, or previously legal actions created gaps that persist despite the fact that current laws are race-neutral. See Chapter 7 for a discussion of the **GI Bill**, the **Federal Housing Administration** (**FHA**), and **redlining**, and their impacts on the current racial wealth gap.

The influences of social norms on policies, and the ways they have changed over time, can be seen in the progression of laws that moved women from being the property of their husbands, to being able to vote, to being able to own property of their own, to holding jobs even after they were married, to becoming members of Congress, and even to becoming Vice President of the United States. However, social norms change slowly. The intransigence of societal norms and their ongoing influence on policy are seen in the continued inability to pass the **Equal Rights Amendment**, which would explicitly grant women equal protections under the law. Policy advocates need to be aware when rights based on societal norms are under threat, because there have been moves to amend or rescind policies in many areas.

So how is it that assumptions become policy? An important part of policymaking is about politics. To convince people to support a candidate, or a lawmaker to support a policy, a story needs to be told that a person or group are like them or not like them, or has some characteristic that make them worthy or unworthy of support. The stories that are told by advocates and dissenters may be different, even on the same issue. These stories, who tells them, and who believes them shape how issues become bills, what is included in those bills, and how politicians vote on those bills. That is how societal assumptions become policy.

The power of stories to shape policy was seen in the lead-up to the passage of the **Patient Protection and Affordable Care Act** (**ACA**). As President Obama was negotiating for its passage, one proposed component would have created a mechanism for recommending the most effective procedures for different medical conditions and populations. Opponents seized this component and used it to tell the story that the ACA would create "death panels," which would decide whether or not your grandmother would get to live. This story, intended to deter legislators and the U.S. population from supporting the ACA, capitalized on societal assumptions that death and aging are to be feared, and that the universal goals of health care are to increase longevity. While not everyone holds these views (see conversations about health vs. life span in Chapter 4), this argument achieved the political goal of excluding that section from the ACA.

If we back up from that specific example and speak more broadly, some societal assumptions are overarching. For example, people hold assumptions regarding the very role of government. Differences in beliefs about the role of government are the original fundamental difference between Republicans and Democrats. Political parties aside, when considering policy advocacy it is important to understand how you, your constituents, and the opponents of the policy understand the very role of government. Fundamental questions include: Should government play a role in redistributing income from those who have to those who are in need? Should government resources go to ensuring that everyone has food to eat, or is that the responsibility of individuals and private charities? And, as is relevant here, what role and how much of a role should government play in the protection and care of older adults? As we will discuss further in the next section, one of the narratives about older adults is that they are frail and vulnerable and therefore require government involvement for their own safety and prosperity. Do you believe that? Do policy makers believe that? It is important to understand who is making which "societal assumptions," in order to advocate effectively for effective policies and programs.

THE STORY TOLD ABOUT AGING IN U.S. SOCIAL POLICY

So far this chapter has hinted at some of the ways that aging is described through the lens of U.S. policy. The passage of the Social Security Act in 1935 occurred in response to the abject poverty of the Great Depression era and a societal belief that older adults were entitled to a certain standard of living in later life. Due to the structure that was established by the Social Security Act, that standard came to be different for different people, and it was not enough for some people. SSI's base level of income suggests that there is a societal belief in there being a minimum by which we hope that older adults will live. By the time SSI came into effect in 1972, a number of states had created a patchwork of systems to provide supplemental funds to bring older adults up to this minimum. SSI legislation brought together this patchwork and extended it, so that older adults in all states would have access to a minimum standard. When SSI was passed in 1972, it provided $130 monthly payments for individuals and $195 for couples (Lyons, 1972). The payment in 2021 is $794 per month for individuals and $1,191 for couples (Social Security, n.d.). The fact that the minimum has not kept pace with the cost of living for older adults suggests that this is no longer the societal belief that it was in 1972.

You can also see societal beliefs in health- and home-care-related policies. There is a belief that people have family available to provide care, with government stepping in only when no other help is available. At the same time, government supports for caregivers are limited. Only recently have we begun to provide governmental support to caregivers, and that support remains inadequate. One of the purposes of the **National Family Caregiver Support Program**, according to the Administration for Community Living (2021), is to "assist family and informal caregivers to care for their loved ones at home for as long as possible" (para. 2), to provide "information to caregivers about available services" (para. 3), and to provide "assistance to caregivers in gaining access to the services" (para. 3). First, this suggests that U.S. societal beliefs are that family and/or other informal caregivers should provide care at home for as long as possible. The alternative to this care at home would be long-term care in a nursing home. As is discussed in later chapters, this alternative is not desired by many who prefer to remain in the community and is extremely costly unless you have spent all of your resources. Second, the reality revealed by this is that aging services are complex and hard to access—so complex that the United States has created a policy to help family caregivers access services created by other policies. Wouldn't it be more efficient to simplify the service delivery system to begin with? If U.S. society valued providing services to older adults, it would not create policies that are this complicated.

TABLE 3.1 Federal Aging Policy Initiatives in the United States

Income	Social Security Supplemental Security Income (SSI)
Community-Based Services	Older Americans Act
Food	Meals on Wheels Older Americans Act
Caregivers	RAISE Family Caregivers Act National Family Caregiver Support Program
Health Care	Medicare Medicaid Patient Protection and Affordable Care Act (ACA)
Energy/Utilities	Low Income Home Energy Assistance Program (LIHEAP) (all ages)
Housing	Housing Choice Voucher Program (Section 8) Section 202 Supportive Housing for the Elderly Low-Income Housing Tax Credit (LIHTC)

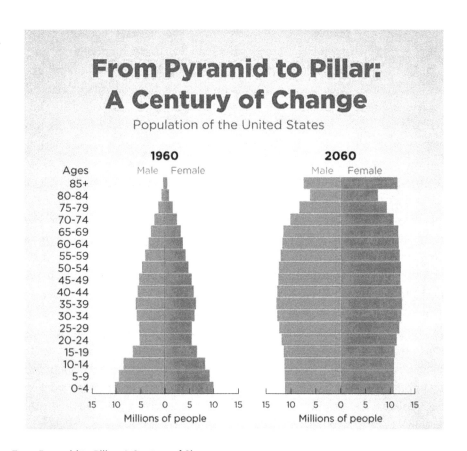

FIGURE 3.1   From Pyramid to Pillar: A Century of Change

SUMMARY

Policies are a reflection of the assumptions or ideals that exist in a society. When it comes to social service policies, ideals about who is worthy or unworthy of assistance are particularly important. These ideals become embedded in policy through the language that is used in the particular policy, the development of inclusion and exclusion criteria, and the messaging that is used to encourage others to support or oppose legislation.

In the United States, societal attitudes toward aging are about wrinkles and gray hair (things to be fixed), technological ineptitude (have to teach grandma how to Zoom!), and frailty. Policy decisions that are based on these attitudes may be fraught with benevolent ageism or paternalistic protectionism, like when older adults are excluded from research studies because it is perceived that participation would be too hard for them. This actually makes drugs and procedures less safe for older adults because they are not tested on them.

At the other end of the spectrum are attitudes that depict older adults as greedy geezers, seeking more than their fair share of the policy pie. This generalization is also not fair, and it results in policies that restrict eligibility, squeezing out those older adults whose incomes or savings are too much and not enough. These individuals have incomes above the eligibility levels for Medicaid or SSI but do not have enough to afford home care or other long-term services and supports, for example, or to pay the high out-of-pocket prescription drug costs that are not covered by Medicare.

The United States is not alone in having societal attitudes that paint an incomplete picture of the story, leading to incomplete policy approaches. All policies everywhere are a result of the societal beliefs in that country. The policy problem in the United States is that a combination of ageism and individualism leaves many older adults without the critical services they need, because they may not meet inclusion criteria that encourage work or have strong work histories. The policies fail to account for the lifelong work of people with low-wage jobs, and people who experienced setbacks in life such as a serious illness or disaster that depleted their savings.

As advocates for older adults and for ourselves, we need to be clear about our own beliefs as well as those in society. To be effective advocates, we have to craft narratives about policy needs that people understand and relate to, including those people in political office. Recently in one state legislature, delegates were debating the merits of a bill that would require in-person driver's license renewals for persons over a certain age. The bill was intended to address some of the sensory changes that sometimes happen in later life, which you will learn about in Chapter 5. The bill did not pass, not because it was a bad bill but because many of the delegates were themselves over that age and did not want to be subject to the conditions of the bill. So who our representatives are can be as important as the societal values they hold, and all must be considered when advocating for important legislation for older adults and for society.

KEY TERMS

Ageism	Digital immigrant
Aid for Families with Dependent Children (AFDC)	Digital native
Benevolent ageism	*Dred Scott v. Sanford*
Civil Rights Act	Equal Rights Amendment (ERA)
Co-morbidities	Federal Housing Administration (FHA)

GI Bill	Redlining
Greedy geezers	Social Security
Housing Choice Voucher Program	Societal assumptions
Low Income Home Energy Assistance Program (LIHEAP)	Stereotypes
Medicaid	Supplemental Security Income (SSI)
Medicare	Systemic racism
National Family Caregiver Support Program	Telehealth
Paternalistic protectionism	Temporary Assistance for Needy Families (TANF)
Patient Protection and Affordable Care Act (ACA)	13th Amendment
	Welfare queen

DISCUSSION QUESTIONS

1. Stereotypes are the way that humans classify information. They only become dangerous when people believe they are always true and fail to see differences between individuals in a group. What stereotypes do you hold? Were you taught them by someone else, or did you draw them based on your observations? Can you think of an example that falsifies the stereotype you hold?

2. Identify an ageist message in a television advertisement, show, or movie. Discuss what is ageist about it. Would that message be socially acceptable if it were about another group? Why or why not?

3. Discuss how policies that are seemingly race-neutral could be applied in ways that have differential effects. Does one group have more access to the opportunity than another? Does that difference in opportunity lead to differences in outcomes? How could we fix that through policy?

4. Consider the monthly SSI payment of $792. Could a single person live on that where you live? What is the average rent? What about heat, groceries, health care, and so on? If someone lived in subsidized housing, their rent would be 30% of their income. Could you pay for everything else on $552 per month? Run some numbers with your classmates and figure out where you could cut corners and where you could not.

Ancillary materials for student practice can be found within Active Learning

REFERENCES

Administration for Community Living. (2021). *National Family Caregiver Support Program.* Retrieved August 2, 2021 from https://acl.gov/programs/support-caregivers/national-family-caregiver-support-program

Benefits.gov. (n.d.-a) *Supplemental Nutrition Assistance Program (SNAP).* Retrieved March 24, 2021 from https://www.benefits.gov/benefit/361

Benefits.gov. (n.d.-b). *Low Income Home Energy Assistance Program (LIHEAP).* Retrieved March 24, 2021 from https://www.benefits.gov/benefit/623

Benefits.gov. (2020, January 22). *An overview of Section 8 housing assistance.* https://www.benefits.gov/news/article/388

Covert, B. (2019, July 2). The myth of the welfare queen. *The New Republic.* https://newrepublic.com/article/154404/myth-welfare-queen

Dred Scott v. Sanford, 60 U.S. 393 (1857). https://www.oyez.org/cases/1850-1900/60us393

Hausknecht, S., Low, L.-F., O'Loughlin, K., McNab, J., & Clemson, L. (2020). Older adults' self-perceptions of aging and being older: A scoping review. *The Gerontologist, 60*(7), e524–e534. https://doi.org/10.1093/geront/gnz153

Inouye, S. K. (2021). Creating an anti-ageist healthcare system to improve care for our current and future selves. *Nature Aging, 1,* 150–152. https://doi.org/10.1038/s43587-020-00004-4

Kurylo, A. (2012). What are *they* like? Non-expert definitions of stereotypes and their implications for stereotype maintenance. *Qualitative Research in Psychology, 9*(4), 337–350. https://doi.org/10.1080/14780887.2010.500517

Lyons, R. D. (1972, October 31). Nixon signs $5-billion bill expanding Social Security. *The New York Times*, A1. https://www.nytimes.com/1972/10/31/archives/nixon-signs-5billion-bill-expanding-social-security-president-signs.html

Medicaid.gov. (2021). *Medicaid.* https://www.medicaid.gov/medicaid/index.html

National Low Income Housing Coalition. (2021). *Out of reach 2020.* Retrieved March 24, 2021 from https://reports.nlihc.org/oor/about

Prieler, M. (2020). Gender representation of older people in the media: What do we know and where do we go from here? *Asian Women, 36*(2), 73–95. https://doi.org/10.14431/aw.2020.6.36.2.73

Social Security. (n.d.). *SSI federal payment amounts for 2021.* Retrieved March 29, 2021 from https://www.ssa.gov/oact/cola/SSI.html

Social Security. (2014). *Social Security quick calculator.* Benefit calculators. https://www.ssa.gov/OACT/quickcalc/

World Health Organization. (2021). *Global report on ageism.* https://www.who.int/teams/social-determinants-of-health/demographic-change-and-healthy-ageing/combatting-ageism/global-report-on-ageism

Credit

Fig. 3.1: Source: https://www.census.gov/library/visualizations/2018/comm/century-of-change.html.

INDIVIDUAL HEALTH IN LATE LIFE

Health Through a Diversity and Intersectional Lens: What Does It Mean to Be Healthy?

INTRODUCTION

How do people define **health**? In 2017, Mike was a 50-something-year-old white man living a middle-class life in a well-to-do suburb. He felt okay most of the time and was moderately active. He rode bikes with his kids and walked throughout his work day, but inconsistent exercise and an unhealthy diet left him more than 50 pounds overweight. In 2018 Mike's health took a significant shift when he was diagnosed with **type 2 diabetes**. **Diabetes** is a medical condition in which your body cannot properly create and/or use **insulin**, a hormone, to process glucose or sugar in the foods you eat, resulting in high **blood sugar**. In type 2 diabetes your body is not able to make or use insulin well (Medline Plus, 2021). Type 2 diabetes is the more common form of diabetes in the United States, with up to 95% of the cases, and nearly one fifth of people over age 65 are thought to have diabetes (Cowie et al., 2018).

For Mike, his diagnosis meant that everything changed. Suddenly his daily routines became much more important to maintaining his health. He had to learn how to eat to manage his blood sugars. Over the course of adjusting to his new diagnosis, Mike learned as much as he could about diabetes, began exercising more consistently, made sure he took his meds on time and as prescribed, and paid attention to his diet. In the first year, he lost his excess weight. Now he walks more than 7 miles a day and runs or bikes whenever he can. So how does Mike's health now compare to his health in 2018? Is he healthier? Sicker? And how does Mike's story relate to older adults?

By the end of this chapter, students will be able to

1. Discuss the differing interpretations of what it means to be healthy.

2. Explain how policies that focus on health care improve or detract from health.

3. Understand how social determinants of health influence overall health.

4. Name three policies that are not "health" policies but influence the health of a population.

Every semester I ask my students what it means to be healthy, and every semester they struggle to come up with a definition. What do you think? My students often struggle with questions like: Can you be healthy with a chronic condition? Is someone with a long-term disability whose condition is stable healthy? Can an older adult with multiple chronic conditions and a long-term disability be healthy? Answers to all of these questions can be both/and, or yes/but. Consider this: There is no ideal or perfect health, and each person may define differently what health means to them. Health may be associated with physical functioning, the presence or absence of pain, and many other factors. How each person defines health may also be shaped by many factors including age, culture, geography, and socioeconomic status.

Health can also be a lifelong prospect. What does that mean? While at any point someone can gain or lose weight, take up an exercise program, or in some other way change their health behaviors, there are factors in younger life that can influence health in later life. Some of these occur before a person is even able to make their own health care decisions, such as prenatal nutrition and substance use, the presence of secondhand smoke in a childhood home, and environmental factors such as proximity to industry or neighborhood air quality. Individual decisions can also influence long-term health. Smoking, for example, is measured in **pack-years**—the number of packs of cigarettes (20 cigarettes) smoked per day times the number of years someone smoked. Pack-years are a prognostic factor in certain types of cancer (Janjigian et al., 2010) and many other conditions. Diet and exercise can have long-term implications as well. Finally, someone's ability to control a chronic condition in younger life impacts later-life outcomes. Uncontrolled type 2 diabetes can result in peripheral vascular disease, neuropathy, end-stage renal disease, poor wound healing, amputation, and early death. Older adults are likely to have one or more chronic conditions. See Figure 4.1 for more information.

How do differences in definitions of health influence policy? People often associate health policy with policies such as Medicare, Medicaid, the Patient Protection and Affordable Care Act (ACA), and other policies that provide access to doctors, hospitals, and medications. Without a doubt, these are important. In Mike's case, his ability to go to a doctor, be diagnosed, and receive medication to control his blood sugar kept him from continuing on an unhealthy path. But as you can also see in Mike's case, there were many other social and policy

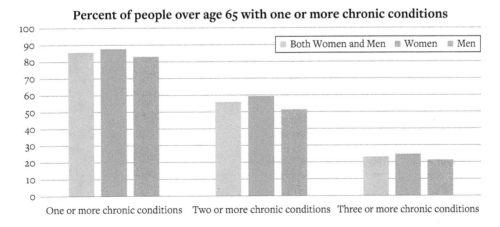

FIGURE 4.1   People Over Age 65 With One or More Chronic Conditions. The CDC collected data on older adults and the occurrence of six possible chronic conditions: arthritis, asthma, cancer, cardiovascular disease, chronic obstructive pulmonary disease, and diabetes

factors that influenced his new, healthier lifestyle. Mike is a college-educated person who was able to research and understand information about diabetes. Mike owned a car that allowed him to go to a grocery store that sold a variety of healthy foods, he could afford those foods, and his health literacy allowed him to learn how to consume those foods in ways that improved his blood sugar control. Mike had sufficient income to purchase a fitness watch to track walking and running distances. He lives in a community with safe sidewalks and pathways for walking, running, and biking. The absence of any one of these things could have negatively impacted Mike's health. They illustrate how education, food, transportation, and economic security policies influence the health of a neighborhood and the people who live there. Those community-based factors are referred to more broadly as social determinants of health.

SOCIAL DETERMINANTS OF HEALTH

Within each of the social determinants of health, the U.S. Office of Disease Prevention and Health Promotion (ODPHP) identifies underlying root causes that can suggest policy solutions to improve health. While the ODPHP materials are developed for the entire population, this chapter will demonstrate ways in which these policies are relevant to older adults.

FIGURE 4.2 Social Determinants of Health Framework

ECONOMIC STABILITY

In the area of economic stability, the ODPHP (n.d.) identified the following subcategories: employment, food insecurity, housing instability, and poverty. Poverty intersects with the other subcategories in this area. Poverty in late life may reflect a lifetime of disadvantage or be something that occurs when an older person's income and retirement assets are inadequate to meet their long-term needs. For many older Americans, Social Security is a key portion of their income and a policy that helps many rise out of poverty. However, there are disparities in the benefits people receive. Employment history influences the level of Social Security benefits to which someone is entitled. Societal norms regarding gender roles and discriminatory hiring policies influenced the types of jobs and the wages paid for women and racial minorities throughout U.S. history. While non-discrimination policies have been developed over the past 50 years, the work histories of current retirees were influenced by these policies and practices, which continue to disadvantage them in late life through lower Social Security benefits. Further, despite the existence of non-discrimination policies, gender wage gaps continue. Women and racial minorities earn less than white men in similar occupations, so these retirement income gaps can be expected to continue.

Health also influences poverty in late life. People with lifelong health challenges have lower lifetime wages. Lower lifetime wages are caused by disruptions to work history and the inability to continue working in later life. As you will learn more about in Chapter 10, the age at which someone accesses their Social Security benefit influences how much money they will get each month. If someone retires early due to poor health, they will receive a smaller monthly Social Security benefit every month for the rest of their life. Thus, Social Security and other income policies have a strong impact on health outcomes for older adults.

Some people supplement their Social Security benefits with retirement savings programs like 401(k) or 403(b) plans, which are defined contribution plans. This means that the money put in by the employer and employee, and any capital gains, are the limits of the benefits. Once the money is gone, it is gone. Chapter 10 provides a more extensive discussion of pensions and retirement income. The point here is that this insecure retirement savings system puts older adults at risk for further income losses at the oldest ages, just when health challenges and other needs may be increasing. Additionally, many people who worked low-wage jobs during their life lacked access to employer-sponsored retirement benefits. Their income made it difficult or impossible to save sufficient funds for retirement in other forms.

Lifelong access to health insurance is related to both economic security and work history. Health insurance is often connected to employment, with most Americans accessing employer-provided health care. Employer-sponsored health plans do not provide full coverage, and out-of-pocket medical expenses have been on the rise. Medical debt is the number one cause of bankruptcy in the United States, often as the result of a major diagnosis or injury. Due to the link between health insurance and employment, people whose health challenges prevent them from working may lose health coverage in the middle of a serious illness or injury, exacerbating risks for medical debt.

Low-wage workers are often not offered health insurance benefits by their employers, and/or people in low-wage jobs do not work enough hours to qualify for benefits, and/or they are unable to afford the employee-contribution portion of the insurance. This lack of insurance may leave individuals unable to manage health conditions over the life span, leaving them at greater risk for complications. **Health care exchanges**, offered by state governments or the federal government through the Affordable Care Act, allow individuals to purchase health insurance outside of employer-provided benefits. The plans offered through these exchanges must provide a variety of plan options at various price points, but low-wage workers may not be able to afford even a basic plan. Additionally, health care exchanges have only been available since 2010, so they are unlikely to have had a large impact on the current generation of older adults.

Food insecurity refers to the inability to consistently obtain adequate food that appropriately meets your nutritional needs. One current population survey estimates that one in 14 seniors are food insecure (Zilliak &

Gunderson, 2020). These data are based on responses to questions such as: "In the last 12 months, were you ever hungry, but didn't eat because you couldn't afford enough food?" and "In the last 12 months, did you ever eat less than you felt you should because there wasn't enough money for food?" Food insecurity among older adults is primarily associated with inadequate income levels, but mobility and transportation access are also factors (Gualtieri, 2018). Food insecurity can result in malnutrition, poor nutritional options, an inability to control chronic conditions, and worse overall health outcomes.

Housing instability refers to the inability to afford to obtain or maintain appropriate housing to meet one's needs. For older adults, this can occur in a variety of ways. In Detroit in the late 1990s, older adults were housing insecure because of a combination of their income and the devaluation of their homes. They lived in single-family homes they had owned for many years, which would suggest adequate housing. However, these homes were often in need of large and costly repairs, such as new roofs to keep the rain out. These older adults did not have adequate income or savings to finance such repairs. A combination of housing policy problems in Detroit had led to their properties being so **devalued** that they could not get home improvement loans, because their houses did not have enough equity (they were not worth enough) to back the loans. Selling the homes would not support a move into apartment housing, because the condition of the homes and the home equity issue would not give them enough money to pay rent. Thus, many were stuck in homes in poor repair that also increasingly did not meet their needs due to accessibility issues such as stairs and inaccessible kitchens and bathrooms.

Even in places without Detroit's economic issues of the late 1990s, some older adults are housing insecure because they are stuck in single-family homes that no longer meet their needs without viable alternatives. In many cities public housing units for older adults have waiting lists, sometimes years long. Older adults with adequate financial resources can go to privately owned senior housing, continuing care retirement communities (also called life care communities), and assisted living facilities, but these are outside the financial reach of many older Americans. Monthly room and board in an assisted living facility averages $4,000 nationally, with regional variation, and can be much higher if additional personal care services are needed. So for older adults with lower incomes, housing insecurity is a significant health factor.

From a policy perspective, there are many ways these disparities in housing security can be addressed. Home modification grant programs, or other home improvement aid, can help older adults repair and/or upgrade existing homes to meet current needs. Public housing policies should ensure that sufficient units exist for those who need housing. While we will discuss nursing home funding further in Chapters 10 and 11, programs that pay for assistance with home-based care for individuals, before they need the level of care that nursing homes provide, should also be considered.

EDUCATION

The ODPHP (n.d.) includes early childhood education and development; enrollment in higher education; high school graduation; and language and literacy under education. It might appear that these areas are not of concern for older adults, but the reality is that they can be huge influencers of health. An older person's history with early childhood education, high school graduation, and higher education are often indicators of the social and economic conditions in which they grew up and the oppressions that existed at the time. For example, many older women may not have advanced degrees, due to expectations around education for women in the past. There are stories of women in higher education programs who were accused of taking spots from men (Read

Ruth Bader Ginsberg's biography if you have any questions about this one). In other cases, older Blacks may not have had opportunities to earn high school diplomas or go to college, due to educational segregation that existed by law prior to 1954 and in practice for many years after that. Historically Black Colleges and Universities (HBCUs) filled some of this gap, but opportunities were limited by discrimination and income. In turn, a person's educational history and achievements may have had lifelong impacts on their job opportunities and income-earning potential.

Additionally, think back to Mike's story. Because of his education, he had a high level of literacy, and was able to research and to understand information about his medical condition that he was able to translate into health behaviors. Literacy is a predictive factor for disparities in knowledge about health conditions, medication compliance, and access to preventive services (Andrulis & Brach, 2007; Kripalani et al., 2006; DeWalt et al., 2004; Berkman et al., 2011). Mike also speaks English, which is an important factor for health outcomes in the United States (Institute of Medicine, 2004). Therefore, policies that influence access to and quality of education are significant predictors of health outcomes.

SOCIAL AND COMMUNITY CONTEXT

The ODPHP defines social and community context as including civic participation, discrimination, incarceration, and social cohesion. This may seem a disparate collection of factors, but they relate to the connection a person feels to their community and their ability to influence change. People who perceive a greater sense of personal control over their environment have higher levels of well-being than those who perceive constraints in their environment (Gore et al., 2016; ODPHP, n.d.). Further, those who live in environments with constrained opportunities such as those related to education, resources, or older age are more likely to blame external factors for outcomes related to physical and mental health (Gore et al., 2016).

Incarceration is both a symptom of discrimination and a disruptor of social cohesion. In the United States, Black men are more likely to be incarcerated than any other group (Fullilove, 2016; Fullilove & Wallace, 2011). This pattern of incarceration is a result of a series of policies and disproportionate application of those policies that have created upheaval and displacement, particularly among people of color in American cities (Fullilove & Wallace, 2011). "Mass criminalization leads to mass incarceration, which has resulted in a disproportionate amount of African American fathers and mothers being placed behind bars—constituting another form of root shock resulting in broken families and broken communities" (Thorpe et al., 2017, p. 18). This discrimination starts young, with children of color being more likely to be punished in school and to enter the justice system for non-violent behavior such as drug offenses. These students then have criminal records, which are held against them in future cases. This pattern of incarceration disrupts communities of color, impacting older adults who have suffered multiple losses by the time they reach older age. Older adults of color are also more likely to be raising grandchildren and other kin due to incarceration and addiction (Backhouse & Graham, 2013). Policies regarding education, drugs, criminal justice, and enforcement all impact opportunities and risks at the community level, which then impact individuals across the life course.

Racial segregation—the result, in part, of policies of **redlining**, **urban renewal**, and deindustrialization—shapes socioeconomic conditions at the community level, which influences socioeconomic mobility at the individual and family levels (Fullilove & Wallace, 2011; Williams & Collins, 2001).

Whole books have been written about each of these topics, and it is difficult to pay them their appropriate respect in one paragraph. For the purposes of this chapter, it is sufficient to know the definitions of these policies and to consider how they influenced the destruction of community connection.

> **Redlining,** instituted by the federal government's Home Owners Loan Corporation (HOLC) in 1937, was designed to steer investment away from risky places. These were defined as those places with older buildings and non-white residents. Literally, the presence of a single Negro family meant that an area was given the worst possible rating, thus setting up the material basis for white flight. (Fullilove & Wallace, 2011, p. 382)

What this meant was that black families were unable to obtain loans to purchase homes, or were only able to do so at inflated rates, due to the risks associated with their neighborhoods. Both of these together devalued the homes they did own and reduced their ability to build generational wealth (that which could be passed from one generation to another).

Urban renewal, or gentrification, is associated with programs that bought or seized land and property that was considered "**blighted**" (in bad or damaged condition) and sold it to developers. The developers "improved" the land, pricing existing residents out of the neighborhood. Nearly a million people were displaced by federally funded urban renewal programs, and nearly 75% of those were people of color (Fullilove & Wallace, 2011). Challenges with gentrification continue to this day. New investment in under-resourced neighborhoods often results in residents being forced to move to make way for development, or needing to leave because of rising costs. These residents include older people who have lived in those communities for long periods of time.

HEALTH AND HEALTH CARE

Health and health care is an important category of the ODPHP (n.d.) social determinants of health matrix. It includes access to health care, access to primary care, and health literacy. While these topics have been discussed throughout this chapter, this section will discuss the quality and competence of the services provided. Bradley and Taylor (2013) sum up the problem when they describe *America's Health Care Paradox,* in which America pays more for health care relative to its **gross domestic product** (GDP, a standard measure of the economic status of a country) compared to other industrialized nations, but yields poorer health outcomes. One of the reasons for this is that other nations invest more money in preventive services on a community level. In the United States, we only provide government-sponsored health insurance to low-income individuals and older adults, missing key opportunities to invest in preventive care.

There are other issues in addition to access. An earlier section of this chapter discussed the importance of Mike's education and literacy in his ability to manage his own health condition. But that is only part of the equation. The linguistic and cultural competency of the provider is also crucial to the health care experience. This ensures that patients and providers can communicate in ways that promote trust and understanding in both directions. Providers also must understand social determinants of health for effective communication and care.

Here's a great example. A sociologist named Marie Gualtieri conducted a focus group project in a community that had a diabetes rate three times the national average. In her study, Black participants reported that when they were discussing their health with white providers, the providers would ask, "Well, why can't you just eat healthier? Why can't you exercise more? Why can't you just eat foods with less sugar?" But the patients didn't have access to those things, because of the policy barriers discussed in this chapter, and because of nutrition literacy. The participants didn't realize that foods like bread converted to sugars, among other nutritional facts, because no one had ever told them. The doctors' lack of knowledge about the barriers made it more difficult for the participants to feel comfortable discussing their realities, because they felt the doctors just didn't get it. This may be why a National Bureau of Economic Research study had similar findings, in which Black men were more likely to trust the recommendations of Black doctors when randomly assigned to a Black or white doctor (Alsan et al., 2018).

These communication barriers, as well as issues with sensory challenges such as hearing and vision, decrease the effectiveness of the health care older adults access, and make it harder for them and their providers to manage their multiple medical conditions.

NEIGHBORHOOD AND BUILT ENVIRONMENT

The category neighborhood and built environment includes access to foods that support healthy eating patterns; crime and violence; environmental conditions; and quality of housing. The importance of some of these is evident in Mike's story. Mike lives in a suburb with a large selection of grocery stores that carry fresh produce, meats, and other foods that contribute to his ability to manage his chronic condition, and he has a private vehicle to get him there. Many urban and rural areas lack even one grocery store in a reasonable distance. People who live in those areas often rely for food on corner stores that do not carry fresh produce or meats, leaving them to consume canned goods and other processed foods. When grocery stores are further away, residents need reliable transportation to get there. Public transportation may not be available, and even when it is, it may be too challenging to complete a food shopping trip if someone is unable to carry heavy bags on a long walk, as is the case for many older adults.

Neighborhood crime and violence impact health in many different ways. Traumatic events, such as exposure to violence across the life span, are linked to negative health outcomes both tied to and independent from health behaviors such as smoking and alcohol/substance use (Lee & Park, 2018). Additionally, neighborhood crime and violence impact residents' ability to have a safe place to be physically active, as opposed to Mike's ability to bike, walk, and run in his community. Statistics show that while older adults are less likely to be victims of crime, they are more likely to fear being victims of crime, which can lead them to being more homebound if they perceive their neighborhood as unsafe. An additional factor for older adults can be neighborhoods that change over time. An older adult may have purchased a home in a neighborhood that at one time was well maintained and safe. As the neighborhood has deteriorated, they may be stuck in place for reasons related to home equity.

Neighborhood environmental conditions are also related to environmental justice issues. Low-income communities are more likely to be located near environmental hazards such as highways, natural gas lines, oil refineries, and other industrial threats. Within these communities, the oldest and the youngest residents are at risk of the greatest adverse health effects. Exposure to pollutants over time is associated with poorer lung function in older adults, with exposure as a function of both concentration and duration of exposure (Eckel et al., 2012).

Housing quality refers to the condition of the dwellings in which people reside. As in the example of Detroit, this can be things like leaky roofs and other large-scale repairs that residents are unable to make. It can also include factors such as lead paint, which is present in many dwellings built before 1978 (when it was banned federally). Lead paint is a concern in public housing, because young children are more likely to put paint chips in their mouths and suffer lead poisoning. Older adults may have been exposed to lead paint or other industrial hazards in their homes and workplaces throughout life.

HEALTH THROUGH A DIVERSITY AND INTERSECTIONAL LENS: AGE

As we will discuss in Chapter 5, the human body undergoes changes as it ages. Humans reach their physical peak in young adulthood, and many view the physical changes that happen after that as decline, and therefore a lack of health. Yet the experience of decline is not universal, and some people take better care of themselves as they age. For example, a 50-year-old man was working three jobs in his 20s, not exercising, and eating poorly. Now he's a personal trainer, eats a regimented diet, and is in the best shape of his life. He is healthier now than he was when he was younger. He's also more resilient, so when he's had to come back from setbacks like musculoskeletal injuries or even cancer surgery, he has been able to quickly return to his former health and stamina. All this to say that while age may be associated with physical function, it is not fate, and aging does not mean poor health.

Age is a factor in ageism that people experience in health systems. Symptoms are often dismissed due to age, such as when someone experiences pain in a joint and is told that it's to be expected as they age. There's a joke where a patient complains about pain in his right knee, and when the doctor says, "Well, you are 75, and so is your knee," the patient responds, "So is my other knee, and it doesn't hurt!" These age-related differences in care were reported often during COVID-19. Some COVID patients experienced confusion, and older patients were released from the hospital despite this symptom, while younger patients were treated for it. In this case, and many other times, physicians believed that confusion is a normal part of aging.

These examples would make it seem like ageism is based on the attitudes of individual physicians, and thus not subject to being changed through policy. Policy is an important place to start. If medical education were restructured, with an increase in the required variety and type of content about the aging body and mind, more physicians would know about symptom presentations more common in older adults and would know what is normal and what is not when it comes to the aging mind. If this content were required to be on medical board exams, those physicians would commit it to memory. Another policy intervention would be to restructure our healthcare payment system, increasing incentives for primary care to provide preventive care. The current system of 15-minute appointments does not allow patients and doctors to get to know each other. A payment system that favored quality and not frequency of encounters would provide opportunities for providers to get to know their patients, so they could understand when something was a change for that person. Within the restructuring of the primary care system, more time should be allowed for visits, to make sure physical, mental, and cognitive concerns can be addressed comprehensively. Other areas where ageism could be addressed through policy would be to change the requirements of the Food and Drug Administration and not approve medications and treatments until they have been tested on patients of all ages.

WHAT CULTURAL FACTORS INFLUENCE THE DEFINITION OF HEALTH?

The discussion of culture and health is one that must be conducted carefully. While some expressed and unexpressed beliefs about health are rooted in culture, it is important to also recognize that people may not act in particular ways because they are of a particular culture. Overgeneralization and misinformation lead to systemic racism, which in turn results in health disparities, such as the disparities in maternal/child health outcomes that exist in the United States. Black mothers are twice as likely to die in childbirth/related causes as white mothers (Tikkanen et al., 2020), and Black infants are more than twice as likely to die in their first year than white infants, holding all other factors constant—meaning that we account for every other similarity and difference (Office of Minority Health, 2019). While this book focuses on older adults, this example of mothers and babies illustrates how systemic racism can impact a population, and when it impacts the youngest of the population, it leads to worse outcomes for people of color across the life course.

These disparities are evident in data regarding the COVID-19 pandemic in 2020. The National Institute for Health Care Management Foundation (NIHCM Foundation, 2020) reported that individuals who identified as Latinx or Native American were hospitalized at 3.9 times the rate of white Americans for COVID-19, and were dying at 1.5 times the rate. The hospitalization numbers were slightly better for Black Americans, at 3.6 times the rate of white Americans, but they were dying at twice the rate of white Americans. Some of these health disparities were the result of disparities in resources, as a result of policy choices. In the first COVID-19 relief package passed by Congress and signed into law by the president, hospital relief funding was distributed proportionally based on revenue, leaving smaller, less resourced hospitals with a smaller proportion of funding—and those hospitals disproportionately served large numbers of racial minority patients, especially Black patients (NIHCM Foundation, 2020).

Systemic racism in healthcare policy exacerbates problems caused by false individual beliefs. For example, a 2016 study revealed that 40% of first-year white medical students and 25% of white residents believed Black people have thicker skin than white people do (NIHCM Foundation, 2020) and thus feel less pain. These biases reinforce themselves when they are used to guide the creation of new health policies.

HOW DO INTERSECTIONAL IDENTITY FACTORS INFLUENCE THE EXPERIENCE OF HEALTH?

Cultural racism refers to stereotypes, stigma, and biases directed towards particular groups by societal structures (Williams et al., 2019). Institutional racism refers to formal structures, such as segregation, that block some groups from opportunities (Williams et al., 2019). Not all institutional structures are based on current laws and policies. Some are the legacies of earlier policies, such as redlining, which have shaped opportunities for earlier generations in ways that are difficult to overcome. Redlining created the Black/white divide in housing that exists in many areas today. Assumptions regarding why people choose to live in certain neighborhoods, and other structural factors, influence the individual discrimination that people experience in life and in health systems (Williams et al., 2019). As discussed in Chapter 1, **intersectionality** (Crenshaw, 1989) describes how identity factors such as age, race, gender, sexual orientation, marital status, and many more overlap or "intersect." People can be the victims of individual discrimination related to any or all of these factors, often at the same time. You can see this in poverty statistics, where the oldest Black women are at the greatest risk of being in poverty; their income levels are often lower than those of other older adults in poverty.

This discrimination plays out throughout all of the social determinants of health, as well as within the healthcare systems themselves. A person has psychological, biological, and behavioral responses to experiences of discrimination. These responses may lead to differences in health care utilization, based on differences in access and differences in levels of trust based on previous, well-founded experiences (NIHCM Foundation, 2020). All of these combine to influence health outcomes (Williams et al., 2019).

SUMMARY

This chapter has demonstrated how the definition of health is multifaceted and complex and includes both individual and societal factors. On the individual level, health can be defined as a combination of health behaviors and function and the individual's definition of adequate levels of each. As demonstrated by this chapter's examples, there are no absolutes, and people of different ages and different diagnoses can be healthier or sicker than their previous selves.

An individual's health status is influenced by multiple societal factors, called the social determinants of health. Social determinants of health include factors of economic stability, education, social community and context, health and health care, and neighborhood and build environment. These factors, and the subcategories within them, encompass a large range of life and many things that people encounter on a day-to-day basis. Each of these is not addressed by specific health or aging policies, but is strongly influenced by policies across the political spectrum, on the federal, state, and local levels.

Ultimately, health is an interaction of all of these things, including individual characteristics, the social environment, and the healthcare systems to which someone has access. To create effective policy that enhances access and addresses barriers, it is important to understand all of these levels.

KEY TERMS

Blighted

Blood sugar

Devalued

Diabetes

Food insecurity

Glucose

Gross domestic product (GDP)

Health

Health care exchanges

Housing instability

Insulin

Intersectionality

Pack-years

Redlining

Social determinants of health

Type 2 diabetes

Urban renewal

DISCUSSION QUESTIONS

1. Define health for yourself. What does it mean to be healthy? What factors are included (e.g., function, diagnoses, activity level)? Compare and contrast with your classmates' definitions.

2. Name the factors within the social determinants of health. Describe one policy that could address a social risk factor.

3. Discuss structural racism in health care, including what it is and how it impacts health.

4. Compare and contrast the benefits of healthcare systems that focus on primary care/prevention versus treatment and cure.

Ancillary materials for student practice can be found within Active Learning

REFERENCES

Alsan, M., Garrick, O., & Graziani, G. (2018). *Does diversity matter for health? Experimental evidence from Oakland* (Working Paper 24787). National Bureau of Economic Research. http://www.nber.org/papers/w24787

Andrulis, D. P., & Brach, C. (2007). Integrating literacy, culture, and language to improve health care quality for diverse populations. *American Journal of Health Behavior, 31*(Suppl 1), S122–S133. https://www.ncbi.nlm.nih.gov/pmc/articles/PMC5091931/

Backhouse, J., & Graham, A. (2013). Grandparents raising their grandchildren: Acknowledging the experience of grief. *Australian Social Work, 66*(3), 440–454. http://doi.org/10.1080/0312407X.2013.817595

Berkman, N. D., Sheridan, S. L., Donahue, K. E., Halpern, D. J., Viera, A., Crotty, K., Holland, A., Brasure, M., Lohr, K. N., Harden, E., Tant, E., Wallace, I., & Viswanathan, M. (2011). Health literacy interventions and outcomes: An updated systematic review. *Evidence report/technology assessment, 2011*(199), 1–941.

Bradley, E. & Taylor, L. (2013) *The American health care paradox: Why spending more is getting us less.* Public Affairs.

Cowie, C., Casagrande, S. S., & Geiss, L. (2018). Prevalence and incidence of type 2 diabetes and prediabetes. In C. Cowie, S. S. Casagrande, A. Menke, M. Cissel, M. Eberhardt, J. Meigs, E. Gregg, W. Knowler, E. Barrett-Connor, D. Becker, F. Brancati, E. Boyko, W. Herman, B. Howard, K. M. V. Narayan, M. Rewers, & J. Fradkin (Eds.), *Diabetes in America* (3ʳᵈ ed., pp. 3-1-3-32). National Institute of Diabetes and Digestive and Kidney Diseases. National Institutes of Health (NIH Pub. No. 17-1468).

Crenshaw, K. (1989). Demarginalizing the intersection of race and sex: A Black feminist critique of antidiscrimination doctrine, feminist theory and antiracist politics. *University of Chicago Legal Forum, 1989*(1), Article 8, 139–167. http://chicagounbound.uchicago.edu/uclf

DeWalt, D. A., Berkman, N. D., Sheridan, S. L., Lohr, K. N., & Pignone, M. P. (2004). Literacy and health outcomes. *Journal of General Internal Medicine, 19*(12), 1228–1239.

Eckel, S., Louis, T., Chaves, P., Fried, L., & Margolis, H. (2012). Modification of the association between ambient air pollution and lung function by frailty status among older adults in the cardiovascular health study. *American Journal of Epidemiology, 176*(3), 214–223. https://doi.org/10.1093/aje/kws001

Fullilove, M. T. (2016). *Root shock: How tearing up city neighborhoods hurts America, and what we can do about it.* New Village Press.

Fullilove, M. T., & Wallace, R. (2011). Serial forced displacement in American cities, 1916–2010. *Journal of Urban Health, 88*(3), 381–389. https://doi.org/10.1007/s11524-011-9585-2

Gore, J., Griffin, D., & McNierney, D. (2016). Does internal or external control have a stronger link to mental and physical health? *Psychological Studies, 61*(3), 181–196. http://doi.org/10.1007/s12646-016-0361-y

Institute of Medicine. (2004). *Health literacy: A prescription to end confusion.* National Academies Press.

Janjigian, Y., McDonnell, K., Kris, M., Shen, R., Sima, C., Bach, P., Rizvi, N., & Riely, G. (2010). Pack-years of cigarette smoking as a prognostic factor in patients with stage IIIB/IV nonsmall cell lung cancer. *Cancer, 116*(3), 670–675. https://doi.org/10.1002/cncr.24813

Kripalani, S., Henderson, L. E., Chiu, E. Y., Robertson, R., Kolm, P., & Jacobson, T. A. (2006). Predictors of medication self-management skill in a low-literacy population. *Journal of General Internal Medicine, 21*(8), 852–856. http://www.doi.org/10.1111/j.1525-1497.2006.00536.x

Lee, S., & Park, C. (2018). Trauma exposure, posttraumatic stress, and preventive health behaviours: A systematic review. *Health Psychology Review, 12*(1), 75–109. https://doi.org/10.1080/17437199.2017.1373030

Medline Plus. (2021). *Diabetes.* Updated August 2, 2021. https://medlineplus.gov/diabetes.html

NIHCM Foundation. (2020, December 1). *Systemic racism & health care, COVID & treatment.* National Institute for Health Care Management. https://nihcm.org/publications/systemic-racism-health-care-covid-treatment

Office of Disease Prevention and Health Promotion. (n.d.) *Social determinants of health.* Healthy People 2030. U.S. Department of Health and Human Services. Retrieved May 14, 2021 from https://health.gov/healthypeople/objectives-and-data/social-determinants-health

Office of Minority Health. (2019). *Infant mortality and African Americans.* U.S. Department of Health and Human Services. https://minorityhealth.hhs.gov/omh/browse.aspx?lvl=4&lvlid=23

Thorpe, R. J., Jr., Griffith, D. M., Bruce, M. A., & Brown, L. (2017). Racism as a fundamental determinant of health for Black boys. In N. M. Finigan-Carr (Ed.), *Linking health and education for African American students' success* (pp. 13–26). Routledge.

Tikkanen, R., Gunja, M., FitzGerald, M., & Zephyrin, L. (2020). *Maternal mortality and maternity care in the United States compared to 10 other developed countries* (Issue brief). The Commonwealth Fund. https://www.commonwealthfund.org/publications/issue-briefs/2020/nov/maternal-mortality-maternity-care-us-compared-10-countries

Williams, D. R., & Collins, C. (2001). Racial residential segregation: A fundamental cause of racial disparities in health. *Public Health Reports, 116*(5), 404–416.

Williams, D. R., Lawrence, J. A., Davis, B. A., & Vu, C. (2019). Understanding how discrimination can affect health. *Health Services Research, 54*(S2), 1374–1388. https://doi.org/10.1111/1475-6773.13222

Credits

What Happens to Physical Health in Late Life?

INTRODUCTION

Every human body starts with a physical baseline—potential strength, height, speed, and other physical characteristics. Some of this is preordained by genetics. If both of your parents are 5 feet tall, the chances of you being able to do things that make you 6 feet tall are slim to none. The rest of it is modifiable, by things like exercise, diet, activity, and so on. As we saw in Chapter 4, some social structures provide greater or lesser opportunities to modify those factors that are modifiable. Those social structures can restrict or enhance the potential someone starts out with, in the form of maternal nutrition, the availability and quality of prenatal care, parental substance use, and stressors that occur during pregnancy.

Social structures aside, this chapter will provide a comprehensive overview of physical changes in later life by body system. Many of those changes appear to be decline, but for the most part, what that means is that a person's physical baseline is lowered as they age, but they continue to have the potential to change their current physical status through their actions. Even something as simple as walking can be significant. Someone who was sedentary at 60 and takes up a walking program can be fitter and faster at 70 than they were at 60.

But the social determinants can impact the physical status at which someone arrives in later life. For example, people who experienced chronic poverty and/or food insecurity may have eaten meals that were less nutritionally dense than those with consistent sources of food. Low-income individuals who lacked health insurance may have untreated chronic health conditions such as poorly controlled diabetes or hypertension, both of which can damage the circulatory and renal systems as well as vision.

MUSCULOSKELETAL

Changes in the musculoskeletal system are some of the most visible and the most stereotyped for older people. Consider the adage, "What animal walks on four legs in the morning, two legs in the afternoon, and three legs in the evening?" The answer, of course, is humans, referring to our progression from crawling, to walking, to relying on a cane in later life. In a well-honed body, muscles and bones work together to create synchronous movement. If either system declines, however, an older person can experience significant changes in mobility and activity status. In later life, muscle tone becomes more difficult to maintain, requiring more exercise to achieve the same levels of muscle maintenance. In a comparison study conducted in Germany, Keller and Engelhardt (2013) found a significant difference in muscular strength between older and younger subjects matched on other physical attributes. Marcell et al. (2014) found in a longitudinal study (the same subjects measured over time) that regular endurance exercise was not enough to maintain muscle strength across the multi-year study period. Weaker muscles make it more difficult to balance, increasing the risk for falls. Bones become thinner, more prone to fracture, and more difficult to heal.

Osteoporosis and **osteopenia** are more common in later life. According to the NIH Osteoporosis and Related Bone Disorders National Resource Center (2019), osteoporosis is a bone disease which causes decreases in bone density and bone mass. Many people who have osteoporosis don't know they do until they experience a fracture from a seemingly minor fall, or from just going about daily activities such as bending or coughing. Increasing age is a risk factor for osteoporosis, particularly for women, who may begin to develop osteoporosis a year or two before menopause. Another individual-level risk factor for osteoporosis besides age and gender is ethnicity. Non-Hispanic white women and Asian women most commonly experience osteoporosis, though people of all races and genders do get it. Family history has more recently been found to be a risk factor, as are certain co-occurring diseases and the long-term use of certain medications (NIH Osteoporosis and Related Bone Disorders National Resource Center, 2019).

Social factors that increase risk for osteoporosis are poor diet, particularly one low in calcium or vitamin D, smoking, and excessive alcohol use (NIH Osteoporosis and Related Bone Disorders National Resource Center, 2019). Diet is both a behavioral risk factor for osteoporosis and a social factor. Excessive dieting to lose weight increases risk, but so do things like poor protein intake over time, which can be related to poverty and/or chronic food insecurity.

Osteopenia is related to osteoporosis, in that it is a bone disease of weakened bones. The risk factors for osteopenia are identical to those for osteoporosis. According to Harvard Health Publishing (2019), osteopenia and osteoporosis are along the same continuum, with osteopenia being the less severe form of bone density decline. "If you think of bone mineral density as a slope, normal would be at the top and osteoporosis would be at the bottom. Osteopenia, which affects about half of Americans over age 50, would fall somewhere in between" (Harvard Health Publishing, 2019, para. 1). Bone density is tested by way of a special type of x-ray, called dual-energy x-ray absorptiometry (DXA or **DEXA**). The National Osteoporosis Foundation recommends **DEXA scan** testing for all women over age 65 and for postmenopausal women younger than 65 with any of the aforementioned risk factors (Harvard Health Publishing, 2019). There are medications that may help with osteoporosis and osteopenia, as well as exercise and diet changes. Older adults with osteoporosis and osteopenia are at significant risk of injury due to falls, which are more common as someone ages.

In any given year, about 28% of adults over 65 fall (Centers for Disease Control and Prevention [CDC], 2020), due mostly to the declines in muscle mass mentioned above, resulting in more than 36 million falls a year. Other causes of falls in older adults include the sensory and cardiovascular declines that we will discuss in subsequent sections. About 8 million of those 36 million falls result in an injury that requires medical treatment and/or limits activity (CDC, 2020). Understanding the causes of falls and knowing how to prevent them is critical. Each year fall injuries result in about $50 billion in health care costs. That's not counting the financial and personal costs of falls, up to and including death. That's right—about 64 older adults per 100,000 die of a fall each year (CDC, 2020). Musculoskeletal health characteristics such as arthritis and osteoporosis increase the risk for falls (Bergen et al., 2019).

Among the most serious types of falls are hip fractures. They are more likely to occur in older adults because progressive weakness makes older adults more likely to fall sideways (CDC, 2016). The risk for hip fracture increases with age; a woman over the age of 85 is 18 times more likely to have a hip fracture than one who is 65 (Sullivan et al., 2016). Consequences of a hip fracture can be severe—many people who fracture a hip are no longer able to care for themselves (CDC, 2016), and nearly one third will die within a year of a hip fracture (Albrecht et al., 2019). Hip fractures are associated with declines in quality of life, increases in depression, and increases in emotional distress (Amarilla-Donoso et al., 2020). In a rather which-came-first conundrum, antidepressant use is associated with an increased risk of hip fracture (Prieto-Alhambra et al., 2014), so it is particularly important to look for ways to decrease the risk of falling in the first place.

Behavioral changes can reduce the risk for falls, as can certain simple home modifications. Evidence-based exercise classes are effective at strengthening and reducing the risk of falls (a full list of programs can be found on the website of the National Council on Aging). A home visit by an occupational therapist can help identify small but important home modifications, such as the removal of throw rugs and the appropriate placement of bathroom grab bars. Too many older adults are injured when they rely on the towel bar in the bathroom or a piece of furniture for balance and it fails, instead of using a properly placed tool made specifically for that purpose.

While falls, fall-related injuries, and death are very serious consequences of the musculoskeletal declines experienced by some older adults, the way society talks about musculoskeletal declines in older adults is often ableist, as well as ageist.

> Ableism is the discrimination of and social prejudice against people with disabilities based on the belief that typical abilities are superior. At its heart, ableism is rooted in the assumption that disabled people require 'fixing' and defines people by their disability. (Eisenmenger, 2019)

When older adults develop physical disabilities in later life and perhaps require assistive devices for the first time, they are seen as declining or failing in the social discourse. This, of course, assumes that in order to be whole one must be physically able, and discounts those who have used assistive devices throughout their lives. It also discounts the episodic use of assistive devices, such as after an injury or a medical procedure.

Arthritis is a joint disease that can happen at any age. **Osteoarthritis** most often occurs in later life. While growing older is the greatest risk factor for arthritis, older adults do not universally experience it. Osteoarthritis was once thought to be a result of wear and tear on joints that builds up throughout a person's life. The current theory is that age-related musculoskeletal changes increase risk but do not cause osteoarthritis. While osteoarthritis can occur in nearly any joint, the most common are the knee, hip, and hands. Osteoarthritis is characterized by joint pain and stiffness, which may result in difficulty with mobility and activity (Anderson & Loeser, 2011). Mobility difficulties often reduce someone's activity level, resulting in greater musculoskeletal declines.

In sum, changes to the musculoskeletal system are common in later life, but they are not destiny. Lifestyle choices across the life course can influence the type and severity of declines, and changes to diet and exercise in later life can help mitigate or reverse changes that do occur. These "choices" assume social structures that provide access to better nutrition and/or exercise options. Left unchecked, these musculoskeletal changes put older adults at risk for falls, fall-related injury, and early death. The messaging about the inevitability of these musculoskeletal changes may lead some to not take action, as they may feel like it is futile.

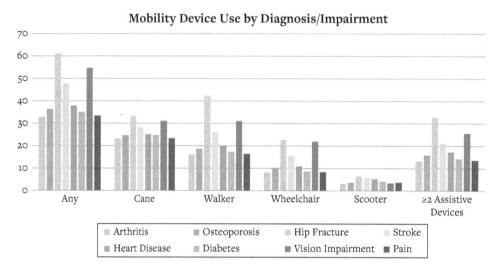

FIGURE 5.1   Mobility Device Use by Diagnosis/Impairment

CARDIOVASCULAR

The cardiovascular system includes the heart and the circulatory system. The heart pumps blood, and the circulatory system consists of the arteries and veins that carry it throughout the body (Medline Plus, 2020a). As people age that system becomes less efficient.

The heart itself is a complex muscle that has a natural **pacemaker** system to control the heartbeat. Over time, this natural pacemaker can be affected by the development of fibrous tissue and other structural changes. These structural changes decrease the pacemaker's functioning, resulting in a slower heart rate (Medline Plus, 2020a). Many older adults address these changes by having an artificial pacemaker implanted in their chest. Artificial pacemakers also help with another age-related change, the development of abnormal heart rhythms, or **arrhythmias**.

In the circulatory system, blood vessels thicken and become more rigid. When the **aorta**—the primary blood vessel that carries blood away from the heart—thickens, the heart has to pump harder. When **capillaries**— the smallest of the blood vessels—thicken, the transfer of nutrients and waste from the blood to the organs and vice versa becomes slower and less efficient. The other thing that happens with blood vessels is that **baroreceptors**, which help blood pressure remain stable and adjust to changes in the environment, become less able to react to change over time. When baroreceptors become less sensitive, some older adults experience changes (drops) in blood pressure when going from sitting to standing (Medline Plus, 2020a). This drop in blood pressure, called **orthostatic hypotension**, also contributes to fall risks for older adults and the resultant complications discussed above. One behavioral change to reduce the risk of falls is to change position slowly. But as you will see in the genitourinary section, many older adults also have greater urgency to use the bathroom, and this is a difficult combination to manage.

Diabetes, a condition we discussed in Chapter 4, causes people to have elevated levels of blood sugar caused by the foods they eat. In someone without diabetes, the pancreas produces insulin, a hormone, which the body uses to turn the glucose in food into energy the body can use. There are two main types of diabetes, type 1 and type 2. In type 1 diabetes, the body does not make insulin. People with type 1 diabetes must rely on synthetic insulin to manage levels of glucose in the blood. Far more common is type 2 diabetes, in which the body does not make or use insulin well (Medline Plus, 2020d). In the United States and around the world, diabetes is extremely common; in fact, it is considered to be one of the most common chronic conditions in existence (Cowie et al., 2018).

Understanding diabetes is critical for those who want to work with older adults and for those who create healthcare policy. Nearly 40% of people who have diabetes are over the age of 65. One in five people over the age of 65 have diabetes, or nearly 8 million people in the United States alone (Laiteerapong & Huang, 2018). As such, many of the costs of diabetes care are borne by Medicare, estimated in 2012 to be $104 billion per year (Laiteerapong & Huang, 2018). While diabetes and the complications from diabetes can impact a person's overall health and well-being in many ways, diabetes is being introduced here in the cardiovascular section because the cardiovascular complications are some of the most visible and disabling. In subsequent sections, you will see some of the other effects as well.

From 10%–20% of people with diabetes experience **peripheral arterial disease** (**PAD**). This condition, which results from the partial or total obstruction of peripheral (outside of the center) arteries, means that circulation to fingers, toes, arms, and legs is reduced or blocked entirely. PAD can cause pain and/or neuropathy. **Peripheral neuropathy**, nerve damage that effects peripheral (outside of the center) nerves or those in the limbs, causes weakness, numbness, and pain in the hands and feet (Mayo Clinic, 2020). This reduction in circulation and nerve damage can result in **diabetic foot ulcers**, or sores on the feet. These ulcers occur because a lack of feeling in the feet keeps people from recognizing when their foot is experiencing pressure or pain, and the lack of circulation inhibits healing of these ulcers once they occur. Complications from diabetic foot ulcers, including infections, often result in lower extremity amputation (Boyko et al., 2018).

Diabetes interacts with social structures and care needs as well. In the United States, there are racial disparities among older adults with diabetes: Black and Hispanic older adults are disproportionately overrepresented (Laiteerapong & Huang, 2018). Diabetes results in increased care needs. Older adults with diabetes are also more likely to experience functional disabilities, such as the inability to walk one quarter of a mile, climb stairs, and do household chores (Laiteerapong & Huang, 2018). Additionally, when older adults with diabetes are dependent on insulin injections, this can impact their ability for self-care, due to the need for visual acuity and manual dexterity to self-monitor blood sugar and inject insulin. As a result, a greater proportion of nursing home residents have diabetes compared to the general population of older adults (Laiteerapong & Huang, 2018).

In sum, changes to the cardiovascular system—including the way the heart pumps blood and the way the body circulates it—may occur in later life, mostly related to the thickening or hardening of vessels and valves. These changes can result in changes to the heart rhythm, increasing the risk for other complications. On a day-to-day basis, changes in blood pressure can increase risk for falls and affect functional status. In addition to changes to the cardiovascular system itself caused by aging, the cardiovascular system can also be damaged by complications caused by diabetes, and diabetes is more prevalent in older adult populations. Complications from diabetes can also decrease functional status and increase morbidity and mortality.

PULMONARY

Pulmonary means related to the lungs. The respiratory system includes the lungs and all of the organs and functions that help someone breathe. As people age, they experience declines in the respiratory system. Beyond the exchange of air, these respiratory system declines also decrease the body's ability to fight off disease in the pulmonary cavity. One of the ways the body fights disease is by expelling foreign objects from the lungs and respiratory system through coughs and sneezes. Some changes to lung function are structural, and are related to musculoskeletal changes that occur in later life. The thoracic cavity, the part of the body that encases and protects the heart and lungs, changes shape, becoming smaller and less elastic (Lowery et al., 2013). The muscles of the body weaken with age, and this includes the muscles that control inhaling and exhaling. This decreases the effectiveness and strength of coughs, impacting the body's ability to clear mucus and foreign objects from the lungs (Lowery et al., 2013). Coughing is also less effective because the nerves that trigger coughing become less sensitive to foreign objects (American Lung Association, 2018).

The lungs of older adults are also at risk due to exposures and health behaviors that occurred across the life course. Smoking is the greatest risk. Smoking is typically measured in pack-years—packs of cigarettes smoked per day, multiplied by the number of years of smoking—so even someone who has smoked rather modestly has accumulated significant ill effects by late life. Lifetime exposure to air pollution is another risk factor. Both indoor and outdoor pollution can damage the lungs (American Lung Association, 2018). Current older adults are at greater risk due to fewer environmental protection standards in their earlier years, and to workplace exposures to asbestos and other chemicals later found to be carcinogenic. People who have lived in poverty are at the greatest risk for environmental exposures, as they are most likely to have worked at-risk jobs, and industrial facilities that release environmental pollutants are more likely to be in poorer neighborhoods.

Chronic obstructive pulmonary disease (**COPD**) is a progressive lung disease that makes it difficult to empty air from the lungs (CDC, 2015). COPD encompasses both emphysema and chronic bronchitis (CDC, 2015). People with COPD are often medically complicated, and their episodes of shortness of breath cause distress in both patients and caregivers (Fried et al., 2012). COPD may interact with physical, psychological, and social conditions including medication side effects, anxiety, and malnutrition (Fried et al., 2012). It is frightening when you feel like you can't breathe! Prevalence of COPD is highest among older adults, though it can occur at any age (CDC, 2015). Across racial and ethnic groups, rates of COPD are highest among those in the lowest-income groups (CDC, 2015), likely reflecting the risk factors outlined in Chapter 4 and some of the social factors that put lung health at risk in general. COPD requires significant medical management, thus is costly to Medicare and to other health systems in general.

RENAL

The term renal means kidney-related but can also refer to the organs associated with elimination, such as the urethra and bladder. In this chapter kidney-related changes will be discussed under renal, and functions associated with elimination under genitourinary. Aging brings both normal, age-related changes to the kidneys and kidney function, and greater risks for several conditions that can impact kidney functioning. The kidney's job is to filter the blood and remove waste from the system. It takes the waste and produces urine, which is stored in the bladder until elimination. The progressive structural deterioration and functional deterioration of the kidney that occur with advancing age are among the most dramatic of any organ system and are in addition to the greater likelihood of kidney injury that comes with growing older (Weinstein & Anderson, 2010). Some normal, age-related kidney changes are related to changes in the cardiovascular system. Older kidneys experience changes in the permeability of capillaries, the smallest of the blood vessels, impacting the rate at which kidneys can absorb waste (Denic et al., 2016). Additionally, arteriosclerosis (hardening of the arteries) in the arteries that feed the kidney can damage the organ itself (Denic et al., 2016). There may be a reduction in the number of functioning neurons in aging kidneys, making them less responsive to changes in the body (Denic et al., 2016). Kidney cysts, non-cancerous growths on the kidney, typically do not interfere with kidney function, but these become more frequent, larger, and more abundant with advancing age (Denic et al., 2016).

The most significant risk to aging kidneys occurs as a result of **diabetes**. One long-term effect of diabetes is kidney damage (American Heart Association, 2020). There are two primary stages: early kidney disease or **renal insufficiency**, when kidney function is reduced by damage such as that from diabetes; and **end-stage renal disease** (**ESRD**) or **kidney failure**, when the kidneys are mostly unable to do their job anymore. Damage to the kidneys occurs as a result of long-term elevated blood sugars (Ghaderian et al., 2015; American Heart Association, 2020) and is also associated with smoking, lack of exercise, and being overweight (American Heart Association, 2020). Renal insufficiency occurs mostly without symptoms and is therefore not diagnosed until the damage is done (American Heart Association, 2020). It is typically diagnosed through the presence of protein in the urine (Ghaderian et al., 2015). It progresses to ESRD when the kidneys are no longer able to do a good job of filtering waste from the blood, such that it builds up in the system (American Heart Association, 2020). People with ESRD require **dialysis**, a procedure in which the blood is filtered by machine. The two types are hemodialysis, which is conducted about three times a week at a center, or peritoneal dialysis, which is done at home. The only permanent solution is a kidney transplant (American Heart Association, 2020). People of any age with ESRD are eligible for Medicare coverage.

GENITOURINARY

Aging can also have an impact on the bladder and the function of elimination. Aging-related changes to muscles and tissues include a decrease in the elasticity of the bladder wall, impacting the ability of the bladder to stretch to contain more urine. Bladder muscles also weaken. Both men and women are susceptible to conditions that may block the **urethra**, the tube that transports urine outside the body. These changes can cause urinary tract infections and bladder control issues (Medline Plus, 2020b). **Urinary incontinence**, a condition in which a person no longer has control over their urination, can decrease quality of life by causing embarrassment or creating reluctance to go out and socialize, for fear that an accident may occur. Urinary incontinence, in conjunction with other disorders mentioned above such as orthostatic hypotension and osteoporosis, can increase risks for falls and injuries.

SENSES

VISION

Late-life changes to vision consist of both general changes and conditions that are more likely to develop in later life. What does this mean? Older adults are likely to experience decreased visual acuity over time (Harvard Health Publishing, 2014) called **presbyopia**, or farsightedness (Medline Plus, 2020c). Like many other conditions, presbyopia is caused by decreases in elasticity in the eye. This makes it more difficult to focus on close objects and to adapt to changes in light (Cavazzana et al., 2018; Medline Plus, 2020c). This difficulty with focusing on nearby objects can make it challenging to participate in lifelong hobbies that require close work, such as needlework, crafts, and the like. In combination with musculoskeletal changes such as arthritis, the loss of these activities can significantly impact quality of life. Problems with glare and with the ability to adjust to changes in light can result in giving up driving, especially at night (Medline Plus, 2020c). Vision changes also create problems with being able to safely get up at night, often to go to the bathroom, and can result in falls.

Older adults are also more likely to develop **cataracts** or **macular degeneration** than younger people (Harvard Health Publishing, 2014). Cataracts cause clouding of the lens of the eye. Macular degeneration is a disease in the part of the eye that is responsible for central vision; this causes vision loss in the central part of the visual field (Medline Plus, 2020c). Older people with diabetes are at risk for additional vision problems related to **diabetic retinopathy**, a disease of the retina which can negatively impact vision (Medline Plus, 2020c).

Vision care in late adulthood is a policy issue. Original Medicare (more on this in Chapter 10) does not cover routine eye exams. Beneficiaries are responsible for the entire cost of the exam and any needed corrective lenses (Medicare.gov, 2020c). Beneficiaries with diabetes are eligible for one annual exam for diabetic retinopathy through Medicare Part B. As with other services covered by Medicare Part B, beneficiaries who do not have supplemental Medicare insurance are responsible for 20% of the cost of services (Medicare.gov, 2020b). This lack of coverage is an issue for older adults, as vision loss can cause significant decreases in quality of life, can compromise the ability to handle instrumental activities of daily living such as medication management, driving, and cooking, and can ultimately impact the ability to live independently.

HEARING

Normal hearing declines begin as early as age 40 or 50. However, they occur gradually, and these declines do not generally impact day-to-day functioning (Harvard Health Publishing, 2014). Hearing loss that impacts social interaction is not normal and can often be treated. Age-related hearing loss is called **presbycusis** (Medline Plus, 2020c). People who experience these losses have challenges hearing high-frequency sounds and differentiating between sounds (Medline Plus, 2020c). Beyond hearing, the health of the ear can impact balance, as key balance receptors are in the ear. Age-related changes to the ear, including an increased likelihood of the buildup of wax, can result in greater fall risk and the aforementioned risks associated with falls. As with vision, Medicare does not cover routine exams for hearing, hearing aids themselves, or visits for fitting/adjusting hearing aids.

Medicare may cover exams ordered by a doctor related to hearing and balance, if the doctor needs them to determine if medical treatment is required (Medicare.gov, 2020d).

TASTE AND SMELL

Taste and smell are different senses, but they often impact people together, as the sense of smell enhances the ability to taste. Smell beings to decline in middle age. This decreased ability to taste may lead to decreased appetite and weight loss, or to increased use of salt and other spices to enhance flavor. While the intake of most spices does not adversely impact health, excessive salt intake can cause elevated blood pressure. Elevated blood pressure increases risks for stroke and heart attack.

While not a sense, eating may also be impacted by changes in dentition. A high percentage of older adults have had at least one cavity (96%) and have gum disease (68%). As a result of these or other dental problems, 13% of people 65–74 and 26% of people over the age of 75 have lost all of their teeth or had them removed. People without teeth and/or those who use dentures may have problems chewing and swallowing fresh, whole foods and may prefer softer, prepared foods (CDC, 2021). Again, Medicare does not cover most dental care. In fact, routine dental care, including cleanings, fillings, tooth extractions, dentures, and more, is not covered at all. According to Medicare.gov (2020a), Medicare will cover hospital care if an older adult needs to be hospitalized for dental care, but it will not cover the dental care itself. As noted, dental problems can cause significant quality-of-life issues as well as weight loss and malnutrition. Low-income older adults are more likely to have challenges in these areas, due to lifelong issues with access to dental care and the inability to afford out-of-pocket costs for dental care in later life.

Policy Spotlight: Medicare and Vision, Hearing, and Dental Coverage

A glaring gap in Medicare coverage exists in the areas of vision, hearing, and dental coverage. None of these are covered under traditional Medicare, leaving some people without the ability to pay for services that have the potential to significantly impact health and quality of life.

Vision: A lack of vision coverage may lead some older adults to delay or avoid routine eye exams, glasses replacement, and treatment for cataracts and macular degeneration. Cataracts and macular degeneration can be treated or slowed, and delayed treatment can result in permanent damage to vision.

Hearing: A lack of coverage for hearing-related services can impact quality of life and cognition. People with hearing loss may be misdiagnosed with cognitive impairment when their responses are incongruous with the questions asked. They may be more likely to develop cognitive loss when they are no longer able to socially engage as well with others. Socialization and cognitive challenges are associated with better brain function in later life.

Dental: A lack of dental coverage may decrease quality of life, and negatively impact health, through poor diet and reduced ability to eat. Lack of dental care can result in pain, self-consciousness about appearance, and malnutrition related to an inability to eat proper foods. Problems with chewing can also increase the risk of choking, especially combined with decreases in cough.

TOUCH

Touch is how your body receives and interprets pain, temperature, pressure, vibration, and body position in the world (Medline Plus, 2020c). As people age, the sensations they experience may be reduced. Some of this change may be attributed to decreased blood flow to nerve endings (a circulatory change) or to health problems such as nutritional deficiencies (Medline Plus, 2020c). Nutritional deficiencies can be caused by social problems such as food insecurity (Chapter 4) or decreased appetite resulting from changes in taste (above). Changes in the sense of touch can increase the risk of injury—for example, burns can occur when the skin is less sensitive to heat/pain and slower to react, and falls can occur when someone has more difficulty sensing the floor or their position in space.

Cavazzana et al. (2018) found that while sense declined overall with age, there were no specific correlations between age and sensory loss, meaning that this loss is not universal, and that not all older adults experience sensory impairment at the same rate. Additionally, their findings suggest distinct causes for each type of sensory decline; someone may have decline in one area but not in another.

Case Study: Marge, Carolyn, and John

Marge worked her whole life as a custodian at an office building and barely made enough to make ends meet. As she entered her 60s, she started to have trouble pushing her cart and standing for her whole shift. She retired and began collecting Social Security. She never owned a car and had to take the bus to go grocery shopping and to the doctor. Her increasing weakness made it harder to carry groceries or walk long distances. Used to being around people all day, she began spending more time at home because it was hard to get around. The lack of mobility meant she was sitting more. She gained weight, which made it even harder to move around. Her weight, her poor diet, and her immobility put her at significant risk for falls.

Carolyn retired from an office job after many years. She exercised regularly and enjoyed an active life of outings with friends, travel, and dinners out. Carolyn didn't know it, but she also had diabetes. The first clue was tingling in her hands and feet. Once she went to see her doctor she was quickly diagnosed, and she had to make substantial lifestyle changes. It was much harder to go out with her friends because she needed to pay close attention to her diet. She found it harder to travel because she relied on insulin, which needed refrigeration. The changes in her life made her very depressed, and she began to isolate herself from her friends.

John's goal was to continue working as long as he could at his job as a high-powered attorney. But his vision was making the work more difficult, and he nearly made a mistake that would have cost his client thousands of dollars when he could not clearly see the page. Luckily a junior attorney with the firm caught the mistake in time, but the incident embarrassed John. John was also starting to have trouble with needing to urgently use the bathroom, and he was always afraid that he would have to go during court hearings. He nearly had an accident one day when a judge didn't call for recess in time. His anxiety about it distracted him from his work and had him starting to think about retiring even though he didn't know what he would do without his work.

SUMMARY

Late adulthood is often seen as a period of decline, and it is understandable that after reading this chapter, you might still hold this view. Aging does increase the risks for decline across a number of body systems, and ill health can often have a cascading effect when decline in one area leads to declines in others—such as an injury leading to a fear of falling, leading to deconditioning, which increases the risks of another fall or of declines in cardiovascular and/or pulmonary health. As this chapter has demonstrated, those risks also interact with the social risk factors discussed in Chapter 4.

Yet not all older adults experience significant decline, and many more people live healthy and independent lives than those who do not. For example, most people think that the majority of older adults live in nursing homes. The truth is that while about a quarter of older adults may end up in a nursing home at some point in their lives, often for rehabilitation and/or recuperation, at any given time less than 5% of people over age 65 live in nursing homes. Many conditions older adults face are chronic conditions, and quality of life is dependent on having access to a coordinated care system that can provide appropriate disease management.

Currently, the policies that regulate healthcare payments and systems (more on this in Chapter 10) are fragmented, leaving older adults and their families to negotiate a system that prioritizes encounters and treatments, and that favors specialists over primary care. While older adults would benefit from more geriatricians who could treat them as whole people, more often they are treated by doctors who see them as the sum of their parts—a cardiologist, an endocrinologist, a pulmonologist, and so on. Effective policy interventions would focus on increasing coordination and decreasing not only costs, but also the burden of navigation, for patients and families.

KEY TERMS

Aorta

Arrhythmias

Arthritis

Baroreceptors

Capillaries

Cataracts

Chronic obstructive pulmonary disease (COPD)

DEXA Scan

Diabetes

Diabetic foot ulcers

Diabetic retinopathy

Dialysis

End-stage renal disease (ESRD)

Kidney failure

Macular degeneration

Orthostatic hypotension

Osteoarthritis

Osteopenia

Osteoporosis

Pacemaker

Peripheral arterial disease (PAD)

Peripheral neuropathy

Presbycusis

Presbyopia

Renal insufficiency

Urethra

Urinary incontinence

DISCUSSION QUESTIONS

1. Some health conditions that older adults face are influenced by access and actions in younger life. How can policy makers create systems that treat health from a life course perspective?

2. Imagine you are a policy maker and could redesign the Medicare system. Based on what you know from this chapter alone, what services would you include?

3. Think about your current home. Would you be able to age in place there? Why or why not? What changes would need to be made for that to happen?

4. Discuss the difference between aging with a disability and becoming disabled in later life. What challenges might each group face, and how can they both be addressed by the same policies?

Ancillary materials for student practice can be found within Active Learning

REFERENCES

Albrecht, J. S., Al Kibria, G., Gruber-Baldini, A., & Magaziner, J. (2019). Risk of mortality in individuals with hip fracture and traumatic brain injury. *Journal of the American Geriatrics Society, 67*(1), 124–127. https://doi.org/10.1111/jgs.15661

Amarilla-Donoso, F. J., López-Espuela, F., Roncero-Martín, R., Leal-Hernandez, O., Puerto-Parejo, L. M., Aliaga-Vera, I., Toribio-Felipe, R., & Lavado-García, J. M. (2020). Quality of life in elderly people after a hip fracture: A prospective study. *Health and Quality of Life Outcomes, 18*(71), 1–10. https://doi.org/10.1186/s12955-020-01314-2

American Heart Association. (2020). *Kidney disease and diabetes.* https://www.heart.org/en/health-topics/diabetes/diabetes-complications-and-risks/kidney-disease--diabetes

American Lung Association. (2018). *Your aging lungs.* https://www.lung.org/blog/your-aging-lungs

Anderson, A. S., & Loeser, R. (2011). Why is osteoarthritis an age-related disease? *Best Practices in Clinical Rheumatology, 24*(1), 15. https://doi.org/10.1016/j.berh.2009.08.006

Bergen, G., Stevens, M. R., Kakara, R., & Burns, E. R. (2019). Understanding modifiable and unmodifiable older adult fall risk factors to create effective prevention strategies. *American Journal of Lifestyle Medicine.* https://doi.org/10.1177/1559827619880529

Boyko, E., Monteiro-Soares, M., & Wheeler, S. (2018). Peripheral arterial disease, foot ulcers, lower extremity amputations, and diabetes. In C. Cowie, S. S. Casagrande, A. Menke, M. Cissel, M. Eberhardt, J. Meigs, E. Gregg, W. Knowler, E. Barrett-Connor, D. Becker, F. Brancati, E. Boyko, W. Herman, B. Howard, K. M. V. Narayan, M. Rewers, & J. Fradkin (Eds.), *Diabetes in America* (3rd ed., pp. 20-1–20-34). National Institute of Diabetes and Digestive and Kidney Diseases. National Institutes of Health (NIH Pub. No. 17-1468).

Cavazzana, A., Röhrborn, A., Garthus-Niegel, S., Larsson, M., Hummel, T., & Croy, T. (2018). Sensory-specific impairment among older people. An investigation using both sensory thresholds and subjective measures across the five senses. *PLoS One, 13*(8), e0202969. https://doi.org/10.1371/journal.pone.0202969

Centers for Disease Control and Prevention. (2015). *Chronic obstructive pulmonary disease among adults aged 18 and over in the United States, 1998-2009.* National Center for Health Statistics. https://www.cdc.gov/nchs/products/databriefs/db63.htm

Centers for Disease Control and Prevention. (2016). *Hip fractures among older adults.* Home and Recreational Safety. https://www.cdc.gov/home-andrecreationalsafety/falls/adulthipfx.html

Centers for Disease Control and Prevention. (2020). *Falls data.* Older Adult Fall Prevention. https://www.cdc.gov/falls/data/index.html

Centers for Disease Control and Prevention. (2021). *Oral health for older Americans.* https://www.cdc.gov/oralhealth/basics/adult-oral-health/adult_older.htm

Cowie, C., Casagrande, S. S., & Geiss, L. (2018). Prevalence and incidence of type 2 diabetes and prediabetes. In C. Cowie, S. S. Casagrande, A. Menke, M. Cissel, M. Eberhardt, J. Meigs, E. Gregg, W. Knowler, E. Barrett-Connor, D. Becker, F. Brancati, E. Boyko, W. Herman, B. Howard, K. M. V. Narayan, M. Rewers, & J. Fradkin (Eds.), *Diabetes in America* (3rd ed., pp. 3-1–3-32). National Institute of Diabetes and Digestive and Kidney Diseases. National Institutes of Health (NIH Pub. No. 17-1468).

Denic, A., Glassock, R., & Rule, A. (2016). Structural and functional changes with the aging kidney. *Advances in Chronic Kidney Disease, 23*(1), 19–28. https://doi.org/10.1053/j.ackd.2015.08.004

Eisenmenger, A. (2019). *Ableism 101: What it is, what it looks like, and what we can do to fix it.* Access Living. https://www.accessliving.org/newsroom/blog/ableism-101/

Fried, T. R., Vaz Fragoso, C. A., & Rabow, M. W. (2012). Caring for the older person with chronic obstructive pulmonary disease. *JAMA, 308*(12), 1254–1263. https://doi.org/10.1001/jama.2012.12422

Ghaderian, S. B., Hayati, F., Shayanpour, S., & Mousavi, S. S. B. (2015). Diabetes and end-stage renal disease; a review article on new concepts. *Journal of Renal Injury Prevention, 4*(2), 28–33. https://doi.org/10.12861/jrip.2015.07

Harvard Health Publishing. (2014). *How our senses change with age.* Harvard Medical School. https://www.health.harvard.edu/healthy-aging/how-our-senses-change-with-age

Harvard Health Publishing. (2019). *Osteopenia: When you have weak bones, but not osteoporosis.* Harvard Medical School. https://www.health.harvard.edu/womens-health/osteopenia-when-you-have-weak-bones-but-not-osteoporosis

Keller, K., & Engelhardt, M. (2013). Strength and muscle mass loss with aging process. Age and strength loss. *Muscle, Ligaments, and Tendons Journal, 3*(4), 346–350. https://pubmed.ncbi.nlm.nih.gov/24596700/

Laiteerapong, N., & Huang, E. (2018). Diabetes in older adults. In C. Cowie, S. S. Casagrande, A. Menke, M. Cissel, M. Eberhardt, J. Meigs, E. Gregg, W. Knowler, E. Barrett-Connor, D. Becker, F. Brancati, E. Boyko, W. Herman, B. Howard, K. M. V. Narayan, M. Rewers, & J. Fradkin (Eds.), *Diabetes in America* (3rd ed., pp. 16-1–16-26). National Institute of Diabetes and Digestive and Kidney Diseases. National Institutes of Health (NIH Pub. No. 17-1468).

Lowery, E. M., Brubaker, A. L., Kuhlmann, E., & Kovacs, E. J. (2013). The aging lung. *Clinical Interventions in Aging, 2013*(8), 1489–1496. https://doi.org/10.2147/CIA.S51152

Marcell, T., Hawkins, S., & Wiswell, R. (2014). Leg strength declines with advancing age despite habitual endurance exercise in active older adults. *Journal of Strength and Conditioning Research, 28*(2), 504–513. https://doi.org/10.1519/JSC.0b013e3182a952cc

Mayo Clinic. (2020). *Peripheral neuropathy.* https://www.mayoclinic.org/diseases-conditions/peripheral-neuropathy/diagnosis-treatment/drc-20352067

Medicare.gov. (2020a). *Dental services.* Medicare. https://www.medicare.gov/coverage/dental-services

Medicare.gov. (2020b). *Eye exams (for diabetes).* Medicare. https://www.medicare.gov/coverage/eye-exams-for-diabetes

Medicare.gov. (2020c). *Eye exams (routine).* Medicare. https://www.medicare.gov/coverage/eye-exams-routine

Medicare.gov. (2020d). *Hearing & balance exams.* Medicare. https://www.medicare.gov/coverage/hearing-balance-exams

Medline Plus. (2020a). *Aging changes in the heart and blood vessels.* U.S. National Library of Medicine. https://medlineplus.gov/ency/article/004006.htm

Medline Plus. (2020b). *Aging changes in the kidneys and bladder.* U.S. National Library of Medicine. https://medlineplus.gov/ency/article/004010.htm

Medline Plus. (2020c). *Aging changes in the senses.* U.S. National Library of Medicine. https://medlineplus.gov/ency/article/004013.htm

Medline Plus. (2020d). *Diabetes.* U.S. National Library of Medicine. https://medlineplus.gov/diabetes.html

NIH Osteoporosis and Related Bone Disorders National Resource Center. (2019). *Osteoporosis overview.* National Institutes of Health, National Institute of Arthritis and Musculoskeletal and Skin Diseases. https://www.bones.nih.gov/health-info/bone/osteoporosis/overview

Prieto-Alhambra, D., Petri, H., Goldenberg, S. B., Khong, T. P., Klungel, O. H., Robinson, N. J., & De Vries, F. (2014). Excess risk of hip fractures attributable to the use of antidepressants in five European countries and the USA. *Osteoporosis International, 25*, 847–855. https://doi.org/10.1007/s00198-013-2612-2

Sullivan, K., Husak, L., Altebarmakian, M., & Brox, W. T. (2016). Demographic factors in hip fracture incidence and mortality rates in California, 2000–2011. *Journal of Orthopaedic Surgery and Research, 11*(4), 1–10. https://doi.org/10.1186/s13018-015-0332-3

Weinstein, J. R., & Anderson, S. (2010). The aging kidney: Physiological changes. *Advances in Chronic Kidney Disease, 17*(4), 302–307. https://doi.org/10.1053/j.ackd.2010.05.002

Credit

Fig. 5.1: Source: https://agsjournals.onlinelibrary.wiley.com/doi/10.1111/jgs.13393.

6

What Cognitive and Mental Health Challenges Can Impact Older Adulthood?

INTRODUCTION

Failing memory in later life is often the punch line of a joke or the inside of a greeting card. When a younger person loses their keys or forgets what they went into a room for, it is called a "senior moment" and laughed off. Ageism, like many other isms, gets under the skin in ways that impact outcomes. If people who believe that failing memory is a part of aging begin to have more forgetful moments, they may avoid talking to their doctor or their family because of stigma or fear. Treatable, reversible causes of memory loss may go unaddressed until it is too late because patients and providers believe they are a normal part of aging. Like physical changes, cognitive changes do occur in later life, but dementia is not a normal part of aging. This chapter will discuss these feared and misunderstood age-related changes, including Alzheimer's disease, other dementias, depression, and delirium, and how policy addresses associated concerns.

CHAPTER-LEVEL LEARNING OBJECTIVES

By the end of this chapter, students will be able to

1. Compare and contrast dementia, delirium, and depression, and explain why it is important to know the difference.

2. Understand normal, age-related cognitive changes and how they are different from dementia, depression, and delirium.

3. Discuss three policies that address cognitive and mental health in later life.

AGE-RELATED COGNITIVE CHANGES

Age-related cognitive changes are those changes that a natural part of growing older. Not all of these changes are bad. These changes do impact memory but not in the stereotypical ways that most people think. They also impact processing speed, executive functioning, and language (Zelinski et al., 2011).

Processing speed is the amount of time it takes someone to perceive and interpret incoming stimuli and react. Changes in processing speed are most visible in situations like driving, where it might take an older person longer to react to changing traffic conditions (Zelinski et al., 2011). When someone is observed as experiencing changes in reaction time, it is important to appropriately assess whether those changes are related to slowing of processing speed, whether they are related to sensory changes such as hearing or vision loss, or whether they are related to musculoskeletal changes. When one is mistaken for the other, appropriate treatments like hearing aids or glasses may not be offered.

Executive functioning, the ability to sequence steps and follow instructions (Hazlett et al., 2015), is required to perform tasks such as Activities of Daily Living (ADLs). This is critical for an older adult's ability to live alone and take care of themselves. Just think about how many steps it takes to get dressed! Well-developed executive functioning allows someone to create a plan, monitor progress, switch between tasks, and control competing responses (Zelinski et al., 2011). Older adults, in general, have demonstrated decreased ability in sequencing and series tasks (Zelinski et al., 2011). For most older adults this decline is mild, and they retain the ability to complete ADLs, and to do sequencing tasks such as following a recipe. When someone is no longer able to do these things, more evaluation is needed, as losing the ability to complete self-care tasks is beyond typical age-related change.

Language challenges in later life are associated with age-related declines in **working memory**. Working memory is the part of thought that allows someone to temporarily store information and manipulate it, like you do when you are learning new information or studying for a test (Zelinski et al., 2011). Declines in working memory make it more difficult for someone to learn new things, particularly things that require memorization. Thus, they can impact someone's ability to take in or to create complex written and spoken language. This does not mean that older adults are unable to learn, write, or speak. It just means that it might take them longer to do these things than it did when they were younger. Depending on their own prior performance levels, older people may still be better or faster than younger people on these tasks. As with executive functioning, when language deficits appear, a person should first be assessed for hearing and vision loss. When someone cannot clearly hear all parts of a conversation, for example, their replies may be unrelated or nonsensical but may not be a product of cognitive decline.

Age-related cognitive changes happen because people experience gradual loss of brain volume over time. Particular deficits are associated with loss of brain volume in particular areas. Specifically, language-related declines are associated with losses in brain volume that occur across many areas of the brain, followed by memory, while other types of decline are associated with brain volume losses in more specific regions (Armstrong et al., 2020). It is important not to treat everyone over the age of 65 the same way. The risk for cognitive impairment increases with increasing age, and cognitive function does not remain the same over time (Huang et al., 2019).

How people feel about or interpret their own memory impairment is often what drives them to seek evaluation at a memory clinic (Haussmann et al., 2018). First-degree relatives, such as children or siblings, of those with Alzheimer's disease are more likely to report memory changes in themselves than people without relatives with Alzheimer's disease. It is not clear whether this greater likelihood to report their own memory changes is related to early stage Alzheimer's disease; depression, which is associated with early dementia; or their own perceptions about their memory loss because of their family history (Haussmann et al., 2018). There is some association between education level and how cognitive impairment manifests. Older adults with higher education levels are more likely to report problems with learning new information, while individuals with less education are more likely to report declines in recall and short- and long-term memory. However, overall, declines in learning are seen as a transitional phase between normal cognitive function and cognitive impairment (Huang et al., 2019).

Physical activity, cognitive stimulation, and socialization are all associated with better cognitive outcomes in older adults, meaning that older adults who are active, physically and intellectually engaged, and involved in interactions with others do better. Meaningful engagement through productive activities enhances self-worth. Socially engaged older adults are also more likely to be physically active. Social engagement helps older adults maintain cognitive status over time (Lee & Yeung, 2019). One study found that different types of activities were more beneficial according to gender (fraternal/alumni organizations for men, and religious activities for women), but this was in a Korean population, so we should be careful not to generalize to other populations (Lee & Yeung, 2019). Religious organizations may have additional benefits, such as community engagement, and socialization is better for cognitive status. The benefits of cognitive stimulation have been observed in both behavioral studies and brain imaging. Duda and Sweet (2020), for example, saw increased activity on the brain following a program of cognitive training.

From a policy perspective, keeping older adults physically and mentally active in the first place is less costly than providing care to those who need assistance due to physical and cognitive impairments. Programs of the **Older Americans Act (1965)** already support many of these types of programs, such as congregate and home-delivered meals, job training, and health promotion, but more funding is always needed (National Council on Aging, 2020). Older Americans Act programs will be discussed in more detail in subsequent units.

ALZHEIMER'S AND RELATED DEMENTIAS

The terms **Alzheimer's disease** and dementia are often misunderstood in that they are mistakenly used interchangeably. Dementia is an umbrella term that encompasses many conditions, including but not limited to Alzheimer's disease. Thus Alzheimer's is always dementia, but dementia is not always Alzheimer's. The Alzheimer's Association (2021f) says the term **dementia** can be used to describe conditions that cause "loss of memory, language, problem-solving and other thinking abilities that are severe enough to interfere with daily life" (para 1). This interference with daily life is the primary way dementia is different than the age-related changes discussed in the last section. Of the dementias, Alzheimer's disease has received the most funding, the most research, and the most publicity. It is also the most common. Other types of dementia include **Lewy body dementia, frontotemporal dementia**, and **vascular dementia. Huntington's disease** and **Parkinson's disease** can also cause dementia or dementia-related symptoms, as can extreme alcohol use (**Korsakoff('s) syndrome**). While each of these dementias is progressive and degenerative, each type has a different presentation and different symptoms and complications.

Senile dementia has long been described as a brain pathology resulting in cognitive, behavioral, and personality changes, but the causes of that senility were generally elusive (Chaufan et al., 2012). Researchers thought then and know now that people with **Alzheimer's disease** develop neurofibrillary tangles, which are accumulations of tau protein inside neurons in the brain, and plaques, which are collections of beta-amyloid proteins between neurons (National Institute on Aging, 2017a). In the 1970s a researcher named Dr. Robert Katzman suggested that what had been diagnosed as senile dementia was really Alzheimer's disease, which then made Alzheimer's disease the fourth or fifth leading cause of death, prompting national attention (Chaufan et al., 2012). Of all the dementias, Alzheimer's disease has received the greatest policy attention, as evidenced by U.S. congressional hearings on the topic as early as 1980 and legislation that supported research into cures. While cures are important, this has kept the policy focus away from the needs of caregivers (Chaufan et al., 2012).

Alzheimer's disease develops gradually; thus, family members and friends may not notice that something has changed until much time has passed. Alzheimer's may present with depressive mood and sometimes with changes to the sleep cycle. The most important symptom is changes in memory that are worse than the person thinks they are, and that do not improve with cueing or prompts (Bottino et al., 2011). People with Alzheimer's disease also experience deficits in executive functioning (Hazlett et al., 2015). Family history is associated with both subjective memory changes (Haussmann et al., 2011) and poorer performance on executive functioning tests (Hazlett et al., 2015). In addition, people with Alzheimer's disease who score better on executive functioning in the early stages of the disease have better rates of survival at 5 years, suggesting that executive functioning is an important component in overall health (Zhou et al., 2010).

Early-onset Alzheimer's disease is that which occurs in people under the age of 65. While there are fewer younger people with early-onset Alzheimer's than older people, and they are outside the scope of this book, they are important to mention when considering policy because they have unique caregiving needs and challenges that older people with Alzheimer's disease do not face, such as work, retirement, and caring for younger children. Among younger people, people with lower cognitive scores or those with a family history of Alzheimer's disease experience worse outcomes (Velayudhan et al., 2020).

Historically, Alzheimer's was only able to be conclusively diagnosed after death when autopsies revealed the signature plaques and tangles in the brain, the long-accepted biomarker of the disease. Also, all dementia that was not due to another apparent cause was labeled Alzheimer's (Knopman et al., 2019). As brain imaging, lab tests, and methods of diagnosing Alzheimer's disease become more advanced, they may lead at some point to a more specific clinical definition of what constitutes Alzheimer's and how it is different than other types of dementia (Knopman et al., 2019). At this point, the types of dementia that we know about beyond Alzheimer's are listed below.

Lewy body dementia is similar to Alzheimer's disease, in that it is a progressive disease and that it is caused by protein deposits in the brain (Alzheimer's Association, 2021d). The Alzheimer's Association (2021d) reports that 5%–10% of all dementia cases are Lewy body dementia, making it the third most common type of dementia, after Alzheimer's and vascular dementia. Symptoms of Lewy body dementia include anxiety, fluctuation in consciousness, **Parkinsonism,** visual hallucinations, and sleep disturbance (Shea et al., 2015). Parkinsonism is a combination of movement symptoms often associated with Parkinson's disease that include rigid muscles, shuffling gait, and problems with starting movements (Alzheimer's Association, 2021d). Lewy body dementia is difficult to diagnose because its symptoms overlap with those of Alzheimer's disease and Parkinson's disease (Vergouw et al., 2020), and many people with Lewy body dementia also have family histories of both Alzheimer's and Parkinson's disease. As with other forms of dementia, proper diagnosis is important, because it suggests appropriate treatments and anticipated course. With advances in science, Lewy body dementia is able to be diagnosed using both clinical and genetic markers (Vergouw et al., 2020). Even with proper diagnosis, survival rates are shorter in those with familial Lewy body dementia.

Frontotemporal dementia is different from Alzheimer's disease and Lewy body dementia because it targets specific areas of the brain. As the name implies, those areas are the frontal lobe (in the front) and the temporal region (around the ears). Since these areas control behavior, behavior changes are an early warning sign. Frontotemporal dementia is also more likely to occur in younger people than Alzheimer's is. While Alzheimer's is most common in people over age 65, frontotemporal dementia is often diagnosed in people between the ages of 40 and 60 (Alzheimer's Association, 2021b). Symptoms of frontotemporal dementia include apathy and behavioral inhibition (Shea et al., 2015). Additionally, people with frontotemporal dementia experience language problems, such as difficulty with making sense when they speak, understanding others, or reading, while people with Alzheimer's disease may have more trouble finding the right word (Alzheimer's Association, 2021b).

Vascular dementia is dementia that is caused by disruptions of blood flow to the brain due to a variety of *vascular*, or blood-vessel-related, conditions (Alzheimer's Association, 2021e; University of California San Francisco, 2021). Conditions that can cause vascular dementia include acute problems such as stroke, or chronic problems such as diabetes, high cholesterol, and high blood pressure (University of California San Francisco, 2021). Vascular dementia is less predictable than other types of dementia, as symptoms vary based on the specific parts of the brain that are affected, and based on whether impacts are the result of a major infarct (stroke) or smaller, less detectable assaults. Stroke symptoms include confusion, disorientation, speech and comprehension problems, and problems with balance and walking (Alzheimer's Association, 2021e). On the other hand, symptoms related to chronic, widespread blood vessel damage include inappropriate or uncontrolled laughing and/or crying, worsening attention span, and problems with word finding (Alzheimer's Association, 2021e). Of the dementias, vascular dementia has the most social and behavioral risk factors, some of which are modifiable and some of which are not. Vascular dementia is associated with age and obesity status. Smoking, lack of physical activity, and unhealthy diet, all risk factors for vascular dementia, may lead to obesity, but they are not all one and the same. Obesity may be related to medical conditions. Health behaviors may be related to social factors discussed in Chapter 4.

Korsakoff syndrome (also written as Korsakoff's syndrome) is a form of dementia caused by vitamin B1 (thiamin) deficiency, most often related to chronic alcohol use and abuse. Symptoms of Korsakoff's syndrome include periodic memory disruptions, uncontrolled eye movements, and gait disruptions. Unique to the memory disruptions of Korsakoff's syndrome are confabulations, when people who do not remember fabricate stories to fill in the gaps (Alzheimer's Association, 2020c; Bottino et al., 2011).

Huntington's disease and **Parkinson's disease** are different from the other conditions discussed here because they are not dementia in and of themselves. Instead, in these conditions, dementia-like symptoms occur as a part of a larger spectrum of disease symptoms. **Huntington's disease** is a progressive, degenerative, genetic disease, most often impacting adults between the ages of 30 and 50 (Huntington's disease Society of America [HDSA], 2021). Huntington's is caused by an error in the DNA replication instructions in the body that, over time, damages the brain. Huntington's has many symptoms that impact movement, gait, personality, and mood. As with dementia, people with Huntington's may develop forgetfulness and impaired judgement. The course of Huntington's typically ranges from 10 to 25 years, meaning that most Huntington's patients do not reach later life (HDSA, 2021). Huntington's patients also almost universally require full-time care for activities of daily living, and due to the typical age of onset, may have young children for whom they are responsible at the time of diagnosis.

Parkinson's disease most often develops around the age of 60, though somewhere between 5%–10% of people with Parkinson's develop it before age 50. That said, Parkinson's mostly impacts older adults. Parkinson's is a brain disease that occurs when neurons in the area that controls movement die out for unknown reasons. Like Alzheimer's symptoms, Parkinson's symptoms develop gradually and might not be noticed at first, and they do get worse over time. Like Huntington's, Parkinson's impacts movement, speech, behavior, and sleep (National Institute on Aging, 2017b). Parkinson's disease is associated with parkinsonism (above), the parkinsonian gait that includes difficulty initiating movement, small steps, and reduced swinging of arms while walking (National

Institute on Aging, 2017b). Important for this chapter are the cognitive and mental health changes associated with Parkinson's. Parkinson's may result in depression, emotional changes, and difficulty with speech and communication (National Institute on Aging, 2017b).

Racial disparities exist in the prevalence of dementia and the prevalence of the risk factors for vascular dementia. These differences may be attributed to many things including biological, behavioral, and socioeconomic factors. Additionally, socioeconomic factors may be attributed to structural racism, which creates differences in opportunities for people of different backgrounds. Without examining the causes, Chen and Zissimopoulos (2018) found that while the prevalence of dementia as a proportion of the population appears to be declining, the rates among some groups, specifically Hispanics, are declining much more slowly than for whites or Blacks. They also found that Blacks are still more than twice as likely to have dementia compared to whites. The National Institute on Aging (2018) estimates that 13% of Hispanics over the age of 65 have some form of dementia; this group's rate of dementia is higher than that of non-Hispanic whites but lower than that of Blacks. Some researchers posit that these differences can be attributed to differences in perceptions of normal, age-related cognitive changes; delays in seeking medical treatment, either because of these perceptions or because of the quality of care available; and the level of trust between patients and their doctors (Chin et al., 2011). All of these reasons have potential policy solutions that should be considered when addressing dementia.

CAREGIVING FOR PEOPLE WITH DEMENTIA

Dementia is of significant concern for caregivers because as a progressive degenerative disease it will, by nature, get worse, and some of those changes may make caregiving very challenging. Dementia caregiving also includes physical, mental, and emotional aspects. Caregiving looks different at the beginning, middle, and later stages of the disease. Because dementia impacts the brain, it impacts decision-making and safety. However, because people with dementia are adults who have been independent for some time, it may be unclear when someone is no longer safe to drive because they might get lost or overwhelmed, or no longer safe to manage money, or no longer safe to cook.

Early-stage dementia refers to the period following diagnosis, when symptoms tend to be mild and the person with dementia is generally able to take care of their daily needs. In this stage, a caregiver generally provides emotional and instrumental support (such as cues and direction) while remaining alert for potential safety concerns and changes in mood or cognition (Alzheimer's Association, 2021a). In this stage it is important for caregivers and people with dementia to engage in planning for the future, such as creating **advance directives** for health care and appointing **power of attorney** for both health and financial decisions. Advance directives, covered more fully in Chapter 11 and in *Policy Spotlight: Advance Directives*, encompass documents in which people can outline their wishes for future health care and appoint others to make decisions for them when they are no longer able. Power of attorney is a particular type of advance directive. While state regulations vary, in most states a person would need to designate someone to make financial decisions and someone to make health decisions separately, even if they are appointing the same person.

The stages discussed in this section generally apply to Alzheimer's disease, as it is the most common type of dementia. Other dementias will have longer or shorter courses or different symptoms, but the caregiving responsibilities, especially in the latter stages, are similar. In the middle stage of dementia, caregiving responsibilities become more regular and more demanding. The person with dementia is likely to need more supervision for safety, and tasks such as driving and cooking may no longer be able to be performed (Alzheimer's Association,

2021a). To an outsider, the person may not appear to be a safety risk, which is why you may see **Silver Alerts**. Silver Alerts are government messages regarding missing older or vulnerable adults, often with cognitive impairment, who are often driving their own cars. Similar to the Amber Alert system for missing children, this policy intervention provides identifying information to the general public in an attempt to locate someone before harm occurs.

Also in the middle phase, people with Alzheimer's may begin to develop personality and behavioral changes and/or aggressive behaviors that caregivers need to be able to manage (Alzheimer's Association, 2021a). They may become frustrated by usual tasks that are more challenging to perform. Caregivers may manage frustration by simplifying instructions or altering the physical environment to make tasks less stressful for the person with dementia (National Institute on Aging, n.d.). Many people in the middle stage of dementia are being cared for at home, so policies that provide respite or access to adult day services are useful to help caregivers from becoming burned out.

People in the late stages of dementia require significant daily care. They may have difficulty walking, lose the ability to eat or swallow regular food, and need total assistance with personal care (Alzheimer's Association, 2021a). Adding to the caregiving burden is the fact that this stage, in cases of Alzheimer's, may not occur until 8–10 years after diagnosis, meaning that the hardest parts don't come until a caregiver's physical, emotional, and sometimes financial resources have been exhausted. In the late stages of dementia, caregivers may seek long-term services and supports, such as home care or residential care in nursing homes or specialized dementia units. Long-term services and supports are covered extensively in Chapter 11.

From a policy perspective, dementia units that are part of assisted living facilities are not regulated by the federal government. Assisted living is regulated on a state-by-state basis, leading to significant variability in structure and quality. In addition, there are no criteria or standard definitions for what a dementia care unit should contain (Blackburn et al., 2018; Lai et al., 2009). Dementia care that is not provided in a nursing home is not covered by any social insurance programs such as Medicare or Medicaid, so the availability of specialized units is limited to those who are able to afford to pay privately for these services. The national average cost of full-time assisted living dementia care is around $5,000 per month. More about the policies that shape long-term services and supports can be found in Chapter 11.

Aggressive behaviors are often associated with dementia and may be made worse in the presence of co-occurring mental health conditions and delirium

> ## Policy Spotlight: Advance Directives
>
> **Advance directives** are documents that adults can complete in advance, detailing their wishes for health care, and designating other adults to make decisions on their behalf when or if they become unable to make them. Advance directive laws are determined on a state-by-state basis.
>
> **Power of attorney** is a document in which an individual cedes legal control of their affairs to someone else. In some cases this may be while they are still able to make their own decisions, such as when a soldier is deployed. The soldier may give a spouse at home power of attorney to handle any legal matters that may arise during deployment.
>
> **Durable power of attorney** is a specific type of power of attorney that remains in effect when the individual is incapacitated or no longer able to make their own decisions. This type is typically used by older adults and their families, particularly following a diagnosis of dementia.
>
> **Power of attorney for health care or health care proxy** (name varies by jurisdiction) is a power of attorney specifically for health care decisions.

(Wharton et al., 2018). For example, traumatic brain injury is a risk factor for developing later dementia (Schaffert et al., 2018). If the traumatic brain injury resulted in a loss of consciousness, the person may show signs of dementia as many as 3 years earlier than average (Schaffert et al., 2018). This is particularly important in populations such as the veteran population, in which the prevalence of both traumatic brain injury and PTSD is high, adding to the caregiving burden.

MENTAL HEALTH

Depression

Depression is a mental health condition marked by sad mood, loss of interest in activities, and changes in appetite and sleep. Depression is not a normal part of aging, but ageism would make many people think so. People often say "of course you're sad, what do you have to live for" or "I would be sad too if I were in your situation." Unfortunately this results in symptoms being disregarded by sufferers and providers alike. The situation is worse for those who live in long-term care settings such as nursing homes, where depression rates are high, as is lack of treatment for it. After all, it wasn't until 2010 that nursing homes were required to assess regularly for depression as part of the Minimum Data Set (Saliba et al., 2012), and it wasn't until 2016 that behavioral health requirements were strengthened (Behavioral Health Services, 2016). Among older adults, one estimate puts prevalence at 6.3% for major depression and 31% for subthreshold depression. Subthreshold depression is when someone has some symptoms of depression, but they are not severe enough to reach diagnostic criteria. It is important to include subthreshold depression in estimates because older adults with subthreshold depression are much more likely to develop major depression within 2 years than those without symptoms (Meeks et al., 2011).

The presence of depression can lead to worse physical health outcomes. This makes sense to most people because everything feels worse when you are sad. Hip fractures are more common in older adults, due to the musculoskeletal changes discussed in Chapter 5, and they are associated with long-term poor outcomes. For older adults a hip fracture may be experienced as a traumatic event, and it may induce psychological distress such as depression and anxiety (van de Ree et al., 2020). In one sample, nearly 70% of those with hip fractures had depression, and depressed hip fracture patients took longer to recover from surgery and were less likely to return to the same level of physical functioning they had before their injury than those who were not depressed (Piscitelli et al., 2012). Decreased physical functioning increases the risk for nursing home placement and death.

Depression in older adults is sometimes confused with dementia, especially with vascular dementia, because they share common features (Bottino et al., 2011). While dementia is uncommon in people under 60, depression can occur at any age, making it more challenging to differentiate in older adults. Symptoms of depression include acute onset, fluctuations in mood, memory complaints, sleep disturbance, and slowed processing speed (Bottino et al., 2011). Any of these, but particularly memory complaint and slowed processing speed, could be mistaken for cognitive impairment. The key difference would be the acute onset, as dementia tends to occur gradually over time.

Delirium

Of the conditions discussed in this chapter, delirium is one of the least discussed and the least understood by medical professionals and members of the public. **Delirium** is a syndrome associated with severe acute-onset confusion (Bottino et al., 2011) that often occurs in the context of a significant change such as a serious illness, a hospitalization, or a change in environment. It can also be brought on by medication changes or drug interactions. People with delirium experience disturbances in consciousness (alertness), orientation (awareness of where they are), memory (recall), thought, perception (interpretation of events and stimuli, sometimes characterized as hallucinations), and behavior (Cole et al., 2012; Bottino et al., 2011). As an example, when one older man had delirium as a result of a drug interaction, he thought he saw cellophane (plastic wrap) all over the house.

Symptomatically, the biggest way delirium is different from dementia is that it occurs suddenly, and symptoms may vary widely (Wharton et al., 2018). However, in settings such as the hospital where new providers (doctors, nurses, social workers) do not know the person's previous cognitive status, they may mistake delirium-related confusion for pre-existing dementia. Ageism exacerbates the occurrence of these assumptions.

This issue is complicated. Despite the fact that dementia and delirium are different, there are associations between the two. Results from one longitudinal study suggested that people who ever experience delirium are at greater risk of developing dementia in the future (Davis et al., 2012). They also found that people who experienced delirium on top of pre-existing dementia experienced greater declines in functional status and greater incidences of mortality than those who did not experience delirium. People who have all three—dementia, delirium, and a history of a mental health diagnosis—have a higher risk of aggressive behaviors during hospitalization than those who do not (Wharton et al., 2018).

Long-term-care nursing home residents frequently experience delirium, and it is associated with negative outcomes (Cole et al., 2012). Yet, at the same time, the presence of symptoms of delirium may signal an underlying problem such as an untreated illness/infection or a dangerous drug interaction (Cole et al., 2012). Proper recognition of these symptoms, such as by using a validated assessment method and/or by having staff that know the residents well and can observe changes in their presentation, can result in appropriate treatment. Proper diagnosis is essential. Delirium is associated with increased mortality—older adult patients diagnosed with delirium are twice as likely to die within 6 months as patients without delirium (Tsai et al., 2013).

DIFFERENTIAL DIAGNOSIS—DEPRESSION/DELIRIUM/DEMENTIA

Depression, dementia, and delirium are the three most common mental health diagnoses among hospitalized older adults, and the top reasons they get referred for psychiatric consultation (Tsai et al., 2013). Depression and dementia often occur concurrently, or one may be an antecedent for the other (Bottino et al., 2011). Understanding which condition a person has is important because they share many common symptoms, and because the correct diagnosis is essential for appropriate treatment. A person's medication regimen must be considered in any thorough assessment of cognitive status and mental health. Older adults are often on multiple medications, and older adults are vulnerable to medication side effects and interactions that sometimes look like dementia (Bottino et al., 2011).

Depression is common in people with dementia, specifically minor depression (Verdaguer et al., 2020). It is not clear what impact this has on outcomes, for either the depression or the dementia, but it is important for treatment considerations to relieve distress. As compared to other symptoms of dementia such as delusions, hallucinations, and agitation, which tend to occur later in the disease process, depression is common throughout the course of dementia, even in very early stages (Lee et al., 2016).

Healthcare professionals who are able to differentiate between depression, dementia, and delirium are essential for maximizing outcomes for older adults, yet there has been a dearth of appropriately trained professionals (Horvath et al., 2017). Education and credentialing policies should ensure the integration of appropriate training into medical, nursing, and social work education. Validated tools should be incorporated into agency-level policies in institutions that care for older adults. For example, the "5D" pocket card was developed to help providers, particularly those who do not work specifically with older adults, to be able to differentiate between dementia, delirium, and depression (Horvath et al., 2017). This instrument brings together a collection of validated rapid instruments for use in busy clinical settings all in one place, along with a straightforward set of references.

The interplay of depression, dementia, and delirium also increases the risks of poor health outcomes. For example, depression is known to increase the risk of medical-related delirium, especially after certain types of procedures. In 2019, Oldham and colleagues showed that pre-operative depression predicted delirium in surgical patients who had a Coronary Artery Bypass Graft (CABG), a common heart surgery in older adults that treats blocked arteries, even when controlling for other known risk factors. Among people who lived in nursing homes, those who had both sub-syndromal delirium and dementia experienced poorer outcomes including functional decline, cognitive decline, and death after 6 months of study than people with either diagnosis by itself (McCusker et al., 2014). Tsai and colleagues (2013) looked at the odds of death among hospital inpatients who had been referred to psychiatry for delirium, dementia, or depression. The delirium group was most likely to die in the first year, followed by the dementia and depression groups, respectively (Tsai et al., 2013). This is in addition to other studies that have shown that older adult patients with delirium, dementia, and depression are more likely to die than patients without any of those conditions.

Depression, delirium, and dementia also influence outcomes in other situations. Each of these conditions, independently and in combination, creates risks in natural disasters and shelter settings. Shelters tend to be large, confusing places that are staffed by non-medical personnel. While the Red Cross provides a majority of these shelters (approximately 60%) and their intake process assesses for self-report of physical and mental health conditions, this is evaluated using one yes/no question with little nuance. Even without prior diagnoses, disaster- and shelter-related conditions can precipitate negative events. Age, cognitive impairment, infections,

Case Study: Dementia, Depression, and Delirium in Practice

Mrs. Johnson is a 67-year-old woman. She lives alone and was found outside near her house, in the winter, in her pajamas. She has no idea how she got there. She presents to the emergency room with some frostbite and is admitted for observation. During her stay she has trouble sleeping and mixes up day and night. She is unsure of where she is and believes that it is her birthday, June 15.

Is this dementia, delirium, or depression?

Dementia, delirium, and depression show similar symptoms when it comes to orientation (awareness of person, place, and time), memory, sleep disturbance, and alertness.

There are differences in onset—delirium comes on rapidly, over hours or days. Dementia develops gradually over months or years. Depression is somewhere in between, coming on and progressing over weeks or months. However, in this case and in many cases, this history is unavailable.

Speech and thinking can be clues to the differences. People with delirium display loud or incoherent speech. People with dementia are more repetitive or have trouble finding words. People with depression do not speak a lot, but their ability to speak is intact.

People with delirium display thinking that is disorganized or hard to follow. Dementia may seem that way, as people with dementia may have trouble finding words or reasoning. People with depression have thinking that is intact, but sad or hopeless.

It is essential to get the diagnosis right. Dementia is progressive and irreversible, but both delirium and depression are treatable. Prompt and appropriate treatment is necessary to avoid permanent harm.

and injuries all predispose older adults to delirium. Add onto that shelter and disaster factors such as lost medication, lost eyeglasses, dehydration, injuries from evacuation, or even disrupted sleep due to shelter conditions (Holle et al., 2019). All of these can put older adults sheltering from disasters at incredibly high risk for delirium. Disaster preparedness and response policies should address delirium assessment and response. Laypeople such as the volunteers in these shelter settings can mistake any of these conditions for other things. Dementia, unfortunately, may be mistaken for normal "old age," thus resulting in individuals with dementia not being given the extra supports they need to be safe in a shelter and post-disaster environment. Depression can be mistaken for general fatigue, fear, or voluntary self-segregation. Best practices are being developed for assessing these populations in emergency/disaster settings (Holle et al., 2019). It is important to remember all at-risk populations when planning for disaster preparedness and response.

MENTAL HEALTH PARITY

Parity is the state of being equal or equivalent. **Mental health parity** refers to insurance coverage that is comparable or equivalent for mental health care and for physical health care. Historically health plans have not been required to provide equivalent coverage. The first federal law to address this issue was not passed until 1996. The **Mental Health Parity Act** required large group health plans, such as those offered by employers, to provide comparable annual and lifetime dollar limits for mental health and physical health (HHS.gov, n.d.). Parity laws have been expanded since 1996 and now include Medicaid managed care plans, federal employees' health plans, and state children's health insurance plans. Most Medicare plans are not required to offer parity for mental health services (National Alliance on Mental Illness, n.d.).

SUMMARY

Cognitive loss is often seen as synonymous with aging, as is physical decline. As you have seen from this chapter and Chapter 5, while some decline is normal, pathological decline that disrupts a person's ability to care for themselves is typically related to a disease process. Dementia is an umbrella term that covers all forms of cognitive impairment that disrupt daily functioning. Alzheimer's disease is by far the most common type of dementia in the United States and around the world, but Lewy body dementia, frontotemporal dementia, vascular dementia, and symptoms caused by Huntington's disease and Parkinson's disease are also widespread.

While older adults may experience the same mental health challenges as younger adults, such as the aging of individuals who have experienced lifelong schizophrenia or bipolar disorder, the most common mental health concerns in older adults are depression and delirium. Delirium is characterized by sudden-onset confusion and hallucinations and usually accompanies another significant change such as a medical illness, a hospitalization, or another severe change in environment. When delirium does occur, it creates significant risk for poorer outcomes related to the original problem.

Depression also causes significant risks for poorer health and social outcomes in older adults. While at any given time, estimates say only 6% of older adults have depression, many more are "subthreshold" or have depressive symptoms without meeting diagnostic criteria. Those older adults are at much greater risk of developing depression in the future. Additionally, depression is greater in certain populations, such as nursing home residents, and needs to be taken seriously. Changes to nursing home regulations that took place in 2016 require greater attention to behavioral health concerns in nursing home residents.

While dementia, depression, and delirium are not the only mental health concerns that impact older adults, they are the most common, and they are some of the most difficult to differentiate from each other. Accurate differential diagnosis is essential for treatment planning and care. Physicians, nurses, social workers, and other health professionals need more education in this area. There are not enough people in any of these professions specializing in geriatrics, so it is essential that policies are developed that require that all professionals be trained in the needs of older adults.

Declines in cognitive and mental health are too often seen as normal parts of aging. This chapter has demonstrated that while age-related risks exist, they are not normal, and they should be properly diagnosed and treated. While dementia is not curable at the present time, large investments in research make more progress towards a cure all the time. In the meantime, we need policies that support caregivers and provide dignity and respect to people aging with dementia.

KEY TERMS

Activities of Daily Living (ADLs)

Advance directives

Alzheimer's disease

Delirium

Dementia

Depression

Executive functioning

Frontotemporal dementia

Huntington's disease

Korsakoff syndrome

Lewy body dementia

Mental health parity

Mental Health Parity Act (1996)

Older Americans Act (1965)

Parity

Parkinsonism

Parkinson's Disease

Power of attorney

Processing speed

Silver Alerts

Vascular dementia

Working memory

DISCUSSION QUESTIONS

1. Describe the symptoms of depression, dementia, and delirium. Discuss how they might be confused with each other and why it is important to know the difference.

2. Together with your classmates, create a policy that addresses the needs of caregivers of people with middle-stage dementia.

3. Imagine that someone in your class has just been diagnosed with dementia. What are three things that person would want to plan ahead for? Research how they would do that in your state and discuss with your classmates.

4. Your grandmother developed confusion following a fall, with a visit to the emergency room. What is her likely diagnosis? Discuss with your classmates.

Ancillary materials for student practice can be found within Active Learning

REFERENCES

Alzheimer's Association. (2021a). *Caregiving.* Retrieved January 14, 2021 from https://www.alz.org/help-support/caregiving

Alzheimer's Association. (2021b). *Frontotemporal dementia.* Retrieved January 12, 2021 from https://www.alz.org/alzheimers-dementia/what-is-dementia/types-of-dementia/frontotemporal-dementia

Alzheimer's Association. (2021c). *Korsakoff syndrome.* Retrieved January 4, 2021 from https://www.alz.org/alzheimers-dementia/what-is-dementia/types-of-dementia/korsakoff-syndrome

Alzheimer's Association. (2021d). *Lewy body dementia.* Retrieved January 12, 2021 from https://www.alz.org/alzheimers-dementia/what-is-dementia/types-of-dementia/lewy-body-dementia

Alzheimer's Association. (2021e). *Vascular dementia.* Retrieved January 13, 2021 from https://www.alz.org/alzheimers-dementia/what-is-dementia/types-of-dementia/vascular-dementia

Alzheimer's Association. (2021f). *What is dementia?* Retrieved January 4, 2021 from https://www.alz.org/alzheimers-dementia/what-is-dementia

Armstrong, N., An, Y., Shin, J. J., Williams, O. A., Doshi, J., Erus, G., Davatzikos, C., Ferrucci, L., Beason-Held, L. L., & Resnick, S. M. (2020). Associations between cognitive and brain volume changes in cognitively normal older adults. *NeuroImage, 223,* 117289. https://doi.org/10.1016/j.neuroimage.2020.117289

Behavioral Health Services, 42 C.F.R § 483.40 (2016). https://www.govregs.com/regulations/title42_chapterIV_part483_subpartB_section483.40

Blackburn, J., Zheng, Q., Grabowski, D. C., Hirth, R., Intrator, O., Stevenson, D. G., & Banaszak-Holl, J. (2018). Nursing home chain affiliation and its impact on specialty service designation for Alzheimer disease. *Inquiry: The Journal of Health Care Organization, Provision, and Financing, 55,* 1–9. https://doi.org/10.1177/0046958018787992

Bottino, C. M. C., Camozzato de Padua, A., Smid, J., Areza-Fegyveres, R., Novaretti, T., Bahia, V. S., and Working Group on Alzheimer's Disease and Vascular dementia of the Brazilian Academy of Neurology. (2011). Differential diagnosis between dementia and psychiatric disorders: Diagnostic criteria and supplementary exams. Recommendations of the Scientific Department of Cognitive Neurology and Aging of the Brazilian Academy of Neurology. *Dementia & Neuropsychologia, 5*(4), 288–296.

Chaufan, C., Hollister, B., Nazareno, J., & Fox, P. (2012). Medical ideology as a double-edged sword: The politics of cure and care in the making of Alzheimer's disease. *Social Science & Medicine, 74*(5), 788–795. https://doi.org/10.1016/j.socscimed.2011.10.033

Chen, C., & Zissimopoulos, J. M. (2018). Racial and ethnic differences in trends in dementia prevalence and risk factors in the United States. *Alzheimer's & Dementia: Translational Research & Clinical Interventions, 4*(1), 510–520. https://doi.org/10.1016/j.trci.2018.08.009

Chin, A. L., Negash, S., & Hamilton, R. (2011). Diversity and disparity in dementia: The impact of ethnoracial differences in Alzheimer disease. *Alzheimer Disease and Associated Disorders, 25*(3), 187–195. https://doi.org/10.1097/WAD.0b013e318211c6c9

Cole, M. G., McCusker, J., Voyer, P., Monette, J., Champoux, N., Ciampi, A., Vu, M., Dyachenko, A., & Belzile, E. (2012). Symptoms of delirium occurring before and after episodes of delirium in older long-term care residents. *Journal of the American Geriatrics Society, 60*(12), 2302–2307. https://doi.org/10.1111/j.1532-5415.2012.04237.x

Davis, D. H. J., Terrera, G. M., Keage, H., Rahkonen, T., Oinas, M., Matthews, F. E., Cunningham, C., Polvikoski, T., Sulkava, R., MacLullich, A. M. J., & Brayne, C. (2012). Delirium is a strong risk factor for dementia in the oldest-old: A population-based cohort study. *Brain: A Journal of Neurology, 135*(9), 2809–2816. https://doi.org/10.1093/brain/aws190

Duda, B. M., & Sweet, L. H. (2020). Functional brain changes associated with cognitive training in healthy older adults: A preliminary ALE meta-analysis. *Brain Imaging and Behavior, 14,* 1247–1262. https://doi.org/10.1007/s11682-019-00080-0

Haussmann, R., Ganske, S., Gruschwitz, A., Werner, A., Osterrath, A., Lange, J., Buthut, M., Donix, K. L., Linn, J., & Donix, M. (2018). Family history of Alzheimer's disease and subjective memory performance. *American Journal of Alzheimer's Disease & Other Dementias, 33*(7), 458–462. https://doi.org/10.1177/1533317518775033

Hazlett, K. E., Figueroa, C. M., & Nielson, K. A. (2015). Executive functioning and risk for Alzheimer's disease in the cognitively intact: Family history predicts Wisconsin Card Sorting Test performance. *Neuropsychology, 29*(4), 582–591. https://doi.org/10.1037/neu0000181

HHS.gov. (2018). *Parity policy and implementation.* U.S. Department of Health and Human Services. https://www.hhs.gov/about/agencies/advisory-committees/mental-health-parity/task-force/resources/index.html

Holle, C. L., Turnquist, M. A., & Rudolph, J. L. (2019). Safeguarding older adults with dementia, depression, and delirium in a temporary disaster shelter. *Nursing Forum, 54*(2), 157–164. https://doi.org/10.1111/nuf.12309

Horvath, K. J., Burns, T., Fernandez, C., Terri Huh, J. W., Moorer, T., Thielke, S., Trittschuh, E., & Cooley, S. (2017). Reevaluation of a clinical resource for assessment of delirium, dementia, and depression. *Gerontology & Geriatrics Education, 38*(3), 245–256. https://doi.org/10.1080/02701960.2014.966905

Huang, F., Zhang, M., & Wang, S. (2019). Changes in cognitive function among older adults: A latent profile transition analysis. *Archives of Gerontology and Geriatrics, 80,* 12–19. https://doi.org/10.1016/j.archger.2018.09.006

Huntington's disease Society of America. (2021). *Overview of Huntington's disease.* https://hdsa.org/what-is-hd/overview-of-huntingtons-disease/

Knopman, D. S., Petersen, R. C., & Jack, C. R. (2019). A brief history of "Alzheimer disease": Multiple meanings separated by a common name. *Neurology, 92*(22), 1053–1059. https://doi.org/10.1212/WNL.0000000000007583

Lai, C. K., Yeung, J. H., Mok, V., & Chi, I. (2009). Special care units for dementia individuals with behavioural problems. *Cochrane Database of Systematic Reviews, 7*(4), CD006470. https://pubmed.ncbi.nlm.nih.gov/19821370/

Lee, J. H., Byun, M. S., Yi, D., Choe, Y. M., Choi, H. J., Baek, H., Sohn, B. K., Kim, H. J., Lee, Y., Woo, J. I., & Lee, D. Y. (2016). Frequency of depressive syndromes in elderly individuals with no cognitive impairment, mild cognitive impairment, and Alzheimer's disease dementia in a memory care clinic. *Dementia and Geriatric Cognitive Disorders, 42,* 135–145. https://doi.org/10.1159/000449155

Lee, Y., & Yeung, W.-J. J. (2019). Gender matters: Productive social engagement and the subsequent cognitive changes among older adults. *Social Science & Medicine, 229,* 87–95. https://doi.org/10.1016/j.socscimed.2018.08.024

McCusker, J., Cole, M. G., Voyer, P., Monette, J., Champoux, N., Ciampi, A., Vu, M., & Belzile, E. (2014). Six-month outcomes of co-occurring delirium, depression, and dementia in long-term care. *Journal of the American Geriatrics Society, 62*(12), 2296–2302. https://doi.org/10.1111/jgs.13159

Meeks, T. W., Vahia, I. V., Lavretsky, H., Kulkarni, G., & Jeste, D. V. (2011). A tune in "a minor" can "b major": A review of epidemiology, illness course, and public health implications of subthreshold depression in older adults. *Journal of Affective Disorders, 129*(1–3), 126–142. https://doi.org/10.1016/j.jad.2010.09.015

National Alliance on Mental Illness. (n.d.). *What is mental health parity?* Retrieved June 2, 2021 from https://www.nami.org/Your-Journey/Individuals-with-Mental-Illness/Understanding-Health-Insurance/What-is-Mental-Health-Parity

National Council on Aging. (2020). *Older Americans Act for advocates.* Retrieved January 8, 2021 from https://www.ncoa.org/public-policy-action/older-americans-act/

National Institute on Aging. (n.d.). *Alzheimer's caregiving.* U.S. Department of Health and Human Services. Retrieved January 14, 2021 from https://www.nia.nih.gov/health/alzheimers/caregiving

National Institute on Aging. (2017a). *What happens to the brain in Alzheimer's disease?* U.S. Department of Health and Human Services. Retrieved January 6, 2021 from https://www.nia.nih.gov/health/what-happens-brain-alzheimers-disease

National Institute on Aging. (2017b). *Parkinson's disease.* U.S. Department of Health and Human Services. Retrieved January 13, 2021 from https://www.nia.nih.gov/health/parkinsons-disease

National Institute on Aging. (2018, December 12). *Studies explore Alzheimer's risk factors, biomarkers in Latinos.* U.S. Department of Health and Human Services. Retrieved May 27, 2021 from https://www.nia.nih.gov/news/studies-explore-alzheimers-risk-factors-biomarkers-latinos

Oldham, M., Hawkins, K., Lin, I.-H., Deng, Y., Hao, Q., Scoutt, L., Yuh, D., & Lee, H. (2019). Depression predicts delirium after Coronary Artery Bypass Graft surgery independent of cognitive impairment and cerebrovascular disease: An analysis of the neuropsychiatric outcomes after heart surgery study. *American Journal of Geriatric Psychiatry, 27*(5), 476–486. https://doi.org/10.1016/j.jagp.2018.12.025

Piscitelli, P., Metozzi, A., Benvenuti, E., Bonamassa, L., Brandi, G., Cavalli, L., Colli, E., Fossi, C., Parri, S., Giolli, L., Tanini, A., Fasano, A., DiTanna, G., & Brandi, M. L. (2012). Connections between the outcomes of osteoporotic hip fractures and depression, delirium or dementia in elderly patients: Rationale and preliminary data from the CODE study. *Clinical Cases in Mineral and Bone Metabolism, 9*(1), 40–44.

Saliba, D., Jones, M., Streim, J., Ouslander, J., Berlowitz, D., & Buchanan, J. (2012). Overview of significant changes in the Minimum Data Set for nursing homes version 3.0. *Journal of the American Medical Directors' Association, 13*(7), 595–601. http://doi.org/10.1016/j.jamda.2012.06.001

Schaffert, J., LoBue, C., White, C., Chiang, H.-S., Didehbani, N., Lacritz, L., Rossetti, H., Dieppa, M., Hart, J., & Cullum, C. M. (2018). Traumatic brain injury history is associated with an earlier age of dementia onset in autopsy-confirmed Alzheimer's disease. *Neuropsychology, 32*(4), 410–416. https://doi.org/10.1037/neu0000423

Shea, Y. F., Ha, J., & Chu, L.-W. (2015). Comparisons of clinical symptoms in biomarker-confirmed Alzheimer's disease, dementia with Lewy bodies, and frontotemporal dementia patients in a local memory clinic. *Psychogeriatrics: The Official Journal of the Japanese Psychogeriatric Society, 15*(4), 235–241. https://doi.org/10.1111/psyg.12103

Tsai, M.-C., Chou, S.-Y., Tsai, C.-S., Hung, T.-H., & Su, J.-A. (2013). Comparison of consecutive periods of 1-, 2-, and 3- year mortality in geriatric inpatients with delirium, dementia, and depression in a consultation-liaison service. *International Journal of Psychiatry in Medicine, 45*(1), 45–57. http://doi.org/10.2190/PM.45.1.d

University of California San Francisco. (2021). *Vascular dementia.* Weill Institute for Neurosciences. Retrieved January 13, 2021 from https://memory.ucsf.edu/dementia/vascular-dementia

van de Ree, C. L. P., de Munter, L., Biesbroeck, B. H. H., Kruithof, N., Gosens, T., & de Jongh, M. A. C. (2020). The prevalence and prognostic factors of psychological distress in older patients with a hip fracture: A longitudinal cohort study. *Injury, 51*(11), 2668–2675. https://doi.org/10.1016/j.injury.2020.07.049

Velayudhan, L., Baillon, S., Daby, L., Suntharamoorthy, P., Kablan, A., Tromans, S., & Lindesay, J. (2020). Predictors of disease progression in early-onset Alzheimer's dementia: A retrospective cohort study. *Journal of the American Medical Directors Association, 21*(11), 1735–1739. https://doi.org/10.1016/j.jamda.2020.05.016

Verdaguer, E. S., Stafford, J., Tuijt, R., & Orgeta, V. (2020). Minor and subthreshold depressive disorders in Alzheimer's disease: A systematic review and meta-analysis of prevalence studies. *Journal of Affective Disorders, 263,* 728-734. https://doi.org/10.1016/j.jad.2019.11.053

Vergouw, L., Bosman, B., van de Beek, M., Salome, M., Hoogers, S., van Steenoven, I., Roks, G., Bonifati, V., van Swieten, J., Lemstra, A., & de Jong, F. J. (2020). Family history is associated with phenotype in dementia with Lewy bodies. *Journal of Alzheimer's disease, 73*(1), 269–275. https://doi.org/10.3233/JAD-190825

Wharton, T., Paulson, D., Macri, L., & Dubin, L. (2018). Delirium and mental health history as predictors of aggression in individuals with dementia in inpatient settings. *Aging & Mental Health, 22*(1), 121–128. https://doi.org/10.1080/13607863.2016.1235680

Zelinski, E., Dalton, S., & Hindin, S. (2011). Cognitive changes in healthy older adults. *Generations Journal, 35*(2), 13–20. https://www.researchgate.net/publication/289229781_Cognitive_Changes_in_Healthy_Older_Adults

Zhou, B., Zhao, Q., Teramukai, S., Ding, D., Guo, Q., Fukushima, M., & Hong, Z. (2010). Executive function predicts survival in Alzheimer disease: A study in Shanghai. *Journal of Alzheimer's disease, 22*(2), 673–682. https://doi.org/10.3233/JAD2010100318

OLDER ADULTS IN FAMILIES AND COMMUNITIES

7

How Do Older Adults Fit Within the Family Structure?

INTRODUCTION

Older adults are talked about as a population sep-arate from the rest. In schools of social work, for example, we often have courses on children and families, and other, separate courses on aging or older adults, as if they were not parts of families. As we will discuss over the next two chapters, older adults are not only part of families, but also engaged in lifelong, reciprocal relationships of caregiving. In

By the end of this chapter, students will be able to

1. Understand the varied ways older adults fit into the family structure.

2. Discuss how family and household structure influ-ences caregiving and family roles.

3. Compare and contrast how policies impact where and how people and families live.

the United States, many people often espouse an ideal of **independence**. Isn't that the supposed goal of every teenager, to leave the house and go off on one's own? But the reality is that people are much more interdependent than they often want to admit. Families support each other in material and non-material ways throughout life, turning to each other when they need an emergency loan or help with care. Policies such as university financial aid assume that people have family members to fall back on to meet their needs when they cannot do it on their own. These and other caregiving policies are problematic because they fail to address situations where families are absent or unavailable, or the family's resources are not sufficient to support additional members.

The challenge to creating policy solutions is the diversity of people's situations. In many places in the United States and abroad, it is not unusual to have three or four generations in the same household, sharing expenses and responsibilities. In recent years young adults have been called the **boomerang generation**, as student loan debt, a stagnant economy, and a poor job market have forced many 20- and 30-year-olds back into their parents' homes, sometimes with a spouse and children in tow (Pew Research Center, 2012). In this chapter we will talk about where and how older adults fit into family structures, and how family dynamics affect where and how someone grows older.

INDEPENDENCE AND THE NUCLEAR FAMILY

Two hundred years ago Americans lived in smaller homes filled with larger, multigenerational families. When the United States was mostly agrarian, survival depended on all members of the household fulfilling their role, and everyone from the children to the oldest grandparent had a job to do, such as tending the youngest children, shelling peas, feeding the animals, or collecting eggs. As the United States developed and industrialized, young people began moving away from the family home to get a factory job in a far-off city, many times sending money back to family remaining in rural areas. In cities, tenements were filled with immigrant families also living in multifamily households, with more established family members helping those more recently arrived in America with jobs, connections, and the means of basic survival. Sometimes workers would bring home "piecework" from factories and sweatshops—where they were paid by the piece—and all family members would work together to maximize the family's income.

But changing social dynamics, world events, and the economy combined to change household and family structure through the ages. The **nuclear family**, parents and children living together by themselves in a household, arose in the post-World-War-II era, along with the baby boom. Soldiers (GIs, short for "Government Issue") returned from the war eager to get on with their lives and start families. The Servicemen's Readjustment Act of 1944 was a series of benefits to help veterans return to civilian life. The so called "**GI bill**" provided education to nearly 70% of men returning from World War II and the Korean War (Chambers et al., 2012), unemployment benefits, and the chance for home ownership through loan guarantee programs (U.S. Department of Veterans Affairs, 2013). The vast numbers of returning servicemen trying to start families created housing shortages, particularly in the cities. Creative developers, boosted by easily available loans, bought large tracts of land far from the cities. With automobiles much more available, people no longer had to live where they worked, and thus the suburbs were born. Mass-produced homes were built on cul-de-sacs and, particularly for white men, these options were attractive.

Policy interventions made home ownership less expensive than renting, for the first time. Two mortgage programs, through the **Federal Housing Administration** (**FHA**) and through the **Veterans Administration** (**VA**) via the GI Bill, gave massive numbers of mortgages using rules developed under the **New Deal** (U.S. Department of Veterans Affairs, 2013; Chambers et al., 2012). These are rules that many modern homeowners know well. For the first time, the term of most mortgages was extended to 30 years, effectively lowering monthly payments. Interest rates were fixed for the duration of the mortgage, allowing people to know what their payment would be. Finally, people could borrow a greater percentage of the value of a home, meaning that they no longer needed to come up with a 50%–60% down payment (Chambers et al., 2012). In addition, a series of changes to the income tax regulations created deductions and benefits to home ownership, increasing the financial benefit of buying a house (Chambers et al., 2012). It financially made sense. In 1949, rent for a New York City apartment was about $50 per month. In the suburbs, under the new programs, someone could buy a home for a $550 down payment, with a mortgage payment of just $29 per month (Daily Beast, 2018).

The GI Bill was not all good for everyone. In the negotiations on the bill, some Southern congressmen feared what these benefits could provide for Blacks. They fought for provisions that allowed states to administer the benefits, as opposed to the federal government. This created discriminatory practices, even though the policy was race-neutral (Blakemore, 2019). Thus, it was more challenging for Black families, even those of returning soldiers, to purchase homes. This uneven administration of GI benefits was coupled with explicit discrimination by the FHA, which gave developers loans to build homes in the suburbs under the explicit provision that they not sell those homes to Blacks. Black veterans attempting to use the GI Bill to finance home ownership found the door to the suburbs sometimes literally slammed in their faces (Blakemore, 2019; NPR, 2017). When they were able to get loans or find homes to buy, they paid higher interest rates. Coupled with continued discrimination in employment opportunities that resulted in lower wages, home ownership was harder to come by for Blacks. Rising home equity is the most significant source of wealth for white families, and the discriminatory practices outlined here created much of the wealth gap that currently exists between Blacks and whites (Blakemore, 2019; Daily Beast, 2018).

Despite housing discrimination, the shifts towards nuclear family households in the American family were happening for both whites and Blacks. Externally, the ideal became a husband and wife, with their children living together in a home. The birth of many children impacted school policies and other government spending. Policies and media images reinforced the nuclear family norms, even when they did not work for all. The baby boomers, those born between 1946 and 1964, were raised in this era and make up many of the current cohort of older adults.

In this era of the nuclear family, men went to work every day, often in the city, and women stayed behind in the suburbs tending to the children and the household. While these women often did not live in intergenerational households, they were available during the day to tend to caregiving duties if someone became ill or injured. Many modern policies are based on this premise: the idea that there is someone available during the day to tend to needs. School policies—from a school day that is shorter than a typical work day, to expectations around volunteerism, to the very idea of a summer break—assume that an adult is available to provide supervision. This ideal was most typically held by middle-class white women. In other subgroups, including low-income families of all races, new immigrant families, and families of color, both men and women have typically worked outside the home. But overall, in the United States in the 1950s, only one in three women worked outside the home (U.S. Bureau of Labor Statistics, 2000).

Policies supported and reinforced this social norm. While some women in this era went to college, they were expected to stay away from the sciences, sticking to literature and language, and it was not unusual for them to leave school with an "M.R.S. degree" (leaving before graduation to get married). At the University of Rochester, in upstate New York, women lived and went to school on a completely separate campus until 1955, and that campus housed the departments that were considered more feminine. Engineering, chemistry, physics, and so on were on the men's campus. In the 1950s and 60s some companies outright refused to hire married women, contributing to the societal expectation that women remain in the home, being supported and directed by their husbands. The expectations were always gendered, and always based on white, heterosexual norms. While nuclear families were separated from their families of origin during this era, Brooks (2020) holds that they replicated those extended families in an interconnected, extended family of neighbors, all brought together by a need for mutual interdependence to help with child rearing.

But the economy changed in the United States over the years, as did how people worked (more on this in Chapter 10). Accompanying these work-life changes were the women's movement and books like *The Second Sex* (de Beauvoir, 1952) and *The Feminine Mystique* (Friedan, 1963). Many women were dissatisfied by the roles offered to them and found suburban, nuclear family life to be stifling. By 1998, three quarters of women aged 25–54 worked outside the home (U.S. Bureau of Labor Statistics, 2000). While the rise of the nuclear family drastically reduced the number of interdependent multigenerational households, the entry of women into the workforce in large numbers has equally influenced how older adults fit into the family structure, both as providers and recipients of care.

With the addition of women to the workplace and the rise of families in which two parents are employed outside the home, child care becomes an important national and state policy issue, as do policies within workplaces. Even in families with parents of two genders who both work (a father and a mother), mothers disproportionately maintain the burden of childcare-related responsibilities. Parents face workplace polices that often do not lend themselves to flexibility, such as needing to leave early to pick up a sick child, attending a concert, or meeting with a teacher (Glynn, 2012). Structural racism is at play here too: Black and Hispanic workers are more likely to be in jobs that lack flexibility and paid leave. Many of these jobs that lack flexibility also pay wages that make it difficult or impossible to afford childcare (Glynn, 2012). There is no comprehensive childcare policy in the United States, and day care options are expensive and limited. In many places it costs more to put a child in day care for a year than it would to put that child through a year of college. Some waiting lists are so long that parents sign up as soon as they learn they are expecting. Thus, many working families rely on older family members, such as the children's grandparents, great-grandparents, aunts, and other relatives, for childcare.

While a diverse array of family members may provide childcare for working parents, for purposes of brevity, this chapter will refer to them as grandparents. These childcare arrangements have rewards and challenges for both the working parents and the grandparents. Grandparents may relish spending time with their grandchildren, particularly if they felt distant or absent because of work or other life circumstances when their own children were young. Others may find reward in being able to help their children in this way. Working parents may be relieved that they can leave their child with a family member rather than relying on strangers in a day care setting. They may also like saving the costs of day care, or be unable to afford day care in the first place. Having grandparents provide care may provide flexibilities that a formal day care center could not. Some shift workers may rely on informal care from relatives because their work schedule does not conform to typical day care hours or changes frequently.

Families who use these arrangements may experience downsides as well. Some family members who provide care may work themselves. They may find themselves juggling part-time or full-time work with childcare, to help other members of the family. Others may find the care of children, particularly if the children are young or have significant needs, to be physically demanding and difficult. Older adults who anticipated freedoms when they left the paid workforce may resent the limitations on their schedule. Working parents may feel uncomfortable leaving their children with relatives, especially if they have disagreed about discipline, meals, safety measures, or other approaches to child rearing, but may feel that they have no choice, due to finances or family pressures. Practices that were common when parents were younger may be no longer recommended. For example, where and how a baby should sleep, and the use of car seats, are things that older family members may have handled differently when their own children were small. A family member may be less likely to accept direction from a parent than a paid caregiver would, particularly if the family member is an experienced parent themselves.

The burdens of grandparent caregivers often increase during crisis situations, as they did during the COVID-19 pandemic. COVID-19-related changes caused shifts in the availability of day care. Some centers temporarily closed for quarantining or reduced capacity to allow for social distancing, and people lost their day care. As people who were able shifted to working from home, some parents pulled their young children from day care due to COVID-19 safety concerns. The financial losses of fewer children were hard on day care centers, and some were forced to close permanently. With the uncertainty of day care—was it safe, was it not, was it even open—some parents relied more heavily than ever on grandparents to provide care, especially if they were able to keep the grandparents in their "pandemic bubble." Employed grandparents faced similar concerns regarding changes to their own paid work and had to balance helping their children with childcare and doing their own paid work.

The entry of women into the paid workforce also decreased the availability of women as **informal caregivers** of older adults. As is discussed in much greater detail in Chapter 8, informal caregivers are family and friends who assist with tasks ranging from grocery shopping, cooking, and cleaning to personal care such as bathing, toileting, and dressing. Of all informal caregivers, 61% of them also work, and of those who work, 60% work full time (National Alliance for Caregiving [NAC] & AARP, 2020). When women went to work, men did not then stay home, so all the adult members of many families work. As a result, potential caregivers of all genders often work. Working caregivers are most likely to be adult children of aging parents. How much caregiving interferes with a worker's job depends on the level of intensity of the caregiving. If caregiving becomes too intense to balance with work, many workers need to leave their jobs, take an unpaid leave of absence, or retire early, because of a lack of paid family leave policy in most states (NAC & AARP, 2020).

DOWNSIZING

As they age, many older adults who raised children in a nuclear family in a large suburban home find themselves in a single-family house that may not be able to meet their changing needs. It may have stairs and inaccessible bathrooms. Older adults need to consider maintenance of their home, and they may not want to deal with snow, lawns, or physical tasks. Some older adults move in response to a health challenge that limits their ability to function in their home, while others move in anticipation of the fact that they will not be able to age where they are (Jungers, 2011). Models of older-adult relocation often discuss push-and-pull factors (Ewan & Chahal, 2013). Younger or more able-bodied older adults may relocate because they are pulled to a community—for warmer weather and available amenities, for example—while other older adults who experience physical challenges in their current space or whose children live far away may be pushed out of their current space, into a space where their needs can be more easily met (Badawy et al., 2019). The accessibility of the home environment is associated with relocating to another location in the same community (Granbom et al., 2019), which suggests that some older adults can remain independent if their environment is able to meet their needs.

When older adults consider downsizing, they need to consider where they want to go. The question of whether a move alone can meet needs is an important one, and if it is, older people are more likely to stay in the same community. More than three quarters of late-life moves are local, within the same county or between counties in the same state (Badawy et al., 2019). Older adults might move further away if they wish to connect with more informal supports, such as their adult children. A planned move, before care is needed, may have greater financial benefits and may leave the older adult feeling more in control of their situation (Ewan & Chahal, 2013).

Affordability is also a concern for relocation. When a house is sold, home equity can support the purchase of a new, smaller home, or pay rent for a period of time, but those funds will run out at some point, and the housing still needs to be affordable when savings are drained. The monthly costs associated with living in senior housing, such as rent and utilities, may be lower than those of living in a single-family house, and thus may serve as a pull factor in relocation (Ewan & Chahal, 2013). One policy option that is sometimes explored is a **reverse mortgage**, a type of loan in which home equity is paid out in monthly payments to facilitate its use by older adults for life and care (Roy et al., 2018). These payments might allow someone to make accessibility modifications that would allow them to stay in the home or to pay for assistive services, but they do use up equity, leaving fewer assets for heirs (Federal Trade Commission, 2015). The factors discussed earlier about discrepancies in wealth related to home equity and housing discrimination mean that there is a significant difference in the ability of Blacks and other groups to use policy tools like reverse mortgages.

CHILDREN MOVING AWAY

Just as people moved from rural areas during industrialization to obtain jobs in major manufacturing cities such as Detroit, Pittsburgh, and Buffalo, many adult children relocate from their childhood home for school, work, or other opportunities. In rural areas the percentage of older adults is much higher than in urban areas due to the exodus of younger people, as discussed below in the section on **brain drain**. Many older adults are left behind without informal supports, in areas with less infrastructure for aging services.

Long-distance caregiving, in which the caregiver lives at a distance from the person receiving care, is the reality for many families. While long-distance caregivers cannot provide day-to-day, hands-on care, they may arrange for paid caregivers, manage appointments, handle finances, order groceries, and provide as many hours of care as local, hands-on caregivers do. Depending on proximity, long-distance caregivers may also

COLORADO'S FIGHT FOR PAID FAMILY LEAVE

By Jennifer C. Greenfield

On November 4, 2020, voters in Colorado approved a ballot measure that created a paid family and medical leave (PFML) program for the state (Legislative Council of the Colorado General Assembly, 2020). Similar proposals had been introduced in the state legislature over several years prior to the ballot measure, with the first legislation introduced in 2015 (Colorado House Bill 15-1258, 2015). Despite growing support for the program across the state's electorate, legislators and the state's governor had been unable to reach agreement on the details of the program, including eligibility, levels of benefits, and, importantly, whether it should be structured as a social insurance program or a mandate for businesses to purchase coverage through the private market. After a final failed attempt to establish a program through legislation during the 2020 legislative session, which was interrupted by the COVID-19 pandemic, advocates collected enough signatures to put a comprehensive social insurance program on the ballot that year. It passed by a margin of 57.75% of voters in favor and 42.25% opposed.

The Colorado program is similar to measures passed in recent years in Oregon, Connecticut, and Washington State (National Partnership for Women and Families, 2021). Importantly, the Colorado program includes a flexible definition of "family member" for the purposes of determining eligibility, such that a worker may take paid time off from work to provide care for a child, spouse, parent, or another individual with whom the worker shares a family-type relationship. This is particularly important for older adults who need help managing a chronic or life-limiting illness, especially when their primary caregiver is a grandchild, other extended family member, or even a close neighbor or friend.

Another important aspect of the new law is that it is structured as a social insurance, not as a mandate for employers to purchase insurance on the private market. Currently, New York is the only state to implement PFML primarily through private market insurance, and the system is successful in New York because it is built upon a well-established disability insurance market, which has been operating since short-term disability insurance was mandated by New York in 1949 (ShelterPoint, 2019). In states like Colorado, without prior short-term disability insurance mandates, establishing a robust private market would likely take significant time and up-front private investments; furthermore, without strict regulations, premiums for private market plans could differ by size of employer, type of labor, and other factors that would risk making PFML insurance unaffordable for some types of businesses. For these reasons, the social insurance model—in which employees and employers pay a small percentage of wages into a single, statewide risk pool—is used by most states to guarantee PFML coverage to workers.

The passage of Colorado's plan was an important victory for the movement to establish a similar federal program, in part because Colorado's electorate is split nearly evenly between Democrats, Republicans, and Independents, and has historically been reluctant to establish new taxes and business mandates. Currently, the only federal mandate regarding leave for workers who experience an illness or need to care for a loved one is the Family and Medical Leave Act of 1996 (FMLA), which mandates that workers at certain businesses must have access to leave with a guarantee of a job upon their return—but there is no requirement that the worker should be paid during their leave. Furthermore, because of the restrictions on eligibility and included businesses, only about 60% of workers nationwide are covered by FMLA, and even fewer can afford to access it because of the lack of guaranteed income. The resounding bipartisan vote of support for paid leave by Colorado's voters, combined with the growing attention on paid leave as a crucial support for workers during the COVID-19 pandemic, have made it evident that paid leave programs are increasingly popular with mainstream voters. Comprehensive paid leave proposals have now been introduced in both chambers of the U.S. Congress and by President Biden as part of his American Families Plan. As of this writing, Colorado joins nine other states and the District of Columbia in offering a paid family and medical leave program, and it may be that a similar program is implemented at the federal level soon.

travel frequently to the care recipient's home, straining finances, leisure, and family time. Long-distance caregiving can be a factor in an older adult or an adult child deciding to make a long-distance move or a move into older-adult housing of some kind. Adding to the complexity is the fact that older adults may be caregivers for their even older parents, and/or they could be the care recipients, both of which factor into relocation decisions (Ewan & Chahal, 2013).

Some older adults may choose to relocate to where their children live. Badawy et al. (2019) found that older adults who move more than 50 miles experience significantly greater expansion of their kinship social network than those who move locally. Moves to senior housing, or closer to children, are often seen as positive, because they help people get the resources they need (Koss & Ekerdt, 2017). However, moves can be quite stressful, particularly if the older person did not feel in control of the factors leading up to the move or the move itself (Ewen & Chahal, 2013).

BRAIN DRAIN—ESPECIALLY IN RURAL COMMUNITIES

The movement of people in and out of rural and metro areas is part of national trends in migration that are driven by people seeking employment, amenities, and lifestyle structures that are different from what is available to them in their current location. Historically, migration patterns have shifted back and forth: from moves out of rural areas and into cities, to the reverse, and back, sometimes very dramatically. Prior to the post-WWII birth of the suburbs, populations were in areas defined as rural or urban, with little to nothing in between. This is a simplified explanation of the patterns, but it reflects some of the larger trends that occurred. In the early days of the United States, people moved west from crowded cities, in search of wide, open spaces and the promises of land that would lead to prosperity. Rural subsistence life was hard, and with industrialization, some people moved back to cities to find jobs. The Great Depression brought all types of migration, including refugees from the Dust Bowl moving west to California. The other large migration is described above, with the exodus of white families to suburbs in the years following World War II. Other, smaller migrations have

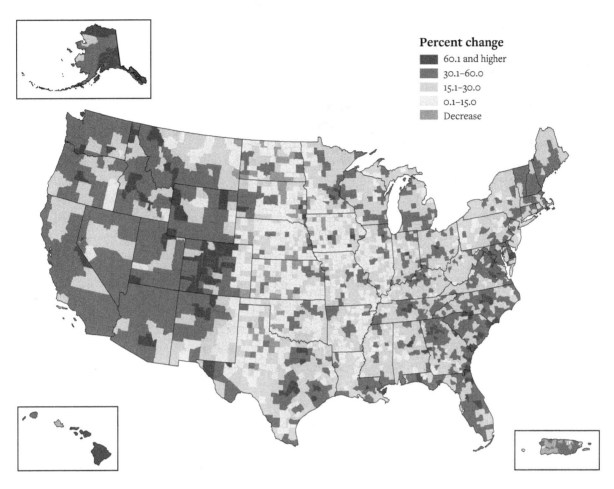

FIGURE 7.1 Older and Growing—Percentage Change Among the 65-and-Older Population: 2010 to 2019

occurred as a result of traumatic events, such as a migration out of New York City into nearby suburbs in the years following September 11, 2001.

Some migration patterns are slower and more insidious. **Brain drain** is the outmigration of younger, educated people, primarily from rural areas (Fiore et al., 2015). The greatest net loss migration that occurs in rural areas is among people between high school graduation and their 20s (Cromartie & Nelson, 2009). In one study conducted in rural Wisconsin, nearly three quarters of high school and college students planned to move to find better job opportunities (Andresen, 2008). There is much less systematic migration in the other direction. Younger older adults, such as those who are recently retired, are less likely to relocate, but if they do, they often choose to move to rural areas for amenities such as recreation and scenic landscapes. Many of the younger people who move away express desires to stay in the area, or to return, but cite career constraints as the primary reason for staying away (Cromartie et al., 2015). Those who return cite family motivations as a primary driver in the decision. In addition to being able to provide informal support to their own family members, these returnees bring crucial experience and education to the workforce (Cromartie et al., 2015).

INTERGENERATIONAL HOUSEHOLDS

Though not discussed in the section above, older adults may already live in, or may choose to move into, intergenerational households. These can happen at any age, in any combination, and may address a variety of needs. Older or younger people could choose to move in with relatives in pre-existing households, or two or more households may decide to combine in a new location. A multigenerational household could be an alternative to the older person selling their home and moving into senior housing or a care setting because they can't manage the home on their own or require care or supervision.

Family members may choose to co-locate for financial reasons, such as with members of the boomerang generation, above, or so that together they can afford a larger home and/or a home in a better location. Sometimes family members co-locate for help with care of older or younger family members or someone who is temporarily or permanently disabled. Whatever the reasons, these arrangements may provide stressors and benefits to all members of the family. Benefits include the sharing of financial and care burdens, as above. Stress may be caused by the adjustment to living with others after being on one's own, or by overcrowding in the new arrangement. One approach to addressing this stress is to create separate spaces within the larger whole.

ZONING LAWS, IN-LAW APARTMENTS, AND GRANNY PODS

Some families look for solutions where both older and younger family members can be in the same place but have their own space. **In-law apartments**, or **accessory apartments**, are smaller dwellings attached to a larger home that often have a separate entrance/exit to allow both families some privacy. In some cities **duplexes**, or "two-family" houses, are common. These often have two similarly sized units, for owner/renter combinations, but families may use them to be near family members who need assistance. A newer model is the idea of the "**granny pod**." A granny pod is a self-contained small home that can be placed on the property of a family member, allowing the older person their own space in easy proximity of people to help. Granny pod options range from the bare essentials—a free-standing bedroom and bathroom—to more elaborate models that provide luxuries such as remote monitoring in case of falls.

The availability of appropriate spaces relies on **zoning laws. Zoning laws**, also discussed in Chapter 9, are local or municipal laws that dictate how land can be used. Single-family home zoning makes it illegal to build anything other than one house on one plot of land (Baldassari & Solomon, 2020). This excludes apartment buildings, duplexes, in-law apartments, and yes, granny pods. Often associated with suburbs, this type of zoning exists widely across both urban and suburban areas. In addition to disadvantaging families who want to or need to live together for care-related reasons, this type of zoning also disadvantages low-income families and contributes to neighborhoods that are segregated based on income, race, and other sociodemographic factors (Baldassari & Solomon, 2020). Diverse neighborhoods are more livable for people of all ages, due to robust community services that lead to better quality of life. This phenomenon is discussed in detail in Chapter 9.

GRANDPARENTHOOD

Becoming a grandparent, at its most basic, occurs when one's child has a child of their own. But this simple definition contains wide variability in experience, age, feelings, and many other factors. Grandparenthood encapsulates all of the other variability that exists in American families, such as single-parent households, delayed childbearing, teen parenthood, surrogacy, adoption, divorce, blended families, and so on. Each of these impacts the experience and the expectations about what it means to be a grandparent. For example, in one extended family, one person became a grandparent at 36, and her father became a great grandparent at 60. In another part of the family, someone else became a grandfather for the first time at 59. Over the past 25 years, the average age at which someone becomes a grandparent has increased (Margolis, 2016). Societal changes, such as more people delaying parenthood or not having children at all, have decreased the likelihood of grandparenthood for some people, while increases in lifespan have increased the likelihood for others (Margolis & Verdery, 2019). Couples who do not have children impact both their parents' and their own experiences of grandparenthood. Timing, or the life stage at which one becomes a grandparent, can have an impact on the experience of grandparenthood, as can culture, familial expectations, and socioeconomic status.

The percentage of adults who have grandchildren has grown over time—from 40%–54% among those born in the 1880s to 60%–80% among those born in the 1930s and 40s (Margolis & Verdery, 2019). The ranges depicted represent variability based on gender and race, with the highest percentages belonging to white women. In some ways this makes sense, as white women have the highest life expectancy, and thus have more time for their children to have children in their lifetime. Life span also influences the average duration of grandparenthood, and thus the number of adults who have living grandparents. As we discuss intergenerational households in this chapter, consider the effects of the presence of grandparents, and the age differences between the generations, on caregiving and resource sharing. Also consider variability of the age differences, such as when one generation had children very young and other generations delayed fertility. Those kinds of gaps can result in more people potentially needing care or resources at one time—older adults and young children, for example—or more people being available to provide care and resources when they are needed.

The role of grandparents in a family varies widely within and between families. What do you believe is the role of grandparents? What has your own experience been? Not everyone has had the opportunity to know their grandparents. Biologically, everyone has had grandparents, but the rest—whether they have been alive in a child's lifetime, whether they are present or local, and the nature of the relationship—is all unique. There are many stereotypes and depictions about what grandparents should and should not be in the media, on TV, and in the movies. Are grandparents like second parents, providing support and discipline when needed? Are grandparents distant figures that you see on holidays? Do grandparents provide treats and indulgences, "spoiling" the kids? Keep in mind that the perception of what grandparents should be may even vary from the perspective of the grandparent, the parent, and the child in the same relationships (Sedano et al., 2020). Grandparents can be all of these: mentors, friends, windows into family history, or even windows into U.S. and global history.

DIVORCE AND GRANDPARENTS' RIGHTS

Grandparenthood may not be an obvious policy issue, but there are growing numbers of cases in which policies and courts have needed to become involved. Two specific examples are: (1) when grandparents become involved in raising their children due to the absence or inability of the children's parents; and (2) the question of whether or not grandparents have the right to visit their grandchildren, particularly if their child is not the child's custodial parent. Grandparent caregiving is discussed in greater detail in Chapter 8. This policy issue of grandparent visitation rights in the United States is under each state's jurisdiction, which means that every state treats the issue differently, and that rights may vary depending on the state of residence of the children and/or of the grandparents.

There are two possible scenarios to consider in regard to grandparent visitation. The first scenario includes cases in which the children's parents are married and involved in the children's lives, yet are estranged from their own parents, the children's grandparents. In general, in those cases, the grandparents do not have a legal right to sue for visitation. The other scenario, in which grandparents have some type of rights in nearly every state, includes cases in which the children's parents are not married to each other, such as in the case of divorce, separation, or death. In those cases, grandparents may be entitled to visitation rights. In California, for example, a grandparent can ask the court for visitation rights if they had a relationship with the child prior to the separation, and it is determined to be in the best interest of the child (California Courts, 2021). In New York, grandparents have a right to ask the courts for visitation, but they do not have a right to it. Also in New York, grandparents who have received a visitation order from the courts have a right to have that order enforced (New York State Kinship Navigator, 2016).

SUMMARY

In the United States many laws are based on the ideal of independence, with the marker of adulthood being a move to independence, often in a physical location separate from one's parents. This chapter has demonstrated that despite our tendency to divide people into groups by age, if we use a life span approach, families are inter-dependent, living situations vary, and age is not the only factor. Older people are not always the recipients of care and often contribute as much as, if not more than, they receive from others.

Many families live in nuclear family arrangements, but there are many times when those arrangements are not flexible or resilient enough to meet all needs. Family members must rely on each other, sometimes combining households into multigenerational arrangements. The generations may work together to provide care for children and older adults, provide other instrumental support, and/or support each other financially, in a variety of ways.

Grandparents play many important roles, acting as mentors, friends, and caregivers of children and other family members. The expected role of grandparents varies based on culture, age, and specific familial context. Many grandparents play essential roles. In most cases, grandparents do not have rights in the courts when it comes to their grandchildren. Dedicated elder-care advocates should be aware of these laws to be able to advocate for grandparents. Social workers and other human services professionals should consider the whole family at all levels, from the individual level to the macro-systems level.

KEY TERMS

Accessory apartment

Boomerang generation

Brain drain

Duplex

Federal Housing Administration (FHA)

GI Bill

Granny pod

Independence

Informal Caregivers

In-law apartment

Long-distance caregiving

New Deal

Nuclear family

Reverse mortgage

Veterans Administration (VA)

Zoning laws

DISCUSSION QUESTIONS

1. Discuss different types of household structures and the benefits and drawbacks of each. Use examples from your own life or from households depicted on television or in the movies.

2. Discuss the differences between aging in an urban area or a rural area, realizing that each area will have its own unique strengths and challenges. Which services would be available in each? Which challenges might be present in one or the other? Which challenges would both face?

3. Imagine you are responsible for designing grandparents' rights legislation for your state. Which factors would you consider? Should grandparents have the right to see their grandchildren? Compare and contrast your responses with those of your classmates.

Ancillary materials for student practice can be found within Active Learning

REFERENCES

Andresen, W. (2008). *Gogebic Range location decision-making survey: Local results.* Retrieved February 9, 2021 from https://iron.extension.wisc.edu/files/2010/05/locationsurvey-finalresults2008-local_3_.pdf

Badawy, P., Schafer, M., & Sun, H. (2019). Relocation and network turnover in later life: How distance moved and functional health are linked to a changing social convoy. *Research on Aging, 41*(1), 54–84. https://doi.org/10.1177/0164027518774805

Baldassari, E., & Solomon, M. (2020, October 5). The racist history of single family home zoning. *KQED News.* https://www.kqed.org/news/11840548/the-racist-history-of-single-family-home-zoning

Blakemore, E. (2019). *How the GI Bill's promise was denied to a million Black WWII veterans.* History Channel. https://www.history.com/news/gi-bill-black-wwii-veterans-benefits

Brooks, D. (2020, March). The nuclear family was a mistake. *The Atlantic.* https://www.theatlantic.com/magazine/archive/2020/03/the-nuclear-family-was-a-mistake/605536/

California Courts. (2021). *Visitation rights of grandparents.* The Judicial Branch of California. https://www.courts.ca.gov/17976.htm?rdeLocaleAttr=en

Chambers, M., Garriga, C., & Schlagenhauf, D. (2012). The New Deal, the GI Bill and the post-war housing. https://economicdynamics.org/meetpapers/2012/paper_1050.pdf

Colorado House Bill 15-1258, A Bill for an Act Concerning the Creation of a Family and Medical Leave Insurance (FAMLI) Program (2015). https://www.statebillinfo.com/bills/bills/15/1258_01.pdf

Cromartie, J., & Nelson, P. (2009). *Baby boom migration and its impact on rural America* (Economic Research Report No. 79). United States Department of Agriculture, Economic Research Service. https://www.ers.usda.gov/publications/pub-details/?pubid=46231

Cromartie, J., von Reichert, C., & Arthun, R. (2015). *Factors affecting former residents' returning to rural communities* (Economic Research Report No. 185). United States Department of Agriculture, Economic Research Service. https://www.ers.usda.gov/webdocs/publications/45361/52906_err185.pdf?v=1275.1

Daily Beast. (2018, September 12). *The postwar housing boom wasn't all sunshine and roses.* https://www.thedailybeast.com/the-postwar-housing-boom-wasnt-all-sunshine-and-roses

de Beauvoir, S. (1952). *The second sex.* Knopf.

Ewan, H. H., & Chahal, J. (2013). Influence of late life stressors on the decisions of older women to relocate to congregate senior housing. *Journal of Housing for the Elderly, 27*(4), 392–408. https://doi.org/10.1080/02763893.2013.813428

Family Caregiver Alliance. (2016). *Caregiver statistics: Demographics.* https://www.caregiver.org/caregiver-statistics-demographics

Federal Trade Commission. (2015). *Reverse mortgages.* https://www.consumer.ftc.gov/articles/0192-reverse-mortgages#how

Fiore, A. M., Niehm, L., Hurst, J., Son, J., Sadachar, A., Russell, D., Swenson, D., & Seeger, C. (2015). Will they stay or will they go? Community features important in migration decisions of recent university graduates. *Economic Development Quarterly, 29*(1), 23–37. https://doi.org/10.1177/0891242414559070

Friedan, B. (1963). *The feminine mystique.* Norton.

Glynn, J. S. (2012, November 20). *Working parents' lack of access to paid leave and workplace flexibility.* Center for American Progress. https://www.americanprogress.org/issues/economy/reports/2012/11/20/45466/working-parents-lack-of-access-to-paid-leave-and-workplace-flexibility/

Granbom, M., Perrin, N., Szanton, S., Cudjoe, T., & Gitlin, L. (2019). Household accessibility and residential relocation in older adults. *Journals of Gerontology: Social Sciences, 74*(7), e72–e83. https://doi.org/10.1093/geronb/gby131

Jungers, C. M. (2011). Leaving home: An examination of late-life relocation among older adults. *Journal of Counseling & Development, 88*(4), 416–423. https://doi.org/10.1002/j.1556-6678.2010.tb00041.x

Koss, C., & Ekerdt, D. (2017). Residential reasoning and the tug of the fourth age. *The Gerontologist, 57*(5), 921–929. https://doi.org/10.1093/geront/gnw010

Legislative Council of the Colorado General Assembly. (2020). *2020 state ballot information booklet* [Research Publication No. 748-1]. http://leg.colorado.gov/sites/default/files/blue_book_english_for_web_2020_0.pdf

Margolis, R. (2016). The changing demography of grandparenthood. *Journal of Marriage and Family, 78*(3), 610–622. https://doi.org/10.1111/jomf.12286

Margolis, R., & Verdery, A. (2019). A cohort perspective on the demography of grandparenthood: Past, present, and future changes in race and sex disparities in the United States. *Demography, 56*(4), 1495–1518. https://doi.org/10.1007/s13524-019-00795-1

National Alliance for Caregiving (NAC) and AARP. (2020). *Caregiving in the U.S.* (2020 Report). https://www.caregiving.org/wp-content/uploads/2021/01/full-report-caregiving-in-the-united-states-01-21.pdf

National Partnership for Women and Families. (2021). *State paid family and medical leave insurance laws.* https://www.nationalpartnership.org/our-work/resources/economic-justice/paid-leave/state-paid-family-leave-laws.pdf

New York State Kinship Navigator. (2016). *Grandparents seeking visitation or custody* [Legal fact sheet]. http://www.nysnavigator.org/wp-content/uploads/2016/01/Grandparents-Seeking-Visitation-or-Custody-KN.pdf

NPR. (2017, May 3). *A 'forgotten history' of how the U.S. government segregated America* (Transcript of *Fresh Air*). National Public Radio. https://www.npr.org/transcripts/526655831

Pew Research Center. (2012, March 15). *Who are the boomerang kids?* https://www.pewsocialtrends.org/2012/03/15/who-are-the-boomerang-kids/

Roy, N., Dube, R., Despries, C., Freitas, A., & Legare, F. (2018). Choosing between staying at home or moving: A systematic review of factors influencing housing decisions among frail older adults. *PLoS ONE, 13*(1), e0189266. https://doi.org/10.1371/journal.pone.0189266

Sedano, S. T., Latia de Roda, P., & Ortiz Soto, P. (2020). Thinking about scenarios of grandparenthood. *Journal of Infant, Child, and Adolescent Psychotherapy, 19*(1), 98–106. https://doi.org/10.1080/15289168.2019.1699755

ShelterPoint. (2019, April 25). *New York Disability celebrates 70 years!* https://info.shelterpoint.com/Blog/new-york-disability-history

U.S. Bureau of Labor Statistics. (2000, February 16). *Changes in women's labor force participation in the 20th century.* https://www.bls.gov/opub/ted/2000/feb/wk3/art03.htm

U.S. Department of Veterans Affairs. (2013). *Education and training: History and timeline.* https://www.benefits.va.gov/gibill/history.asp

Credit

Fig. 7.1: Source: https://www.census.gov/library/visualizations/2020/comm/map-popest-65-and-older.html.

Who Takes Care of Whom?

INTRODUCTION

The root of caring takes place in a family structure. While the make-up of any given family varies, an infant receives sustenance, clothing, diaper changes, and—in the right circumstances—support for healthy cognitive and emotional development from the adults in their life. In previous generations, the societal assumption was that female household members were the primary providers of this care, and many policies were structured that supported this arrangement.

By the end of this chapter, students will be able to

1. Describe the ways families care for each other across the life course.

2. Explain the influence of policy on caregiving arrangements.

3. Compare and contrast the influence of two caregiving policies on day-to-day experiences.

The Social Security Act, passed in 1935, is a prime example. In the **Social Security Act**, only women were entitled to survivor's benefits. This additional benefit assumed that they were at home, caring for the children, and was given to them so that they would be able to continue providing for their children if their husband died. In 1973, a widower named Stephen Wiesenfeld sued the Social Security Administration to obtain these benefits on behalf of himself and his newborn son. Bucking the societal assumption, his wife had been the primary earner. He wanted to be able to remain home and care for his son after his wife died. *Weinberger v. Wiesenfeld* (1975) was a landmark case for gender discrimination in policy, argued by Ruth Bader Ginsburg (who would later become a Supreme Court justice) when she was the head of the American Civil Liberties Union's Women's Rights Project. This case is important to our discussion of elder care because it provides an illustration of a situation in which policy assumptions impacted caregiving in a family and thus demonstrates how policies impact caregiving arrangements.

CARING FOR ELDERS

While the vast majority of older adults will independently care for themselves until the end of their lives, many older adults will require some assistance with daily needs due to declining physical and/or cognitive health. (See Chapter 5 for more on physical health and Chapter 6 for more on cognitive health.) **Instrumental Activities of Daily Living** (**IADLs**) are independent living tasks such as medication management, finances, grocery shopping, chores, laundry, meal preparation, and transportation. IADLs are those things that someone needs to do to be able to live independently. They are also tasks that people in a household may do cooperatively. People of all ages may obtain outside assistance with IADLs, such as hiring a house cleaner or using a ridesharing service like Uber. **Activities of Daily Living** (**ADLs**) are personal care tasks, such as bathing, grooming, dressing, toileting, and feeding, which are typically done by adults for themselves.

When an older adult requires assistance, informal caregivers—family members or friends—provide the majority of this care, unpaid. In 2015, just over 34 million Americans provided care to someone aged 50 or older, and nearly half of these (15.7 million) provided care to someone with Alzheimer's or another dementia (Family Caregiver Alliance, 2016). Statistics that report on the number of caregivers use a wide range of activities and varying amounts of time in their identification of caregivers. Caregivers can live with their care recipient or not. Some caregivers live at a distance (more than an hour away) and provide support such as researching local services, managing finances, arranging appointments, and, of course, offering emotional support. Other caregivers co-reside with their care recipient and provide hands-on care around the clock. There is also a vast array of caregiving that goes on in between these extremes. Eighty-five percent of all caregivers are family members (Family Caregiver Alliance, 2016). They care for parents (42%), adult children (14%), in-laws (7%), and grandparents/grandparents-in-law (7%). The division of labor is often gendered, with female caregivers providing more hands-on care and male caregivers helping more with finances (Family Caregiver Alliance, 2016).

Caregivers are most likely to be children caring for one or both of their aging parents, with daughters providing more hours of care than sons (Family Caregiver Alliance, 2016). Seventy percent of people caring for their parents are between the ages of 50 and 64, which has significant implications for their own ability to save and invest for their retirement during the latter years of their working life and impacts their ability to accept higher-paying, more demanding jobs. Employed family caregivers often experience role conflict and make employment adjustments such as retiring early or reducing hours to resolve this conflict (L. Li & Lee, 2020). L. Li and Lee (2020) found that making employment adjustments has an adverse effect on mental health and life stress that is directly related to how many employment adjustments a caregiver makes.

Caring for aging parents often causes tension between siblings, who must negotiate both division of labor and determining what is in the best interest of the parents (Jacobs, 2013). This negotiation is often fraught with the ghosts of Christmases past (proverbially), and siblings may be unconsciously responding to years of perceived hurts and slights in the context of the situation before them (Lashewicz & Keating, 2009). Families with histories of trauma, such as abuse, neglect, or other adverse childhood experiences, may have additional challenges in negotiating caregiving situations, particularly if the person in need of care perpetrated any of the adverse experiences. These families may need the help of a professional counselor to address their caregiving challenges. Overall, there is some evidence that sibling relationships that were strong to begin with are strengthened by caregiving, while those that were strained become more strained (Lashewicz & Keating, 2009). Issues specific to caregiving tend to stem from expectations regarding which siblings should provide care, sometimes based on geography or gender, equity/fairness in division of labor, and perceptions that one sibling appears to be taking control and/or making all the decisions (Jacobs, 2013; Lashewicz & Keating, 2009). Some of these issues may be universal, while others are rooted in culture.

IN WHAT WAYS DOES CULTURE INFLUENCE CAREGIVING?

Culture is "the customs, arts, social institutions, and achievements of a particular nation, people, or other social group" (Oxford Languages, n.d., definition 2). As this chapter began, we discussed the American cultural assumptions of women as caregivers that became rooted in policy. Like other policies, these were written by whites, most often men, most (if not all) of whom were born in the United States. As such, the policies may not account for the realities of non-white, non-majority cultures and women. **Intersectionality** (Crenshaw, 1989), discussed in Chapter 1, refers to the ways various aspects of identity overlap or "intersect." Crenshaw (1989) originally used it to describe the case of a Black woman who sued a factory for discrimination in hiring. The court ruled against her, saying that both Blacks and women were being hired, disregarding the fact that the roles in which Blacks were hired excluded women and the roles in which women were hired excluded Black people. Factors such as age, race, gender, sexual orientation, marital status, and many more may lead to privilege and disadvantage in different contexts and spaces, often at the same time. How is this relevant to caregiving? Different cultural groups may have differing expectations around caregiving. These expectations may interact with policies and laws in unexpected ways.

Caregiving Expectations and Intersectional Factors

The **Family and Medical Leave Act** (**FMLA**) (U.S. Department of Labor, n.d.) is the only federal law in the U.S. that provides any kind of leave for caregiving responsibilities. It provides up to 12 weeks of unpaid, job-protected leave each year for employees who meet certain criteria and who work for employers who meet certain criteria. Employees must: have worked for the covered employer for at least 12 months, have worked at least 1,250 hours in the preceding 12 months for that employer, and work at a location where the employer has at least 50 employees within 75 miles. Employers covered under FMLA are all local, state, and federal employers, schools, and private sector companies who employ 50 or more workers for at least 20 weeks of the year. Many people associate FMLA with maternity leave, and one of its primary provisions is for the birth or adoption/fostering of a child and bonding with that child. FMLA is one of the only ways someone can take time off for childbirth.

FMLA has significant implications for caregiving too. One of the lesser known provisions is that FMLA can be taken "to care for an immediate family member (spouse, child, or parent—but not a parent 'in-law') with a serious health condition" (U.S. Department of Labor, n.d., question 5). Yet, many times, the caregiving needs of aging parents are far longer than the 12 weeks allotted by FMLA. The average duration-of-care provision is 4 years (Family Caregiver Alliance, 2016), and while not all of that time may be intensive, daily, hands-on care, it is nearly impossible to predict whether caregiving responsibilities that preclude working can be completed in 12 weeks. Family/work role conflict has been shown to result in poorer mental health outcomes for caregivers (L. Li & Lee, 2020).

Specific provisions of the law provide specific challenges for some groups. For example, the scope of the law that only permits employees of certain types of businesses favors industries that have been historically dominated by whites and by men. The narrow definition of family favors those in legally defined family structures such as marriage, including marriage by the caregiver's parents. According to the FMLA,

> Parent means a biological, adoptive, step or foster father or mother, or any other individual who stood ***in loco parentis*** [italics original, bold added] to the employee when the employee was a son or daughter (as defined by the FMLA). This term does not include parents-in-law. (FMLA, 1993)

In loco parentis means that the person acted in the role of a parent to the worker/caregiver, and as far as the FMLA is concerned, when that worker was of a dependent age. Family members who came into the picture later, such as a parent's longtime partner, would not be included in this definition. This provision also excludes extended family members, such as aunts or uncles who may not have children of their own, and **fictive kin**—close friends who are family in all ways but blood.

The provision that FMLA leave is unpaid unfairly disadvantages low-wage workers. Finances have been shown to drive who is able to take family leave and how long those leaves are (Armenia & Gerstel, 2006). Additionally, data shows that caregivers with a spouse present—even an ex-spouse who provides support—are much more likely to take leave, suggesting that workers who take unpaid leave need to have someone else available to provide financial support (Armenia & Gerstel, 2006). Armenia and Gerstel (2006) also found that people with higher family income were more likely to take leave. Taking leave, reducing hours, or otherwise adjusting employment to meet caregiving demands is likely to result in concerns about current and future financial security (L. Li & Lee, 2020). Across the board, only 46% of all workers are eligible for FMLA leave. Hispanic workers have the least access, as only 41% work in eligible jobs. Additionally, all groups experience disparity between those who are eligible for FMLA and those who can afford to take it. Hispanic workers have the lowest eligibility and affordability, at 29% of all workers, while African American workers have the greatest disparity between those who are eligible and those who can afford to take FMLA leave (Joshi et al., 2020). Lower-wage workers who take leave have greater odds of having difficulty making ends meet during their leave than higher-wage workers (Vohra-Gupta et al., 2020).

Caregiving statistics suggest that Hispanic and African American caregivers experience higher caregiving burden than their white counterparts do—57% of African American caregivers and 45% of Hispanic caregivers provide an average of 30 hours per week of care, yet Armenia and Gerstel (2006) found they are no more likely to take FMLA leave, suggesting differences in their ability to take leave (Family Caregiver Alliance, 2016). Unfortunately this finding was supported nearly 14 years later, when Vohra-Gupta and colleagues (2020) found that African American respondents had the highest rates of needing leave, and the highest proportion of those not taking leave for financial reasons, as compared to both Hispanic and white workers.

The FMLA was intended to be gender neutral, yet women are nearly twice as likely as men to take FMLA leave (Armenia & Gerstel, 2006). Some of this can be attributed to the FMLA provisions related to childbirth and bonding with a newborn, but not all of it. Armenia and Gerstel (2006) found that men were likely to take longer leaves than women when caring for a sick parent, suggesting that men take leave in a crisis and women handle more routine care, but this finding is skewed by the low numbers of men taking long caregiving leaves in the first place. Some states are making strides toward creating caregiving leave of their own, such as Colorado, as illustrated in Figure 7.1. The only other federal legislation related to caregiving is the **RAISE Family Caregivers Act**, discussed further in *Policy Spotlight: RAISE Family Caregivers Act*.

Policy Spotlight: RAISE Family Caregivers Act

The "Recognize, Assist, Include, Support, and Engage (RAISE) Family Caregivers Act" of 2017 became law in January 2018. It creates an advisory council whose role is to develop a national family caregiving strategy. The advisory council includes a diverse array of organizations including MHP Salud, the National Asian Pacific Center on Aging, the National Indian Council on Aging, the National Caucus & Center on Black Aging, and SAGE Advocacy & Services for LGBT Elders. In November of 2020 the council approved five goals and 26 recommendations to submit to Congress (Administration for Community Living, 2020).

   Goal 1: Family caregivers' physical, emotional, and financial well-being will improve as a result of expanded awareness, outreach, and education.

Goal 2: Family caregivers are recognized, engaged, and supported as key partners with providers of health care and long-term services and supports.

Goal 3: Family caregivers have access to an array of flexible person- and family-centered programs, supports, goods, and services that meet the diverse and dynamic needs of family caregivers and care recipients.

Goal 4: Family caregivers' lifetime financial and employment security is protected and enhanced.

Goal 5: Family caregivers are engaged stakeholders in a national research and data gathering infrastructure that documents their experiences, translates evidence into best practices, develops person- and family-centered interventions, and measures progress toward the National Family Caregiver Strategy.

The complete list and other resources can be found at the RAISE Family Caregiver Resource and Dissemination Center. https://www.nashp.org/the-raise-family-caregiver-resource-and-dissemination-center/

Ethnicity and Gender and How They Shape Caregiving Responsibilities

The idea of cultural influences on caregiving was introduced in Chapter 1 when we discussed **filial piety**, a concept derived from Confucian teaching that emphasizes intergenerational relationships and the good of the family (Lai, 2010). Some caregivers interpret filial piety as an obligation to care for, "assist, respect, obey, please, and maintain contact with elderly parents" (Lai, 2010, p. 209). When considering any cultural influence, it is important to remember that not everyone in a cultural group shares a belief. Lai (2010) found that respondents who identified more closely with elements of filial piety experienced less caregiving-related burden than those with lower scores on a measure of filial piety. But this may not tell the whole story. What happens in families in which siblings, caregivers, and care recipients feel differently about filial piety? We must ask ourselves whether these are different from the instances discussed above, in which siblings disagree about the care of their aging parents or parents and children disagree about care needs.

Case Study: Culture-Specific Aging Services

In areas where there is an enclave of people from a particular cultural group, aging services can be customized to address the culture-specific needs of that population. One example is the existence of Korean-specific aging services in an area in central Maryland. In this area, there is a sizeable population of Korean families, many of whom are aging or who have aging relatives living in multigenerational families. Many of the Korean elders prefer to speak their native language and to reside with their families when they are in need of care.

In response to the size of the population of Korean elders, the county has a Korean-speaking social worker on staff at its Office of Aging and Independence. This social worker provides most of the department's services in Korean, such as information and referral, health insurance counseling, and community living programs. These services allow Korean elders to remain in the community in their own homes or in the homes of family members for as long as possible, as is culturally appropriate.

Another community-based service that serves Korean elders is Korean-specific adult day care. These programs support elders and their caregivers by providing daytime supervision and socialization. They allow adult children to work without worrying about a parent who should not be left alone, and to delay or eliminate the need for institutionalization, which supports filial piety values.

Finally, if institutionalization is required, there is one nursing home in the area that has a Korean-specific, long-term care unit. This unit provides person-centered, culturally specific services. The staff all speak Korean. The activities are culturally appropriate, and the food is prepared by a particular chef. While many Korean families avoid nursing home placement, this option is available if they have no other choice.

Native Americans are another cultural group discussed in Chapter 1. As with Chinese families, it is important to consider in-group as well as between-group diversity. Native populations consist of many different tribes with different customs and beliefs (Brown & Gibbons, 2008). Despite this intergroup variability, as in Chinese culture, respecting and caring for elders is a nearly universal view (Brown & Gibbons, 2008). Native communities experience many structural barriers to formal caregiving due to the rurality of reservations and the chronic underfunding of the **Indian Health Service** (Brown & Gibbons, 2008). The Indian Health Service is an agency of the U.S. Department of Health and Human Services that is primarily responsible for providing health services to American Indians and Alaska Natives (Indian Health Service, n.d.). As a result of these structural challenges, informal family caregivers provide the majority of long-term services and supports (Jervis et al., 2002). Despite high rates of chronic health conditions in Native and Indigenous communities, elders report high rates of social support (Conte et al., 2015). In some communities and tribes there are fewer family members present to provide care, and one tribe reports success with a small assisted-living facility (Brown & Gibbons, 2008). As the number of Native elders grows, other communities may need to consider developing formal support structures to provide care, and policy makers will need to ensure that policy structures support and do not hinder this development.

Policy Spotlight: On Lok, and Ethnic and Economic Factors of the Origins of PACE

The unique needs of ethnic minority elders have sometimes led to national programs that have benefitted all, as in the case of On Lok. On Lok was developed in the 1970s in San Francisco in response to the needs of seniors in the community who wanted to age at home, and whose needs did not require a nursing home level of care (G. K. Li et al., 2009). The Immigration Act of 1965 removed restrictions on immigration from certain areas, including China, which resulted in unprecedented growth in the Chinatown neighborhood of San Francisco (Lehning & Austin, 2011). Many of the immigrants were single men who had come to work and were now aging in place. In response to the growing population, the Chinatown-North Beach District Health Committee of the San Francisco Public Health Department conducted a needs assessment and found many frail elders whose needs were not being met by existing services yet who wanted to remain in the community (G. K. Li et al., 2009; Lehning & Austin, 2011). It was determined that the types of services they needed, such as meals, socialization, and medical care, could be provided by specially designed adult day services at a much lower cost than the cost of nursing home care. The initial program received a demonstration grant from the Administration on Aging aimed at producing cost-effective alternatives to nursing homes (Lehning & Austin, 2011). This On Lok demonstration project resulted in the creation of Program of All-Inclusive Care for the Elderly (PACE), a Medicare- and Medicaid-supported nursing home without walls that has been replicated across the country (G. K. Li et al., 2009). PACE participants must be over the age of 55, live within a designated PACE catchment area, be nursing home eligible, and be able to live safely in the community (G. K. Li et al., 2009). In 2020, 53,000 people were enrolled in PACE (National PACE Association, 2020). More information on PACE is provided in Chapter 11.

ELDERS CARING FOR OTHERS

Much of the discussion about caregiving revolves around the idea that older adults are the recipients of care, but seldom the givers of care. This section seeks to dispel those myths. Aside from sharing statistics on older adults who care for other older adults such as spouses, this chapter will cover two specific populations: kinship caregivers and the parents of aging people with disabilities. According to the Family Caregiver Alliance (2016), 34% of all caregivers are over the age of 65 themselves. Older caregivers, those over the age of 75, spend an average of 34 hours a week providing care, which is higher than the average across all caregivers.

GRANDFAMILIES AND THE POLICIES THAT INFLUENCE THEM

Kinship caregiving is care provided to children by non-parental relatives. The literature discussing grandfamilies is vast. This section is intended to provide a snapshot of the types of situations covered in this area and to suggest areas for policy interventions. **Grandfamilies** is a blanket term referring to households where a child lives with at least one grandparent and no parents. Other people, such as the grandparent's spouse and the child's aunts, uncles, and/or cousins, may also be present in the household (Pilkauskas & Dunifon, 2016). Compared to children in non-relative homes, foster children who reside in kinship arrangements, including with grandparents, have better outcomes (Harnett et al., 2014). Grandparents, on the other hand, experience higher levels of parenting stress than foster parents, mostly due to a lack of practical support (Harnett et al., 2014; Backhouse & Graham, 2013). Grandparents often receive fewer instrumental supports than non-relative foster parents do, and they may not be eligible for stipends. Grandparents may also choose not to take formal custody to avoid conflict with their own children, but such arrangements leave grandparents ineligible for many resources.

Grandparents also report lower perceived emotional support than foster parents do (Harnett et al., 2014; Backhouse & Graham, 2013), which may be because they are out of sync with their same-aged peers, who are no longer dealing with child-rearing concerns. Grandparents also may have little in common with their grandchildren's friends' parents. This lack of emotional support is an important factor for grandparent health, as greater social support predicts better health among grandparent caregivers (Hayslip et al., 2015), suggesting potential policy and program interventions for better outcomes (Chan et al., 2019).

The circumstances that lead grandparents to be primary caregivers are often complex and include drug and alcohol addiction, mental illness, incarceration, domestic violence, and serious illness (Backhouse & Graham, 2013). Depending on the reason, grandparents may experience financial issues, legal battles, and conflict with the child or children's parents as they try to negotiate the caregiving situation (Backhouse & Graham, 2013). They may lack the financial resources for developing written legal plans or formalizing custody (Peterson, 2018). There may be multiple grandchildren in the household with varying legal situations. Grandparents who raise grandchildren due to the drug use of the child's parent experience more instability in the household than those who provide care for other reasons. In fact, in some cases, the incarceration of the parent increases the stability of the grandparent-headed household, particularly if the parent was disruptive (Yancura, 2013).

Grandparents often report concerns about the future, including insecurity about their own health, issues such as the grandchildren's education and raising teenagers, and what would happen to the children if they became unable to provide further care (Backhouse & Graham, 2013). Caregiving responsibilities may preclude grandparents from being able to participate in leisure activities as they turn over their spare time to instrumental activities of caregiving and running a household. Some fear they will be unable to sustain these activities as they grow older (Marken & Howard, 2014), or that they will die before their grandchildren are able to live on their own (Peterson, 2018). Those who do try to plan for their grandchildren's futures often have trouble identifying potential back-up caregivers due to the age and other responsibilities of family members and trusted others (Peterson, 2018).

Grandparents often struggle with grief and conflict relating to the situation that led to their own child being unable to care for their children (Backhouse & Graham, 2013). In addition, children are often placed with a grandparent as a result of household instability or trauma, resulting in behavioral issues in the child. Children's behavioral or emotional issues are associated with greater depression and distress in the grandparents (Doley et al., 2015). African American solo grandparents experience worse health than similarly situated white single parents, and often experience depression (Whitley & Fuller-Thomson, 2017). A similar study of Hispanic solo grandparents found a high prevalence of multiple chronic medical conditions in the grandparents (Whitley & Fuller-Thomson, 2018), which may have implications for both their future care needs and their ability to continue to care for their grandchildren. There are evidence-based practices shown to decrease behaviors in the grandchildren, suggesting interventions that could provide benefits to both grandchildren and the grandparents (Chan et al., 2019). These practices could be incorporated into policy solutions to support grandfamilies.

Some studies have suggested there are cultural influences on the decision to raise grandchildren, particularly in the domains of responsibility and custom, though these differed based on the reasons that the child's parents were absent (Yancura, 2013). In some Native populations, grandparents provide a central role in children's lives even in the absence of grandparent caregiving (Lewis et al., 2018). Yup'ik Alaska Natives report that when they are raising their grandchildren, those roles expand to include family provider, teacher of appropriate behavior, role model, and wisdom bearer (Lewis et al., 2018). Among African American communities, nearly half of grandparents who co-reside with their grandchildren have primary responsibility for their care, and most are raising the children in the absence of the custodial parent (Whitley & Fuller-Thomson, 2017). However, patterns of responsibility and custom are complex and are not easily explained by white versus racial/ethnic minority divisions (Yancura, 2013). Suffice it to say that culture should be considered when developing policy for, and working with, grandparents who are raising their grandchildren.

AGING DISABLED CHILDREN AND THE INTELLECTUAL AND DEVELOPMENTAL DISABILITY SERVICE SYSTEM

The Family Caregiver Alliance (2016) reports that there are an estimated 641,000 adults over the age of 60 who are living with intellectual and developmental disabilities such as cerebral palsy, autism, epilepsy, and traumatic brain injury. This population is growing at an unprecedented rate, due to general improvements in health outcomes and the health-related benefits of deinstitutionalization (McGinley, 2016). Over the 20th century, for example, the life expectancy of someone with Down Syndrome rose from age 9, in 1920, to age 56 in 1993 (McGinley, 2016).

In addition to the new aging of this population, the movement of this population has contributed to the scope and scale of this caregiving challenge. Currently, about three quarters of individuals with developmental disabilities live in the community, and nearly a quarter have a family caregiver who is over the age of 60 (Family Caregiver Alliance, 2016). Prior to about 1990, this was less of a problem, because the majority of these adults did not live as long as they do now; in addition, this problem was invisible, as the majority of these adults were institutionalized (McGinley, 2016).

What Happens When the Aging Parents Are No Longer Able to Care?

At a time when people with intellectual disabilities died in their teens, 20s, and 30s, the aging of their parents was essentially a non-issue, particularly if they lived in institutions. However, the combination of deinstitutionalization and increased life expectancy has created a perfect storm. Most of the literature on older parents of aging children with disabilities focuses on what will happen when the parents are no longer able to care. Some research suggests that aging parents of adults with disabilities are simultaneously anxious about the future and reluctant to plan for if and when they become unable to care (Pryce et al., 2015). Some parents believe there is no viable alternative, either because existing service structures are too mired in bureaucracy to negotiate or because they do not trust the quality of the services provided (Walker & Hutchinson, 2018).

Some parents believe that the sibling(s) of the person with an intellectual disability will step in when the parents are no longer able to care, without ever having checked with the siblings (Walker & Hutchinson, 2018), leading to a lack of alternative planning and a crisis situation when something happens to the parent(s). Researchers have found that individual-level factors on the part of both the person with an intellectual disability and their non-disabled siblings influence whether or not the sibling is available for care. These include demographic characteristics such as the gender of the sibling (female siblings are more likely to provide care), birth order, and whether or not they are the only sibling. Other factors include the financial stability of the sibling, other life expectations and circumstances of the sibling such as marriage and children, employment status, and the availability of community resources and support. The final set of factors is comprised of individual-level factors on the part of the individual with the intellectual disability, including the degree and type of disability and the lifetime relationship between the person with the disability and their sibling (Saxena, 2015).

Coyle et al. (2014) examined key themes in the transition of a sibling to the role of caregiver once parents were no longer able to care. The first was the role of aging—their own aging, the aging of the person with the intellectual disability, and the aging of parents and others in the support network. The transition to caregiving for a sibling with an intellectual disability often takes place during the mid-life period, and the caregiving sibling may be caring for their parents at the same time. Issues related to aging and the disease process for the person with intellectual disabilities may make caregiving and this transition more challenging, for example, as people with Down Syndrome are more likely to develop dementia (Coyle et al., 2014).

Siblings whose parents engaged in advance planning were more prepared for caring, both emotionally and functionally, and adjusted better to the transition. This may be an area for policy development: to encourage more advance planning for this population. Many siblings find that once they become caregivers, planning continues to be important, especially if they feel that there is no one to take over for them if they are unable to care (Coyle et al., 2014). Siblings may be unfamiliar with formal service delivery systems, and the aging service and disability service systems are remarkably disconnected. This is another area for policy advocacy: to make transitions between the two systems more seamless.

SUMMARY

Caregiving is often discussed on a policy and programming level as a one-dimensional model, with one caregiver and one care recipient. The reality is much more complex, with care being delivered and received in many different directions for multiple people, often at the same time. Thus, the needs of caregivers are also multidimensional, and policies need to consider many different needs. For the nation as a whole, greater attention needs to be paid to family leave, enhancing options for paid leave and providing more flexibility for caregivers in diverse situations. More attention is needed to address the concerns of specific types of caregivers, such as grandparents who are raising grandchildren and individuals who are caring for adults with intellectual and developmental disabilities. Unpaid, informal caregiving is estimated to have an economic value of nearly $500 billion per year. It is time that policy takes caregiving seriously, as it does for other issues of such great import.

KEY TERMS

Activities of Daily Living (ADLs)

Family and Medical Leave Act (FMLA)

Fictive kin

Filial piety

Grandfamilies

Immigration Act of 1965

Indian Health Service

Instrumental Activities of Daily Living (IADLs)

Kinship caregiving

On Lok

Program of All-Inclusive Care for the Elderly (PACE)

Social Security Act

Weinberger v. Wiesenfeld

DISCUSSION QUESTIONS

1. Who takes FMLA leave to care for family members, and how can you account for between-group differences in the opportunity to take leave?

2. If you could design a policy for your state to provide leave for family caregivers, what would it need to contain? How would you balance the needs of caregivers and employers? Compare and contrast with the plans created by your classmates.

3. Grandparents raising their grandchildren often face dilemmas related to custody, support, and other legal matters. Research two programs that require someone be a legal guardian for children in order to receive services, and discuss how these policies can be modified to increase access.

4. Compare and contrast the needs of older adults caring for their children with developmental disabilities with the needs of siblings providing the same care.

Ancillary materials for student practice can be found within Active Learning

REFERENCES

Administration for Community Living. (2020). *Family Caregiving Advisory Council: Final recommendations*. https://acl.gov/sites/default/files/RAISE_SGRG/RAISE%20RECOMMENDATIONS%20FINAL%20WEB.pdf

Armenia, A., & Gerstel, N. (2006). Family leaves, the FMLA and gender neutrality: The intersection of race and gender. *Social Science Research*, *35*(4), 871–891. https://doi.org/10.1016/j.ssresearch.2004.12.002

Backhouse, J., & Graham, A. (2013). Grandparents raising their grandchildren: Acknowledging the experience of grief. *Australian Social Work, 66*(3), 440–454. http://doi.org/10.1080/0312407X.2013.817595

Brown, C., & Gibbons, J. (2008). Taking care of our elders: An initial study of an assisted-living facility for American Indians. *Journal of Applied Gerontology*, *27*(4), 523–531. https://doi.org/10.1177/0733464807313403

Chan, K. L., Chen, M., Lo, K. M. C., Chen, Q., Kelley, S., & Ip, P. (2019). The effectiveness of interventions for grandparents raising grandchildren: A meta-analysis. *Research on Social Work Practice, 29*(6), 607–617. https://doi.org/10.1177/1049731518798470

Conte, K., Schure, M., & Goins, R. T. (2015). Correlates of social support in older American Indians: The Native Elder Care Study. *Aging & Mental Health, 19*(9), 835–843. http://doi.org/10.1080/13607863.2014.967171

Coyle, C. E., Kramer, J., & Mutchler, J. E. (2014). Aging together: Sibling carers of adults with intellectual and developmental disabilities. *Journal of Policy and Practice in Intellectual Disabilities*, *11*(4), 302–323. https://doi.org/10.1111/jppi.12094

Crenshaw, K. (1989). Demarginalizing the intersection of race and sex: A Black feminist critique of antidiscrimination doctrine, feminist theory and antiracist politics. *University of Chicago Legal Forum, 1989*(1), Article 8, 139–167. http://chicagounbound.uchicago.edu/uclf

Doley, R., Bell, R., Watt, B., & Simpson, H. (2015). Grandparents raising grandchildren: Investigating factors associated with distress among custodial grandparent. *Journal of Family Studies, 21*(2), 101–119. http://doi.org/10.1080/13229400.2015.1015215

Family and Medical Leave Act, 29 U.S.C. § 825.122 (1993). https://www.govinfo.gov/content/pkg/CFR-2010-title29-vol3/xml/CFR-2010-title29-vol3-sec825-122.xml

Family Caregiver Alliance. (2016). *Caregiver statistics: Demographics.* https://www.caregiver.org/caregiver-statistics-demographics

Harnett, P., Dawe, S., & Russell, M. (2014). An investigation of the needs of grandparents who are raising grandchildren. *Child & Family Social Work, 19*(4), 411–420. https://doi.org/10.1111/cfs.12036

Hayslip, B., Jr., Blumenthal, H., & Garner, A. (2015). Social support and grandparent caregiver health: One-year longitudinal findings for grandparents raising their grandchildren. *Journals of Gerontology: Series B, 70*(5), 804–812. https://doi.org/10.1093/geronb/gbu165

Indian Health Service. (n.d.). *About IHS.* U.S. Department of Health and Human Services. Retrieved December 30, 2020 from https://www.ihs.gov/aboutihs/

Jacobs, B. (2013, July 29). *Getting along to care for mom.* AARP. Dying and Death Talk. https://dyinganddeathtalk.com/getting-along-to-care-for-mom-by-barry-jacobs/

Jervis, L. L., Jackson, M. Y., & Manson, S. (2002). Need for, availability of, and barriers to the provision of long-term care services for older American Indians. *Journal of Cross-Cultural Gerontology*, *17*(4), 295–311. http://www.doi.org/10.1023/a:1023027102700

Joshi, P., Baldiga, M., & Huber, R. (2020, January 16). *Unequal access to FMLA leave persists* [Data visualization]. Diversitydatakids.org. https://www.diversitydatakids.org/research-library/data-visualization/unequal-access-fmla-leave-persists

Lai, D. (2010). Filial piety, caregiving appraisal, and caregiving burden. *Research on Aging, 32*(2), 200–223. http://doi.org/10.1177/0164027509351475

Lashewicz, B., & Keating, N. (2009). Tensions among siblings in parent care. *European Journal of Ageing, 6*, 127–135. https://doi.org/10.1007/s10433-009-0109-9

Lehning, A. J., & Austin, M. J. (2011). On Lok: A pioneering long-term care organization for the elderly (1971–2008). *Journal of Evidence-Based Social Work, 8*(1–2), 218–234. https://doi.org/10.1080/15433714.2011.541828

Lewis, J. P., Boyd, K., Allen, J., Rasmus, S., & Henderson, T. (2018). "We raise our grandchildren as our own": Alaska Native grandparents raising grandchildren in southwest Alaska. *Journal of Cross Cultural Gerontology*, *33*(3), 265–286. http://www.doi.org/10.1007/s10823-018-9350-z

Li, G. K., Phillips, C., & Weber, K. (2009). On Lok: A successful approach to aging at home. *Healthcare Papers*, *10*(1), 44–49. http://www.doi.org/10.12927/hcpap.2009.21222

Li, L., & Lee, Y. (2020). Employment adjustments and mental health of employed family caregivers in Canada. *Aging & Mental Health*, *24*(12), 2073–2081. https://doi.org/10.1080/13607863.2019.1647136

Marken, D., & Howard, J. (2014). Grandparents raising grandchildren: The influence of a late-life transition on occupational engagement. *Physical & Occupational Therapy in Geriatrics*, *32*(4), 381–396. https://doi.org/10.3109/02703181.2014.965376

McGinley, J. (2016). From nonissue to healthcare crisis: A historical review of aging and dying with an intellectual and developmental disability. *Intellectual and Developmental Disabilities*, *54*(2), 151–156. https://doi.org/10.1352/1934-9556-54.2.151

National PACE Association. (2020). *PACE by the numbers* [Infographic]. Retrieved December 30, 2020 from https://www.npaonline.org/policy-and-advocacy/pace-facts-and-trends-0

Oxford Languages. (n.d.). *Culture.* Retrieved December 30, 2020 from Google at https://www.google.com/search?client=firefox-b-1-d&q=culture

Peterson, T. (2018). Future care planning by older grandparents raising adolescent grandchildren. *Families in Society: The Journal of Contemporary Social Services*, *99*(1), 67–77. https://doi.org/10.1177/1044389418756615

Pilkauskas, N. V., & Dunifon, R. E. (2016). Understanding grandfamilies: Characteristics of grandparents, nonresident parents, and children. *Journal of Marriage and Family*, *78*(3), 623–633. https://doi.org/10.1111/jomf.12291

Pryce, L., Tweed, A., Hilton, A., & Priest, H. M. (2017). Tolerating uncertainty: Perceptions of the future for ageing parent carers and their adult children with intellectual disabilities. *Journal of Applied Research in Intellectual Disabilities*, *30*(1), 84–96. https://doi.org/10.1111/jar.12221

Saxena, M. (2015). Variables that can enhance and complicate sibling caregiving of individuals with intellectual and developmental disabilities. *Journal of Policy and Practice in Intellectual Disabilities*, *12*(3), 210–219. https://doi.org/10.1111/jppi.12127

U.S. Department of Labor. (n.d.) *FMLA frequently asked questions.* Wage and Hour Division. Retrieved December 29, 2020 from https://www.dol.gov/agencies/whd/fmla/faq

Vohra-Gupta, S., Kim, Y., & Cubbin, C. (2020). Systemic racism and the Family Medical Leave Act (FMLA): Using critical race theory to build equitable family leave policies. *Journal of Racial and Ethnic Health Disparities.* Advance Online Publication. https://doi.org/10.1007/s40615-020-00911-7

Walker, R., & Hutchinson, C. (2018). Planning for the future among older parents of adult offspring with intellectual disability living at home and in the community: A systematic review of qualitative studies. *Journal of Intellectual & Developmental Disability*, *43*(4), 453–462. https://doi.org/10.3109/13668250.2017.1310823

Weinberger v. Wiesenfeld, 420 U.S. 636 (1975). https://www.oyez.org/cases/1974/73-1892

Whitley, D. M., & Fuller-Thomson, E. (2017). African-American solo grandparents raising grandchildren: A representative profile of their health status. *Journal of Community Health*, *42*, 312–323. https://doi.org/10.1007/s10900-016-0257-8

Whitley, D. M., & Fuller-Thomson, E. (2018). Latino solo grandparents raising grandchildren: Health risks and behaviors. *Hispanic Health Care International*, *16*(1), 11–19. https://doi.org/10.1177/1540415318757219

Yancura, L. (2013). Justifications for caregiving in White, Asian American, and Native Hawaiian grandparents raising grandchildren. *Journals of Gerontology: Series B*, *68*(1), 139–144. https://doi.org/10.1093/geronb/gbs098

How Does Community Policy Shape the Aging Experience?

INTRODUCTION

Unit 2 of this book described the physical (Chapter 5) and psychological (Chapter 6) changes that may occur as someone grows older. The other chapters in Unit 3 discussed social changes that may occur as someone ages, particularly as they relate to family and caregiving. This chapter explores a central tenet to social work practice, person-in-environment, and discusses how community environmental factors impact individuals even as they are experiencing the physical, psychological, and social changes that may accompany aging. The community factors considered here impact people of all ages, including older adults. This chapter will discuss how macro-level practitioners such as community organizers and politicians can improve the lives of older adults by considering things that improve life for all.

CHAPTER-LEVEL LEARNING OBJECTIVES

By the end of this chapter, students will be able to

1. Describe how community-level livability factors impact the lives of older adults.

2. Define "food desert" and name three ways in which the availability of food impacts aging.

3. Compare and contrast the reasons community planners would plan services for older adults versus for the whole community.

COMMUNITY WALKABILITY

People in the United States used to live where they worked. If you have ever traveled to Europe, you may have seen that in most European cities, people still get places on foot, by bike, or via public transportation. In the United States, that is often not the case. Over decades our housing and transportation policies have combined to create communities that leave us ever more car dependent and that leave those without cars lacking access to basic resources. Consider the neighborhood you grew up in and the one where you live now. Can you walk anywhere? Are there sidewalks? Is there lighting? If you can walk safely, where can you get to in a reasonable distance? Are there restaurants? Grocery stores? Pharmacies? Chances are high that if you live in the United States, you answered "no" to many if not all of these questions. Chances are also high that policies, which you may or may not know about, have combined to create that situation.

Zoning policies are municipal or local laws that limit how land can be used. In general, the more populated an area, the more zoning laws exist. Zoning laws define areas as residential, industrial, and commercial and determine what combination of these activities may occur in a given area. There are benefits and drawbacks to zoning laws, especially as they relate to the walkability of a community. On the one hand, zoning laws keep industries that may be harmful to residents' health or safety from building in residential neighborhoods. On the other hand, when neighborhoods are zoned residential only, it increases the distance between houses and businesses, increasing the need to rely on a car.

The walkability of a neighborhood has additional meaning for older adults. Walkability includes not just distances to locations, but other physical factors dictated by policy, that shape a neighborhood. As discussed in Chapter 4, while not all older adults experience physical decline, increasing age increases the chance of developing mobility issues. For those with mobility issues, walkability includes considerations such as the presence or absence of curb cutouts for wheelchairs or walkers, timing of traffic lights to allow enough time for safe passage across busy streets, and the state of repair of the sidewalks.

A "**walk score**" is a rating system that aggregates the walkability of a given house or neighborhood. It evaluates walking routes to nearby amenities and awards points based on the distance to amenities within different categories. The maximum score is 100. Walk scores are available for any address in the United States and Canada. In general, major cities tend to have the highest walk scores, due to the near-universal presence of sidewalks and the presence of mixed-use neighborhoods. In 2020, the top five scores were in New York City, San Francisco, Boston, Philadelphia, and Miami (Walk Score, 2020). However, in large cities, the walk score can vary across neighborhoods; even within cities with high walkability, there can be pockets where communities, particularly low-income communities, lack access to services and resources. For example, in New York City, residential areas of Manhattan such as Greenwich Village and Chelsea have many businesses and restaurants in close proximity to housing, and many transit options, including both buses and trains, which provide access to many areas of the city. Residential areas in Brooklyn and Queens tend to be much more isolated, with greater distances to businesses and fewer transit options.

FOOD DESERTS

A **food desert** is an area that lacks access to food. According to the U.S. Department of Agriculture, more specifically, a food desert is a census tract that is low income, in which a substantial proportion of the population is unable to get to retail stores that sell healthy and affordable food. A **census tract** is a small area within a county that contains an average of 4,000 residents. Census tracts are used in government assessment and reporting. A low-income census tract has a poverty rate of more than 20%, or a median family income less than 80% of the region's median. In urban areas, food deserts have no grocery stores within 1 mile of a third of the census tract's population. In rural areas, the measure is no grocery store within 10 miles (Ver Ploeg et al., 2011).

Lack of access to food, or food insecurity, is discussed more in depth in Chapter 4. Food deserts represent a specific type of food insecurity in which individuals may want to purchase healthy food, and have the money to do so, but experience barriers in getting to the grocery store because of where it is. In addition, the food that is available where they live, via corner/convenience stores, is unhealthy and less affordable than it would be if purchased in a grocery store. Older adults, particularly low-income older adults, may face particular challenges with transportation and mobility. Transportation will be discussed in detail in the next section. Mobility can be a limiting factor for older adults in being able to walk or use public transportation to get to available food stores. While a physically able person might be able to walk 1 mile to a grocery store and carry home a few days' worth of food, the physical limitations that sometimes accompany late life (refer to Chapter 5) make this more difficult for some older adults. The same concerns arise for being able to walk to and wait for public transportation and to carry groceries home on said transportation. Combatting food deserts and increasing access to healthy foods improves the health of older people, people with disabilities, and families with children— really, the whole neighborhood.

TRANSPORTATION INFRASTRUCTURE

Community walkability and food deserts both describe the ability for someone to get the things that they need from where they live. For people who can afford to own and maintain their own car, walkability and distance to stores may impact quality of life, but they are less likely to impact health and length of life. For people without cars, access to safe, reliable transportation or the lack thereof affects their ability to buy food, see a doctor, get medication, and obtain and maintain gainful employment (Dabelko-Schoeny et al., 2021). Both walkability and transportation are essential infrastructure contributors to quality of life.

The quality of public transportation often depends on who is perceived as having a need. Like in other policy decisions, who has the power to define the problem? In large cities, where traffic and parking make driving impractical and car ownership more expensive, a wider cross-section of the population becomes potential consumers of public transportation. As the costs of owning a car decrease in smaller cities and rural areas, the potential consumers of public transportation are lower income, and the availability, frequency, and reliability of public transportation decline. The acceptability of using and willingness to use different transportation types depends in part on availability and quality, and in part on individual-level factors such as comfort with such systems and the perceived availability of alternatives (Dabelko-Schoeny et al., 2021).

The same group that publishes Walk Score data also has a metric called **Transit Score**. This measure calculates the "usefulness" of the transit routes in an area, taking into consideration the quality factors we've discussed: frequency, type (rail, bus, etc.), and distance to the nearest stop (Walk Score, 2020). It should be no surprise that four of the cities with the top five walk scores appear on the list of cities with the top five transit scores: New York, San Francisco, Boston, Washington DC, and Philadelphia. It is important to note that with Transit Score, as with Walk Score, quality is not the same across the region, even in high-scoring cities. For example, as stated in the previous section, residents of New York City's Manhattan will find it much easier to get to a bus or a train than residents in the far reaches of Staten Island or Queens will.

Transportation infrastructure impacts older adults in much the same ways that it affects younger people—in terms of access to other goods and services. Older adults who miss trips miss out on socialization, medications, groceries, and needed medical tests (Fields et al., 2021). Some trips can be easily rescheduled, such as going to Walmart on a different day. But when medical appointments must be cancelled at the last minute due to transportation issues, in addition to missing out on the necessary medical care, older adults risk an array of negative outcomes like being charged for a missed appointment, facing extended delays in being able to reschedule with a specialist, and/or being labelled as a no-show and getting dropped by that medical provider. While these may seem like severe consequences, all of these have happened, and more.

Older adults and persons with disabilities face additional transportation barriers due to not being able to use regular cars, and having difficulties boarding traditional buses or trains. There are policies that allow for transportation for this population; however, specific services for older adults and persons with disabilities are sometimes contingent upon the existence of transportation infrastructure. According to the Disability Rights Education & Defense Fund (DREDF) and TranSystems Corporation (2010), public transit companies are required under the **Americans with Disabilities Act** (**ADA**) to provide paratransit to persons unable to ride the fixed-route system due to one of three reasons: an inability to navigate the bus or train independently, a need for an accessible vehicle, or some obstacle that prevents the person from reaching the bus or the train. Available transportation is paramount to the provision of paratransit because the ADA requires that paratransit be provided within the areas served by public transportation (42 U.S.C. § 12143(c)). In one medium sized city this meant that someone could be picked up for a paratransit ride within three-quarters of a mile of any fixed bus route (there were no trains in that city). Thus, areas with limited public transportation also lacked paratransit options for disabled persons.

Transportation services for older adults may extend beyond the transportation infrastructure available within a community. There may be public, private, or volunteer entities that provide transportation for older adults. Who provides them determines the policy implications. Door-to-door wheelchair transportation services are often provided by private medical transportation companies. These rides are very costly, and many seniors cannot afford to take them often. Some Medicaid programs cover rides such as these, but to medical appointments only, leaving physically challenged older adults increasingly socially isolated. In addition, those who become wheelchair dependent in later life may live in houses that are less than accessible, making it especially difficult to get in and out of the house to use the transportation that is available. The **Older Americans Act** is one source of older-adult-specific transportation. More information on Older Americans Act transportation can be found in Chapter 12.

THE ROLE OF LOCAL CONTEXT IN SHAPING AGING IN COMMUNITY: WHO 8 FACTORS OF LIVABILITY

The World Health Organization (WHO, 2007) developed a paradigm describing eight factors that make communities more livable for all people. It so happens that addressing these factors also makes it easier for older adults to age in community. Each of these factors can be addressed by local, state, or federal policy, or a combination. The first factor is public gathering spaces—including green space, safe streets, sidewalks, places to sit outdoors, and accessible buildings (AARP, n.d.). The presence of green spaces can be impacted by conservation laws and development laws, just to name two. Conservation policies designate areas as unable to be developed to protect natural features or wildlife. Development policies can be designed such that they require developers to maintain certain amounts of green space per number of houses. Access to public green spaces is associated with better mental health (Wood et al., 2017). Wood and colleagues (2017) also found that for each additional park, well-being scores increased incrementally. Thus, policies that promote green spaces can improve the overall health of a community.

Safe streets can be created through a range of policies that address safety from crime, but also safety from traffic and other hazards. Local policies on policing and the existence of neighborhood watch/associations

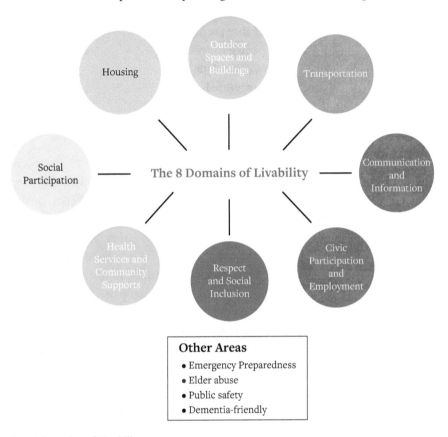

FIGURE 9.1 The 8 Domains of Livability

can both enhance and detract from the safety of a community. Some communities experience over-policing, which can decrease safety more than it can enhance it. Laws such as "Stand Your Ground" increase the power of community watch, but they can decrease safety for some groups within communities, such as when George Zimmerman, a neighborhood watch captain in Sanford, Florida, shot an unarmed young black man, Trayvon Martin. Safe streets for older adults are as much about perception as they are about safety: Older adults are less likely to be victims of crime, but many older adults perceive themselves to be at greater risk and alter their activity patterns accordingly.

Safe streets also include the presence of sidewalks and bike paths, which allow pedestrians to get where they need to go away from speeding traffic. Traffic lights and crosswalks can enhance safety, while their absence can make an area practically unwalkable, reducing access to needed businesses and services. Some communities use a variety of traffic-calming interventions such as speed bumps and traffic islands to reduce the speed of vehicles in residential and pedestrian areas. Sidewalks alone are not sufficient. They must be designed in such a way as to facilitate use by people using walkers, wheelchairs, strollers, and other devices, and be wide enough to accommodate the pedestrian flow. Both design and state of repair are local policy issues. It is up to municipalities to decide how to design sidewalks and to budget for maintenance.

Places to sit outdoors are design features that enhance the ability of older people and people with disabilities to walk. These underappreciated features allow people to rest while walking, perhaps then walking greater distances. Some areas discourage the development of outdoor seating because of concerns that seating areas will encourage groups to congregate, or that people who are homeless will use the spaces for sleeping. But for a safer community, instead of not building outdoor seating, the community should provide safe and interesting activities for groups of all ages and create policies to address issues related to homelessness, such as permanent housing, temporary shelter, and health care services.

The second WHO factor of livability is transportation (AARP, n.d.). Transportation infrastructure is covered in depth in the section above. Expanding transportation makes a community more livable for people of all ages, as it increases mobility and access to jobs, education, and recreation. Transportation is particularly important for older people because of the physical changes outlined in Chapter 5. Older adults who drove in their younger years may reduce the times and distances they drive or stop driving all together. Visual changes, including the generalized decreased acuity of presbyopia and conditions such as cataracts, macular degeneration, and glaucoma, can make it difficult to see adequately enough to drive. They can make it difficult to drive in the dark, due to glare and difficulty adjusting to changes in light, leading many older adults to stop driving at night. Transportation options for older adults can be limited by difficulties exiting their homes and/or difficulties getting in and out of certain types of vehicles. Access to some types of transportation, such as app-based rideshare services like Uber and Lyft, can be difficult due to disparities in technology access and literacy.

The third livability factor is the availability of housing that is adaptable—designed or able to be modified, to allow people to age in place—and of a variety of affordable housing options in different shapes and sizes (AARP, n.d.). Federal policies such as the housing choice voucher program (Section 8) provide housing assistance to low-income families, older adults, and people with disabilities. The housing choice voucher program allows eligible individuals and families to rent any property that meets minimum health and safety standards whose landlord agrees to accept the voucher (U.S. Department of Housing and Human Development [HUD], n.d.). In general, rent subsidies allow voucher participants to rent moderately priced housing in a given area and to pay no more than 30% of their income towards rent (HUD, n.d.). However, in some areas, rents may be higher than the "payment standard" determined by HUD (n.d.), landlords may not accept the vouchers, or zoning laws (covered above) may only allow single-family housing and/or not permit renters. Older adults may also be particularly hampered by the presence of years-long waiting lists for housing vouchers in many locations and limited accessible units to rent.

Zoning laws that permit accessory or in-law type units are more welcoming to older adults, who may want to co-locate with family members but have access to separate space. A new trend called "**granny pods**" (Coppa, 2020) is increasing options for older family members. These are small home units that could be placed on the property of a family member and hooked up to existing utilities, so that someone who required care could live in close proximity to caregivers (Coppa, 2020). While there are many barriers to these units including cost and rules regarding zoning and homeowners' associations, they do provide options for family members who wish to care for an aging or disabled person, but whose homes are not accessible for someone in need of care or do not have adequate space.

The fourth livability factor is the availability of accessible, affordable, and fun social activities that provide opportunities for social participation (AARP, n.d.). Activities specifically for older adults can be run by local departments of recreation, by federal Older Americans Act funds that support senior centers, by both, and/or by others. Some places have community college programs tailored for older adults. But accessible, affordable, fun activities do not have to be specifically created for older adults. This factor can work in combination with the first factor. If there are community spaces in which people can gather, groups can be encouraged to hold events and activities there. Any type of religious organization, club, or interest group can create accessible, affordable, and fun activities. These activities may be lifelong activities older adults have enjoyed for many years. Some older adults who are able to retire use the time to pursue activities they did not previously have time for, while others devote more time to usual activities.

The fifth livability factor is respect and social inclusion (AARP, n.d.). One way for people to feel included is through intergenerational activities that allow people of different ages to feel valued. Like the accessible, affordable, and fun activities of the fourth factor, these can be specifically designed to bring generations together, or they can be activities that have a larger draw. For example, outdoor music could be an accessible, affordable, and fun community event, but the type of music played might draw one generation or another. However, a community chorus or orchestra might draw musicians of different ages who want to play music together. Other types of intergenerational activities are those that bring people of different ages together to learn from each other, with each bringing a skill or talent that the other desires. Some successful groups have had older people helping children with reading, younger people helping older adults navigate electronic devices, and people of all ages learning how to cook together or teaching each other different types of cuisines. Like many of the other factors discussed in this chapter, this type of programming is typically regulated on the local level.

The sixth livability factor is opportunities for a variety of employment options, where older adults can continue to work for pay if they want, move to a part-time employed role, volunteer, or remain engaged in community life in other ways (AARP, n.d.). The presence or absence of job opportunities in general is tied to the economic health of a community. Policies at all levels (federal, state, and local) can impact the health of the economy and the presence or absence of jobs. This factor, however, refers to specific types of jobs, where people of all ages, but especially older adults, can choose how much they want to be engaged in the workforce, with professional and non-professional part-time options.

This factor also calls for the existence of volunteer opportunities that value the skill and experience of the older person. In Amherst, NY (near Buffalo), The Town of Amherst Center for Senior Services provides a great example of doing this well. The senior center has a full-time social worker employed as a volunteer coordinator. That person helps match seniors with all types of volunteer opportunities, both in the senior center itself and throughout the community (Town of Amherst, n.d.). These volunteer opportunities vary in experience needed, level of commitment, time required, and so on. The center serves as a clearinghouse for organizations in need of all types of volunteer assistance, providing area non-profits with a way to recruit qualified volunteers and providing seniors with the opportunity to find the right volunteer position, from those who want to use their lifelong expertise to those who want to try something completely different.

The seventh livability factor, communication and information (AARP, n.d.), recognizes that not everyone has access to the internet and/or broadband. Communities that possess this factor disseminate information through a variety of channels. This should be a priority for everyone who disseminates information to the public. For example, many job applications are now completely online, preventing those who do not have access to a computer or the internet from applying to needed jobs. Some groups may only be able to access computers available in public spaces such as schools, public libraries, and senior centers. This became a serious issue during the COVID-19 pandemic, when libraries and public schools in many jurisdictions were closed for extended periods. The digital divide worsened, as all groups lacking internet were disadvantaged. Children could not access virtual lessons, older adults could not interact with friends and family, people of all ages could not access telehealth services, and people who had lost jobs due to the pandemic had difficulty accessing job postings and applications. Government agencies must also consider this issue—for example, when they disseminate voting materials, they must include information about when, where, and how to register to vote and to cast a ballot. Other information includes tax forms, announcements of public meetings, and other opportunities for civic engagement. The reliance on the internet for information dissemination disadvantages particular groups—those who are economically disadvantaged, people in rural areas for whom broadband is not available, and many older adults.

The eighth and final WHO livability factor is health services and community supports (AARP, n.d.). While healthcare policies are discussed in more detail in Chapter 11, and social determinants of health in Chapter 4,

UNIQUE CHALLENGES OF RURAL AGING

By Beth Prusaczyk

Knowing local context is critical for developing effective aging policy in every community and that is especially true in rural areas. In some ways, aging policy may be more important for rural areas as rural areas have a higher proportion of older adults than urban areas (17.5% of the population in rural areas as compared to 13.8% in urban areas) (Smith & Trevelyn, 2018), and this disparity is compounded by the scarcity of resources in rural areas (Morken & Warner, 2012). Aging in place and age-friendly communities are particularly challenging concepts in rural areas for multiple reasons.

First, while many rural residents own their own homes, the housing stock is overall older and needs more modifications to be age-friendly (Housing Assistance Council, 2014). If older adults cannot stay in their own homes, there are very few options in the community such as apartment buildings, senior or retirement communities, assisted living facilities, and nursing homes (Housing Assistance Council, 2014). Second, there are few home- and community-based services in rural areas (Morken & Warner, 2012) and those that exist may be considerable distances from an older adult's residence. This is related to a third reason why aging in place is challenging in rural areas—transportation. Public and mass transportation is extremely limited and disjointed in rural areas, meaning older adults who no longer drive face challenges to accessing services (Morken & Warner, 2012).

These and other challenges facing older adults in rural areas can be overcome through aging policy that is not **place-neutral** (Rhubart et al., 2021). Place-neutral policies are written to be the same for everyone everywhere, without considering the differential impact of the policy on rural or urban areas despite knowing aging is very different in rural versus urban areas. Avoiding place-neutral aging policies and instead creating and evaluating policies specifically for rural areas is essential for creating age-friendly communities that help older adults age in place in rural areas.

There are several aging policies that could have a significant impact on rural areas. First, policies that help older adults remain in their homes are needed, given the shortage of alternative options in the community. One way to do this would be to provide more funding to bolster existing home modifications programs for rural older adults so that their homes can be made safer and more accommodating for their changing needs (Housing Assistance Council, 2014). Second, the COVID-19 pandemic has presented an opportunity to create and expand policies related to tele-services, services provided over the telephone or through the internet, such as telehealth. Tele-services have the potential to address multiple challenges for rural older adults by supplementing the scarce home- and community-based services and by alleviating barriers to in-person services such as long distances and lack of transportation (Ewing, 2014). A third area of aging policy that could specifically target rural older adults would be to create and fund incentives for health and social service providers to operate in rural areas (Ewing, 2014). The lack of providers in rural areas exacerbates all of the other challenges faced by rural older adults and their caregivers and the benefits of increasing the number of services would be far-reaching.

this factor refers to the availability of medical services themselves. In some communities, access is increasing through the presence of urgent care centers and clinics at pharmacies that offer access to vaccinations and medication reviews. These are important sources of care, particularly in areas with limited numbers of primary care physicians, as they provide important preventive care and keep people from seeking routine care in emergency rooms. But a fully functioning community medical infrastructure should have primary care physicians (PCPs) for everyone, including specialist PCPs such as pediatricians, geriatricians, and family physicians. It should have adequate numbers of specialists so that consults can be obtained in a reasonable time frame. These services should accept insurance and/or be affordable for those without insurance.

"AGE-FRIENDLY" POLICIES

Up to this point, this chapter has discussed community-level policies that improve quality of life for people of all ages, and how implementing these policies also improves quality for older adults. Age-friendly policies are those macro- (community-) level policies that are designed specifically to improve quality of life for older adults. The World Health Organization's Global Network of **Age-Friendly Cities** and Communities strives to make their cities friendlier places in which to grow old. Washington, DC joined this group in 2012 (DC.gov, n.d.).

In 2015, the Washington, DC mayor's office and Age-Friendly DC began the Block-by-Block Walk program (DC.gov, n.d.). They recruited multigenerational teams of volunteers to walk roughly three- to five-block areas of their immediate neighborhoods to identify issues that presented challenges for older residents. Most volunteer teams included older residents and people with disabilities. Each team observed structural and behavioral factors

Case Study: The Impacts of Age-Friendly Factors on Day-To-Day Life

Margo retired from her job as an elementary school teacher last year. She lives in a suburban neighborhood that is surprisingly walkable, with paths leading from houses to small shopping areas sprinkled throughout the community. There are buses every hour, from the shopping areas to a larger mall down the road. Her community has a volunteer driver service in which volunteers are matched with older adults who need rides to doctor's appointments and such. Margo volunteers for this program but also knows that if she were to need to give up her car, she would be able to get rides from it too. Margo also volunteers 3 days a week during the school year at the library, where many retired teachers help elementary students with reading and homework after school. Margo and her wife have a strong social network of people of all ages, and they can rely on them for help with heavier chores they no longer feel comfortable doing themselves. Margo feels active and engaged in her community and can't wait to see what comes next. She may even take a cooking class offered by the local grocery store!

Joanne moved to a 55-and-over community a couple of years before her retirement from the corporate world. Her neighborhood is filled with small, single-family houses that stretch as far as the eye can see. The neighborhood is quiet but lacks amenities such as a grocery store or a hairdresser. She has tried to find someone to help her with yardwork, but as the whole community is 55 and over, there are no teenagers looking to make a few extra dollars. The community bus goes to the local shopping center on Wednesday afternoons. Joanne tried going with them once but felt rushed because she had to be back on the bus at a particular time and was afraid she was going to be stranded if she missed it. Her community has a small senior center with activities, but Joanne doesn't want to be around all those old people. She feels like all they do is talk about their aches and pains, and she doesn't want to play bingo again. Joanne's husband doesn't drive anymore, and with the lack of local activities, Joanne feels increasingly isolated.

to consider whether pedestrians could safely access needed services and amenities. They considered whether traffic lights allowed adequate time for crossing, whether there was a safe place to pause if the light changed mid-crossing, whether design or structures inhibited pedestrian or driver visibility, and whether sidewalks were in good repair. Participants reported the issues to DC government using the 311 mobile app, which allowed them to geo-tag the location and open a ticket for the issue to be addressed. Although the formal evaluation has ended, community members are still encouraged to report problems using the mobile app. They can also use the Vision Zero map, which allows the reporting of issues such as chronic speeding behavior, a stop sign that is not well used, or a traffic light that does not allow sufficient time for crossing.

SUMMARY

The factors of livability discussed in this chapter are unique in two ways, as compared to those in the rest of this book. First, these factors are not policies, but they can be fostered by policies that address day-to-day living and shape the ways people interact with their local environment. Second is the idea of staying local. Each of these factors is impacted by decisions that are made inside the community by locally elected officials and appointees. In the United States, we often focus on large national elections such as presidential races and senate races and fail to participate in local elections. In many communities, turnout for midterm elections is less than 25% of registered voters. Yet these are the elections in which city council members, school board representatives, mayors, governors, state delegates, and other local officials who impact day-to-day life are chosen.

For older adults, the ability to remain living in the community they want to live in, and their quality of life in that community, are shaped by policies around housing, transportation, activities, services, and safety. This chapter also demonstrates that things that make a community livable for older adults also make it more livable for everyone else. This idea is catching on. There is a new non-profit helping with city planning in Canada that talks about 8 80 cities—the idea is that if we plan cities for 8-year-olds and 80-year-olds, they will be good for everyone (8 80 Cities, n.d.). City and neighborhood planning is an aging policy issue.

KEY TERMS

Age-friendly cities

Americans with Disabilities Act (1990)

Census tract

Food desert

Granny pods

Housing choice vouchers

Older Americans Act	Transit Score
Place-neutral	Walk Score
Section 8	Zoning

DISCUSSION QUESTIONS

1. Choose one domain of livability and discuss the ways your community achieves or does not achieve this goal.

2. Identify three ways to make your college campus more age-friendly. Compare your responses with a classmate.

3. Compare and contrast the community-level needs of 8-year-olds and 80-year-olds. Decide whether you agree with the idea that if we plan cities for 8-year-olds and 80-year-olds, they will be good for everyone. Why or why not?

Ancillary materials for student practice can be found within Active Learning

REFERENCES

AARP. (n.d.). *The 8 domains of livability: An introduction.* AARP Network of Age-Friendly Communities. https://www.aarp.org/livable-communities/network-age-friendly-communities/info-2016/8-domains-of-livability-introduction.html

Americans With Disabilities Act of 1990, 42 U.S.C. § 12143(c) (1990). https://www.ada.gov/pubs/adastatute08.htm

Coppa, C. (2020, June 22). 'Granny pods' allow elderly family members to live in a high-tech backyard cottage. *Country Living.* https://www.countryliving.com/home- design/a37788/granny-pods/

Dabelko-Schoeny, H., Maleku, A., Cao, Q., White, K., & Ozbilen, B. (2021). "We want to go, but there are no options": Exploring barriers and facilitators of transportation among diverse older adults. *Journal of Transport & Health, 20,* 100994. https://doi.org/10.1016/j.jth.2020.100994

DC.gov. (n.d.). *Age-friendly DC.* https://agefriendly.dc.gov/page/age-friendly-dc-block-block-walk

Disability Rights Education & Defense Fund (DREDF) & TranSystems Corporation. (2010). *Eligibility for ADA paratransit.* https://dredf.org/ADAtg/elig.shtml

8 80 Cities. (n.d.). *Creating cities for all.* https://www.880cities.org/

Ewing, J. (2014). *Helping rural seniors age in place.* National Conference on State Legislatures. https://www.ncsl.org/documents/health/RuralSeniorsAge814.pdf

Fields, N. L., Cronley, C., Mattingly, S. P., Roark, E. M., Leat, S. R., & Miller, V. J. (2021). Transportation mobility and health among older adults: Examining missed trips and latent demand. *Journal of Transport & Health, 21,* 101069. https://doi.org/10.1016/j.jth.2021.101069

Housing Assistance Council. (2014). *Housing an aging rural America: Rural seniors and their homes.* http://www.ruralhome.org/storage/documents/publications/rrreports/ruralseniors2014.pdf

Morken, L., & Warner, M. (2012). Planning for the aging population: Rural responses to the challenge. Department of City and Regional Planning, Cornell University. http://cms.mildredwarner.org/p/146

Rhubart, D. C., Monnat, S. M., Jensen, L., & Pendergrast, C. (2021). The unique impacts of U.S. social and health policies on rural population health and aging. *Public Policy & Aging Report, 31*(1), 24–29. https://doi.org/10.1093/ppar/praa034

Smith, A. S., & Trevelyan, E. (2019). *The older population in rural America: 2012-2016.* U.S. Department of Commerce, Economics and Statistics Administration, U.S. Census Bureau. https://www.census.gov/library/publications/2019/acs/acs-41.html

Town of Amherst. (n.d.). *Town departments.* http://www.amherst.ny.us/content/departments.php?dept_id=dept_19&menu_id=menu_06

U.S. Department of Housing and Human Development. (n.d.) *Housing choice vouchers fact sheet.* https://www.hud.gov/topics/housing_choice_voucher_program_section_8

Ver Ploeg, M., Nulph, D., & Williams, R. (2011). *Mapping food deserts in the United States.* U.S. Department of Agriculture, Economic Research Service. https://www.ers.usda.gov/amber-waves/2011/december/data-feature-mapping-food-deserts-in-the-us/

Walk Score. (2020). *Cities and neighborhoods.* https://www.walkscore.com/cities-and-neighborhoods/

World Health Organization. (2007). *Global age-friendly cities: A guide.* http://www.who.int/ageing/publications/Global_age_friendly_cities_Guide_English.pdf

Wood, L., Hooper, P., Foster, S., & Bull, F. (2017). Public green spaces and positive mental health – investigating the relationship between access, quantity and types of parks and mental wellbeing. *Health & Place*, *48*, 63–71. http://dx.doi.org/10.1016/j.healthplace.2017.09.002

Credit

FEDERAL AGING POLICIES IN THE UNITED STATES

CHAPTER 10

What Goes Out Must Come In: How Income Policies Influence Late Life in the United States

INTRODUCTION

The nature of work has evolved over the course of U.S. history. At the country's founding, the United States was predominantly agrarian, with most people living in rural areas and engaged in work related to farming. Whether you owned the farm, or worked on that of another, was tied to social class, poverty, and of course, in the case of slavery, to race. Fast-forward to the Industrial Revolution in the mid-1800s, when growing numbers of people moved to cities, particularly in the northern states, to work in factories. As with the agrarian society, one's place in life had a lot to do with social class and race. People of color, particularly Blacks, and women worked in the worst conditions and the most dangerous jobs. Policies in some cases, and the absence of policies in others, exacerbated these conditions.

Work in the modern sense did not begin to emerge until the mid-1900s. In the early 1900s factories were not subject to safety regulations, and there were few limitations on working hours. While accidents were common, the scope and scale of this lack of regulation was brought to life on March 15, 1911 when a fire broke out in the **Triangle Shirtwaist Factory** in New York City. The factory employed mostly young women, who worked at long tables with poor ventilation (Smith, 2011). The fire took place on a Saturday, when workers had already put in nearly 50 hours for the week (Glick, 2011). Workers were locked in during the workday to reduce theft (Smith, 2011). The factory was housed on the top three floors of a 10-story building. The building had one fire escape that did not go all the way to the ground. Fire ladders were not tall enough to reach trapped workers. The lack of an effective fire escape and the locked doors prevented many from being able to escape the fast-moving flames, which fed on the fabric scraps that were everywhere. In total, 146 people died in the fire that day.

By the end of this chapter, students will be able to

1. Describe three different ways in which older adults disengage from the workplace.

2. Discuss the non-financial benefits of work.

3. Understand the role of Social Security, savings, and pensions in late-life income.

4. Name the three legs of the "three-legged stool" and describe how those have changed over the last 50 years.

You may be wondering what that has to do with retirement. This fire, and industrial accidents that resulted in dismemberment and death, propelled the development of labor unions, who fought for policies that improved workplace safety and conditions of work. Some of the policies that came out of this fight shaped how people work today, such as building policies that regulate fire exits, child labor laws that prevent children under a certain age from working, minimum wage laws, and stipulations regarding overtime pay (Henning, 2011; Seminario, 2011; Glick, 2011). Frances Perkins, who became the Secretary of Labor under Franklin Delano Roosevelt, witnessed the **Triangle Shirtwaist Factory Fire**, and some say that led her to support New Deal standards for wages, hours, and working conditions, and the right to collective bargaining (Henning, 2011). The New Deal also brought forth the **Social Security Act**, in 1935. This act provided lifetime income to retirees in certain job categories who met employment requirements. Later in this chapter we will talk more about who was excluded from the Social Security Act, and about some of the societal assumptions associated with those choices.

As these policies were developing, **life expectancy** was also increasing. Life expectancy is an estimation of how many more years someone will live from their current age. Many life expectancy tables show life expectancy from birth, and from 1900–2000 in the United States, significant gains were made in life expectancy from birth. At birth in 1900, a child could expect to live 46 years (for males) and 48 years (for females). By 1950, males could expect to live 66 years from birth, and females 71 years. By the year 2000, life expectancy from birth was 76 years for men and 81 years for women. Much of this improvement came from reduced infant and child mortality. Due to improved sanitation and treatments for infectious disease, such as the discovery and proliferation of antibiotics, many more children survived to adulthood (Schanzenbach et al., 2016), increasing the age to which one could expect to live. You should also note that when the Social Security Act was written in 1935, retirement age was set at 65. Compare that to the life expectancy ages noted in this paragraph.

When, where, and how someone works, and how long they expect to live after they stop working, have significant implications for expectations about what they will do and what their expenses will be. Retirement policies influence the income they have available at that time. Once someone survives to later life, they are more likely to live to an even greater age than their life expectancy at birth predicted, because they have been fortunate enough to escape the many causes of death that could have happened at younger ages (Schanzenbach et al., 2016). That is, your chances of living longer extend with every year that you live. Yet life expectancy is also influenced by social factors such as income and by health behaviors such as smoking and drug use. A 40-year-old female at the highest levels of income might reasonably be expected to live to age 89 (87 for a male), while her counterpart at the lowest levels of income would be expected to live to age 79 (72 for a male) (Schanzenbach et al., 2016). This difference can be seen in cities like Baltimore, where the differences in life expectancy between richer or poorer areas of the city are close to 20 years (age 84, and under age 70, respectively) (Baltimore City Health Department, 2017). Perceived life expectancy and health expectancy impact if and when someone retires, while actual life expectancy and health impact financial needs in retirement, and affect how people spend their retirement years.

WHO IS ABLE TO RETIRE?

The idea of retirement, a time of leisure following many years of work, is filled with assumptions based on life course experiences. Despite changes in the structure and nature of work, including more protections than existed a hundred years ago, there is still significant disparity in who is able to retire. Retirement is reserved for those who have the financial stability to sustain their life without income from a job. As you will read later in this chapter, financial stability depends on both retirement income and savings, and there are many factors—both individual and societal—that contribute to the availability of income and savings. Additionally, some people may be able to sustain life in retirement but are unable to sustain their previous lifestyle, causing loss of status and/or situation, and people in certain groups are more likely struggle than others. The image presented of retirement is of a time to enjoy things such as traveling or visiting grandchildren. These require both health and income, which are often interdependent.

INCOME IN RETIREMENT

Where does income come from in retirement? Retirement income may consist of many sources: Social Security, public or private pensions, retirement savings, investment income, real estate, or other assets.

Social Security

The Social Security system as we know it was created by the **Social Security Act of 1935**. Social Security provides monthly payments to retirees and disabled persons who meet work-related criteria, and spouses and dependents of deceased workers who met those criteria. Many people believe that the Social Security taxes people pay during their working years are deposited into an account for their sole use in retirement. This is false. Workers pay taxes into Social Security, which are used to pay the benefits of current recipients. Any excess is put into a Social Security trust fund to pay future benefits.

The amount of someone's monthly Social Security benefit is calculated based on the worker's highest 35 years of earnings. A person born after 1929 has to have worked at least 40 quarters (10 years) in a covered line of work to be eligible for benefits. A worker is eligible to receive their "full" benefit at age 67. Workers can retire as early as age 62, but workers who elect to do this receive a reduced monthly benefit for life. Alternately, workers can defer collecting Social Security until age 70 and receive a larger monthly benefit for life.

Because workers receive payments based on lifetime earnings, many women receive lower Social Security payments than men. Historically women worked in occupations that were lower paid than men's occupations—particularly when it was legal to discriminate on the basis of sex. Still, in 2019, white women earned 82 cents for every dollar that white men earned (American Association of University Women, 2020). The numbers were even worse for non-white women relative to white men—Black women (62 cents), Hispanic women (54 cents), Native Hawaiian/Pacific Islander women (61 cents), and American Indian/Alaska Native women (57 cents) (American Association of University Women, 2019). Workers who earned low wages throughout their lives and are female, Black, and/or Latinx have significantly less saved for retirement than whites, and report a much bleaker outlook for the future (Gatta, 2019).

The Social Security Act attempted to address some of this gender disparity through spousal rules. Married individuals can access Social Security benefits based on their own work record or that of their spouse. A spouse is eligible if they are over the age of 62 or caring for a dependent child—one who is under age 16 or receiving Social Security disability benefits themselves. The spouse's benefit is up to one half of the retiree's (the person with the work record)'s benefit. If the spouse, often the wife, is eligible for their own benefit, they are able to collect whichever benefit is higher (their own or half of their spouse's). Finally, the same rules for early collection apply. If the spouse has not yet reached full retirement age when they begin to collect, they will receive a reduced benefit for life (Social Security Online, 2013). These rules were designed to be heteronormative, favoring mixed-gender couples, and they rely on the existence of a traditional marriage, which was denied to same-sex couples until 2015.

Pension Plans

Pensions are retirement funds provided by an employer. Traditional pension plans, or **defined benefit plans**, used to be the most common plan. These plans guaranteed a fixed income, either for life or for a predetermined number of years, to retirees who met certain criteria, such as length of employment. These plans had many benefits for employees—they were certain about how much income they would have in retirement, and they did not have to make any decisions about where and how to invest the money (Pension Benefit Guaranty Corporation [PBGC], 2000). These plans were popular at a time when workers would spend their entire career at one company. However, the drawback of these plans is that workers are putting all of their eggs in one proverbial basket. If a company fails or is unable to meet their financial promises, retirees can lose everything. This happened in 1963 to Studebaker auto workers, and despite law changes intended to protect workers, it also happened in the early 2000s to retirees of Eastman Kodak Company.

Employee Retirement Income Security Act

One of those law changes was the passage of the **Employee Retirement Income Security Act (ERISA) of 1974.** This act clarified the expectations for companies that hold pension plans, requiring them to create funding and vesting plans, to create clear criteria for qualification, and to manage the pension funds appropriately (PBGC, 2000). These changes were supposed to make pensions more secure for workers, to ensure their income in retirement.

The Wobble of the Three-Legged Stool

The **"three-legged stool"** of retirement financing refers to a retirement that is secure, seated upon a combination of Social Security income, pension income, and personal savings. This concept came from a time when many people worked for the same employer for their entire career, and retired with a defined benefit pension plan sponsored by the employer or their labor union. This is no longer the reality for most workers. Starting in the early 1980s, there was a change in how people worked.

Manufacturing declined as production became more automated and more global. Jobs were outsourced to countries with lower labor costs. The types of work available to people with less than a college degree moved into the service and care industries. These industries pay far less than manufacturing jobs, thus many Americans work low-wage jobs. These are jobs in which full-time work may not allow someone to afford life's basics. These workers often need to balance multiple jobs or rack up credit card debt to make ends meet (Gatta, 2019). Low-wage jobs frequently offer no sick time, no paid vacations, and no benefits (Gatta, 2019; Butler, 2013). In the professional sphere, some jobs became more contract-based, with workers "consulting" rather than being employees of a company. Consulting is appealing to some because it gives workers more flexibility, but it takes away protections such as job security and benefits. These changes made people more mobile across their work lives, which impacted retirement savings and benefits. With people no longer working for the same company their entire career, pension structures changed too.

By the year 2000 there had been a large increase in **defined contribution plans** such as 401(k)s, with some companies eliminating their traditional pension plans entirely (PBGC, 2000). In defined contribution plans, workers and/or employers may contribute tax-deferred money into retirement accounts on the worker's behalf. These plans give employees more control over the amount they save for retirement, though there is a cap on the percentage of salary that can be invested tax free, and most employers who match have a cap as to how much they will contribute. This move decreased individual worker retirement security and adversely affected some more than others (Morrissey, 2016). In theory, these plans have the potential for greater returns, depending on how the money is invested; however, they are subject to the vagaries of the market and can vary significantly over time (Butrica et al., 2009). Employers who participate in these plans are also not required to contribute anything. In some cases they will only contribute as a match to anything the employee invests, which is a perfect storm in a country where many workers are unwilling or unable to invest in their retirement savings (Morrissey, 2016). In fact, nearly half of working-age people in the United States have no retirement savings, and families in the highest income quintile are 10 times more likely to have retirement savings than people in the lowest quintile (Morrissey, 2016).

Low-Wage Workers and Retirement

Many low-wage workers arrive at retirement age having worked a variety of jobs, all of them for low wages. As one participant in Butler's (2013) study said, "You name it, I've done it" (p. 304). Butler's study collected the experiences of older home care workers, many of whom have worked in other types of direct care for children, older adults, and people with disabilities, cleaned other people's houses, and worked in factories, stores, and restaurants, and on farms (Butler, 2013), none of which provided long-term employment or any type of retirement or pension plan. These workers continued to work in home care despite their own advancing age (the oldest worker was 80) because they needed the money, and the job provided other benefits, such as schedule flexibility and choice about which cases to accept (Butler, 2013).

This history of low-wage work often has taken its toll on the bodies of workers. Low-wage jobs tend to be the most physically demanding. According to the Bureau of Labor Statistics, the job category including nursing assistants had the second highest rates of illnesses and injuries. Truck drivers had the highest rates (Squillace et al., 2009). Low-wage workers often have no control over their schedules, go to work sick because they lack sick leave and can't afford to take time off without pay, and may be forced into early retirement because of the physical demands of the job or a workplace injury (Gatta, 2019; Glick, 2011). Social Security benefits are based on the highest 35 years of wages, with the expectation that wages will rise over the course of a career. For most low-wage workers, wages remain flat or even decrease in their spending power over a lifetime.

PUBLIC BENEFITS FOR LOW-WAGE RETIREES

Supplemental Security Income (**SSI**), **Temporary Assistance for Needy Families** (**TANF**), and **Supplemental Nutrition Assistance Program** (**SNAP**) are public programs not specifically designed for older adults, but they do benefit low-income older adults. Older adults are the main recipients of SSI. Other beneficiaries are those who are blind and those who have a documented disability that is expected to keep them from working for a year or more. As with many needs-based programs, eligibility for SSI benefits is based on a combination of income (money coming in) and assets (things of value someone owns, or cash reserves). Income requirements vary by state. Asset limits for eligibility are $2,000 for an individual and $3,000 for a couple, not counting a house if the applicant lives in it, and in many cases, one car. Federal SSI payments are low—$783 for an individual, and

$1,175 for a couple, per month. States may add to this federal SSI benefit. However, they may reduce the benefit if someone has other income. People may only get SSI if they have exhausted all other sources of income, such as Social Security and pensions, and any other payments for which they might be eligible (Social Security Administration, 2020). A person can get both Social Security retirement or disability payments and SSI. People who receive both are those whose Social Security payments are low enough to fall below the income requirements for SSI. SSI benefits are adjusted based on all other income, including Social Security payments.

Most older adults are not eligible for **Temporary Assistance for Needy Families** (**TANF**), but for older adults who are raising extended family members such as grandchildren, TANF can be a lifeline, as the children or household may qualify if the family is in extreme poverty. Grandparents raising grandchildren may be retired, relying on Social Security income themselves, and be financially unprepared to take on unexpected child rearing. (See Chapter 8 for more on these families.) TANF is a federal program that is funded through grants to states, which gives states flexibility on how it is implemented (Center on Budget and Policy Priorities, 2020). There are two types of grants: family grants and child-only grants. The family grant program was designed for low-income single mothers with few assets and was designed to be time-limited, to encourage participants to become self-sufficient through employment; it has work requirements (Beltran, 2014). Grandfamilies, or kinship caregivers, are more likely to take advantage of the child-only benefits, which only take into consideration the child's income. However, people who apply for TANF are required to seek all other forms of income before eligibility, and grandfamilies may not want to seek child support from absent parents because of tenuous situations that led to the children being in the household in the first place (Beltran, 2014). TANF benefits in general, and child-only benefits more specifically, are also extremely low and do not raise recipients out of poverty (Center on Budget and Policy Priorities, 2020). Grandparents may feel they are not worth the effort of applying.

The **Supplemental Nutrition Assistance Program** (**SNAP**), formerly known as food stamps, is the last defense for many food-insecure people, including older adults, against hunger. As eligibility for SNAP is determined at the household level, it is challenging to discuss the distinct impact SNAP has on reducing hunger in older adults, since older adults may reside in multigenerational households. SNAP eligibility requirements operate on the assumption that people who live together purchase and prepare food together (Dean et al., 2020). In 2018, the most recent year for which data is available, nearly half (44%) of SNAP households included someone 50 or older, and three quarters (75%) of SNAP households that included an older adult were single-person households (Dean et al., 2020). What this means is that older adults are likely to be among those who are food insecure, and living alone increases that risk. While SNAP is an essential lifeline for the households that receive it, there are important limitations. The SNAP amount is based on the Department of Agriculture's Thrifty Food Plan, an extremely low estimation of the amount of money it takes to provide adequate caloric and nutrient intake (Dean et al., 2020). One third of households with an older adult received the maximum monthly benefit, and three quarters of the households that received the minimum benefit contained an older adult. The maximum benefit comes out to about $2.13 per meal per person, and the minimum benefit only covers about five meals per month (Dean et al., 2020).

STOPPING WORK VERSUS STEPPING BACK

Many retirement policies, including Social Security, have an all-or-nothing approach to work—meaning you are either retired or not retired—which has implications for income and for life purpose. Social Security considers someone to be retired as soon as they begin receiving benefits. If recipients choose to continue to work after receiving benefits, which is allowed, there are limits on the income they can earn while under the full retirement age. People between the ages of 62 and 67 who have begun collecting Social Security can only earn $18,240 in income before their Social Security benefit is reduced (Social Security, n.d.). Once someone reaches full retirement age, they can continue to work without it having an impact on their Social Security benefits (Social Security, n.d.). This policy disadvantages lower-income retirees. For reasons discussed above, low-wage workers may seek early retirement due to health concerns but then may return to work to supplement their income, because they are less likely to have retirement savings or pensions. This reduction in benefits adversely affects their overall income at a time when it may be most needed. Higher-wage workers may choose to delay collecting Social Security until they reach full retirement age because they do not need the additional income, and may be able to continue working after they reach full retirement age because their jobs may be less physically demanding.

The decision of when and whether to retire may fall anywhere from needing to work for financial reasons, to staying in the workforce for personal fulfillment, to retiring as soon as one can to maximize years spent in leisure, to needing to retire for the worker's health or to care for a relative or friend in poor health (Choi et al., 2018). In recent years some people have sought options that allow them to reduce their work hours or stress level while remaining engaged in the workplace. A worker's ability to do this varies due to macro factors such as policies in the workplace or industry, and individual factors such as the need to replace income. Offering flexible work arrangements can help companies retain the knowledge and experience of more seasoned workers (Choi et al., 2018).

"Consulting"

Professionals who leave full-time employment may sell themselves as consultants in their previous industries. This option allows them to share their long-earned expertise and remain engaged in the industry while being able to manage their own priorities and schedules. Finance magazines such as *Kiplinger* and *Fortune* offer articles on how to successfully negotiate the transition, reaping all of the benefits and none of the drawbacks. One consultant highlighted in a *Fortune* article sees himself as working part-time, as opposed to being retired, and chose that route due to both being financially secure already and thinking he had maximized opportunities in his previous job (Chew, 2017). A *Kiplinger* article is more cautious, highlighting the benefits that can be obtained from consulting, such as focusing only on those areas which ignite passion, while emphasizing that planning is necessary to successfully achieve one's goals (Lewis, 2020).

Workplace Policies

The ability to consult, or to step back from work in a part-time way, is contingent on workplace policies. As discussed in Chapter 9, the World Health Organization posits that having options for working full- or part-time, or volunteering, makes a community more age-friendly. But the ability to choose when and where to work has not always been age-friendly, and age discrimination remains a workplace issue. **Mandatory retirement**, often at age 65, was the norm for many years. In 1967 the **Age Discrimination in Employment Act (ADEA)** prohibited discrimination in employment based on age, specifically for individuals ages 40 to 65. It did not prohibit discrimination against those over age 65, and it allowed mandatory retirement policies to remain in place (Workplace Flexibility 2010, 2010). The ADEA was amended in 1978 to extend protections to people up to age 70 (Workplace Flexibility 2010, 2010). This change did not ban mandatory retirement policies, but in practice, it did eliminate policies that mandated retirement at age 65 (Lazear, 1979).

Arguments for mandatory retirement suggest that without it, younger workers would not have opportunities for advancement. These arguments are bolstered by the ageist and unsupported view that older workers are less productive and/or less able to keep up with new technologies in the workplace. Companies may favor mandatory retirement because older workers are often paid higher wages (Olsen, 2017), and hiring a younger worker to do the same job may save them money. Immediately following the passage of the ADEA, Lazear (1979) concluded that both firms and workers benefitted when mandatory retirement policies were in place. The ADEA was amended again in 1986 and 1994, eliminating mandatory retirement and protecting all workers over age 40, with no upper limit (Workplace Flexibility 2010, 2010). Despite this, there are exceptions. Mandatory retirement policies remain in many fields (Hannon, 2015).

TABLE 10.1 Mandatory Retirement

A sample of industries that have mandatory retirement ages:

Industry	Age
Law enforcement officers (federal)	50 or as soon thereafter as 20 years of service are reached.
Firefighters (federal)	50 or as soon thereafter as 20 years of service are reached.
Air traffic controllers	50 or as soon thereafter as 20 years of service are reached.
Other law enforcement	Varies
Commercial pilots	60
Judges	Varies by state; upon completion of the latest elected term after age 70 in Alabama; 70 in Maryland

(Alabama Code Title 12, 2019; DCPAS, 2017; Hannon, 2015; Maryland Const. Art. IV § 3, 2015; Part 121 Pilot Age Limit, 2009)

It is not only mandatory retirement policies that impact older workers. Age discrimination in hiring is a significant barrier to employment in later life. One *New York Times* article found that nearly half of workers over age 50 lose their longtime jobs before they are ready to retire and are never able to return to a job with similar pay (Cohen, 2019). This type of discrimination in hiring is, of course, illegal (U.S. Equal Opportunity Employment Commission, n.d.) but is notoriously difficult to prove (Cohen, 2019; Olson, 2017). Those who are unable to regain paid employment experience decreases in quality of life and purpose, and also experience irreparable harm to retirement savings and investments (Cohen, 2019; Yang, 2020). Workers who enjoy their jobs and feel valued are more likely to stay in the workplace than those who do not. Those who feel like they are being treated differently because of their age may choose to retire or leave work, even if they do not lose their jobs as a result of discrimination (Choi et al., 2018).

Feeling valued and having options appear to be key to satisfaction and health, as they relate to choosing to retire or choosing to stay in the workplace. It turns out that value is essential to well-being in retirement as well.

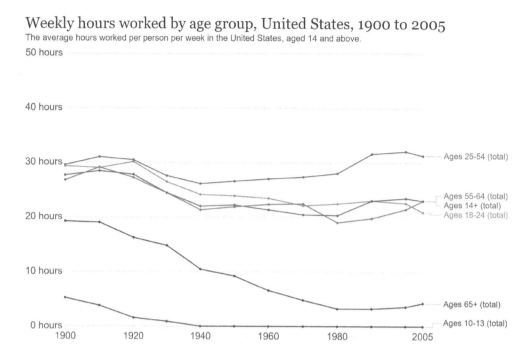

FIGURE 10.1   Hours Worked by Different Age Groups, United States

Volunteerism: Work and a Sense of Purpose

For some retirees the loss of paid employment means a loss of routine and purpose, and that loss of routine and purpose is associated with depression and physical and cognitive decline. **Formal volunteering**, participating in a constructive activity on behalf of a person or group, has been shown to buffer ill effects for older adults who have experienced losses, such as unplanned job losses and interpersonal losses such as that of a spouse (Jang et al., 2018; Yang, 2020). In fact, Yang (2020) found in a nationally representative sample of people over 50 that volunteering an average of 2 hours per week decreased depressive symptoms in those who were unemployed and those who worked part-time. Research on Alzheimer's disease has suggested that engaging the brain may delay the onset of cognitive decline. One such study, using longitudinal data from the Health and Retirement Survey, found that formal volunteering may slow cognitive decline even in those with a genetic predisposition for Alzheimer's (Han et al., 2020).

Older adults relocate for a variety of reasons after retirement—from desired moves to places with more amenities, to moves precipitated by declines in income and health status, which may be less than planned. Gonzales et al. (2019) found partial support for their hypothesis that formal volunteering buffered the effects of relocation. Further, volunteering may impact health and disability. Volunteers in their sample had better health and functional status on IADLs and ADLs than non-volunteers, but the authors acknowledge that this could have made those participants more able to volunteer in the first place (Gonzales et al., 2019). Carr et al. (2018) further supported this claim when they found that people who volunteered more than 100 hours a year experienced 63% less loss of physical function than non-volunteers. The spot, or "dose," of volunteering that appears to result in the best outcomes is somewhere between 40 and 100 hours per year (Morrow-Howell, 2010).

Retirement is often a precursor to starting volunteering. Once older adults begin volunteering, they tend to stick with it. One study found that older adults who volunteered at the first time point measured were still actively engaged 8 years later (Morrow-Howell, 2010). This commitment, coupled with the "dose" response to volunteering, has the potential to suggest policy interventions that can lead to improved outcomes for older adults.

Work Without Income

The ability to volunteer may be associated with socioeconomic status. One might think that higher socioeconomic status would allow more time for volunteering, especially in late life, when people with higher incomes/assets are more likely to be able to retire. Yet findings suggest that people with fewer financial resources volunteer more of their time (Johnson et al., 2018). It may be that they are less able to make financial donations, so they give what they have—time. Another theory posits that lower socioeconomic status may be associated with lower levels of volunteerism because lower-income communities have less infrastructure for volunteering, leading to less recruitment of lower-income elders (Cho et al., 2020).

Three important federal programs that promote volunteerism among low-income older adults are the **Foster Grandparent program**, the **Retired Senior Volunteer Program** (**RSVP**), and the **Senior Companion program**. Two of these pay a small stipend to volunteer participants, while the other reimburses expenses (Americorps, n.d.-b; Cho et al., 2020). They support specific types of volunteerism.

The **Foster Grandparent** program matches older adult participants with children and youth to serve as mentors, tutors, and caregivers (Americorps, n.d.-a). Each state's program looks a little bit different. For example, in New York the focus is on young people with special needs (New York State Office for the Aging, n.d.-a). Foster Grandparent volunteers must commit to serving between 15 and 40 hours per week, and be over age 55 (New York State Office for the Aging, n.d.-a). Foster Grandparent volunteers are able to receive a small monetary stipend if they meet financial guidelines. Eligible participants earn less than 200 percent of the poverty line, after certain medical expenses are deducted (Americorps, 2021). As in many federally funded programs, states are able to supplement the federal dollars with state funds to support the Foster Grandparent program.

The **Retired Senior Volunteer Program** (**RSVP**) is broader than the Foster Grandparent program and more flexible. RSVP volunteers are assigned to work in a variety of human service settings and can choose where, when, and how to volunteer (Americorps, n.d.-b). Additionally, the hours requirements are less stringent, ranging from "a few hours" (New York State Office for the Aging, n.d.-b, para. 1) to 40 hours per week. As in the Foster Grandparent program, RSVP volunteers must be over age 55. Unlike in the Foster Grandparent program, RSVP volunteers receive no direct financial stipend. They are reimbursed for out-of-pocket costs associated with their volunteer work.

The **Senior Companion** program allows older adults to help other older adults remain in their own homes. Senior Companion volunteers are assigned to other older adults to help them with Instrumental Activities of Daily Living (IADLs) such as shopping or paying bills (Americorps, n.d.-c). Since volunteers may be handling other older adults' financial records, a criminal background check is required for this program. Volunteers in this program can also receive stipends. As in the Senior Grandparents program, to be eligible for a stipend, the volunteer needs to have an income below 200 percent of the poverty line (Americorps, 2021b). In addition, Senior Companion volunteers are eligible to receive accident insurance, liability insurance, and excess automobile liability insurance if they are going to be driving as part of their volunteer requirements (Americorps, 2021b). Together these programs provide opportunities for people of limited financial means to engage in volunteer work in their communities.

SUMMARY

Paid work provides income to sustain life and lifestyle. It may also provide structure, routine, and purpose. Retirement, a period of time after someone exits the paid workforce, is seen as a time of relaxation and leisure, a reward for a lifetime of hard work. Yet not everyone is able to retire to a life of leisure. The ability to retire depends on having adequate income in retirement. Retirement income for most Americans consists of Social Security and pensions. Social Security is a federal system that workers pay into, which provides monthly payments in the event of retirement or disability. Payments are calculated based on prior earnings, leaving many low-wage earners with unsustainably low Social Security payments. Social Security was never intended to be the sole source of retirement income.

Retirement income used to rest steadily on a "three-legged stool" of Social Security payments, pensions, and savings. Over the course of time, through policy changes and changing employment patterns, pensions moved from defined benefit plans to defined contribution plans, meaning that workers no longer could count on knowing what they would get in retirement. On the positive side, they were no longer relying on just one company for retirement security—a risk that Studebaker or Kodak employees could tell you all about. But defined contribution plans do not require employers to contribute, and many of them rely on workers making contributions, which employers then match. Overall, Americans have far less in savings than they did a generation ago; this trend has been exacerbated by recessions, stagnant wages, and fewer well-paying opportunities for high school graduates. Retirement is no longer secure.

Low-wage workers may lack an opportunity to retire at all, needing to continue to work well into "typical" retirement age in order to have necessities like housing and food. The social safety net for older adults is minimal. Supplemental Security Income is available only to the lowest-income seniors, and SNAP benefits may help a little but typically do not cover the costs of putting food on the table, due to the structure of the policy and how benefits amounts are calculated. Seniors in the unexpected situation of raising dependent children such as grandchildren, nieces, and nephews in the absence of their parents may qualify for TANF, but complicated qualification rules make this challenging, if not functionally impossible, to access.

Some workers are able to negotiate part-time work, stepping back from the full-time grind but staying intellectually challenged, socially engaged, and financially secure. Others may choose volunteer work for the challenge and engagement aspects. But the ability to volunteer also depends on the availability of resources to cover the costs of volunteering. Federal policies support some low-income older adults in their ability to volunteer. Volunteering is associated with physical and mental health benefits. Polices that support engagement of older adults with the community should be encouraged.

KEY TERMS

Age Discrimination in Employment Act (ADEA)

Defined benefit plans

Defined contribution plans

Employee Retirement Income Security Act (ERISA) of 1974

Formal volunteering

Foster Grandparent program

Life expectancy

Mandatory retirement

Retired Senior Volunteer Program (RSVP)

Senior Companion program	Supplemental Security Income (SSI)
Social Security	Temporary Assistance for Needy Families (TANF)
Social Security Act	Three-legged stool
Supplemental Nutrition Assistance Program (SNAP)	Triangle Shirtwaist Factory fire

DISCUSSION QUESTIONS

1. Describe the differences between defined contribution and defined benefit pension plans. Which would you rather have, and why?

2. What is meant by the "three-legged stool" of retirement? Describe what has changed to cause this analogy to not work anymore.

3. Compare and contrast Social Security and Supplemental Security Income.

4. Discuss three benefits older people get from volunteer activities.

Ancillary materials for student practice can be found within Active Learning

REFERENCES

Alabama Code Title 12, Courts, Ala. Stat. § 12-18-7 (rev. 2019). https://codes.findlaw.com/al/title-12-courts/al-code-sect-12-18-7.html

American Association of University Women. (2019). *The simple truth about the gender pay gap: Fall 2019 update.* https://www.aauw.org/resources/research/simple-truth

American Association of University Women. (2020). *The simple truth about the gender pay gap: 2020 update.* https://www.aauw.org/app/uploads/2020/12/SimpleTruth_2.1.pdf

Americorps. (n.d.-a). *AmeriCorps seniors Foster Grandparent program.* Retrieved March 8, 2021 from https://americorps.gov/serve/fit-finder/americorps-seniors-foster-grandparent-program

Americorps. (n.d.-b). *AmeriCorps seniors RSVP.* Retrieved March 8, 2021 from https://americorps.gov/serve/fit-finder/americorps-seniors-rsvp

Americorps. (n.d.-c). *AmeriCorps seniors Senior Companion program.* Retrieved March 8, 2021 from https://americorps.gov/partner/how-it-works/americorps-seniors-senior-companion-program

Americorps. (2021a). *Senior corps: Stipend distributions – Foster Grandparents.* Retrieved March 8, 2021 from https://www.nationalservice.gov/sites/default/files/resource/rr11-sc-stipends-fgp-ho2_4-13-12%20%281%29.pdf

Americorps. (2021b). *Senior corps: Stipend distributions – Senior Companion.* Retrieved March 8, 2021 from https://www.nationalservice.gov/sites/default/files/resource/rr11-sc-stipends-scp-ho1-4-13-12.pdf

Baltimore City Health Department. (2017, July 7). *20-year gap in life expectancy between richer, poorer areas of Baltimore (CBS).* https://health.baltimorecity.gov/news/news-coverage/2017-07-07-20-year-gap-life-expectancy-between-richer-poorer-areas-baltimore-cbs

Beltran, A. (2014). *Improving grandfamilies' access to temporary assistance for needy families* [Policy brief]. Generations United. https://www.gu.org/app/uploads/2018/05/Grandfamilies-Report-TANF-Assistance-Policy-Brief.pdf

Butler, S. S. (2013). Older women doing home care: Exploitation or ideal job? *Journal of Gerontological Social Work*, *56*(4), 299–317. https://doi.org/10.1080/01634372.2013.773392

Butrica, B., Iams, H., Smith, K., & Toder, E. (2009). The disappearing defined benefit pension and its potential impact on the retirement incomes of baby boomers. *Social Security Bulletin, 69*(3), 1–27.

Carr, D. C., Kail, B. L., & Rowe, J. W. (2018). The relation of volunteering and subsequent changes in physical disability in older adults. *Journals of Gerontology: Series B, 73*(3), 511–521. https://doi.org/10.1093/geronb/gbx102

Center on Budget and Policy Priorities. (2020). *Policy basics: Temporary Assistance for Needy Families.* Retrieved December 28, 2020 from https://www.cbpp.org/research/family-income-support/temporary-assistance-for-needy-families

Chew, J. (2017, December 13). Why consulting can be better than retiring. *Fortune.* https://fortune.com/2017/12/13/working-retirement-consulting/

Cho, J., Kim, B., Jeon, J., & Park, S. (2020). Perceived usefulness and easiness of information and communication technologies and volunteering among older adults. *Journal of Gerontological Social Work, 63*(5), 428–446. https://doi.org/10.1080/01634372.2020.1760992

Choi, E., Ospina, J., Stenger, M., & Orsi, R. (2018). Understanding work enjoyment among older workers: The significance of flexible work options and age discrimination in the workplace. *Journal of Gerontological Social Work, 61*(8), 867–886. https://doi.org/10.1080/01634372.2018.1515140

Cohen, P. (2019, June 8). Nice résumé. Wait, you're how old? *The New York Times*, B1.

Dean, O., Flowers, L., & Figueiredo, C. (2020). *Millions of adults ages 50 and older rely on the Supplemental Nutrition Assistance Program (SNAP)* [Fact sheet]. AARP Public Policy Institute. https://www.aarp.org/content/dam/aarp/ppi/2020/07/millions-of-adults-rely-on-snap.doi.10.26419-2Fppi.00106.001.pdf

Gatta, M. (2019). Rescuing retirement: Diane's story. *LERA: Perspectives on Work, 23*, 30–33.

Glick, D. J. (2011). Protecting workers today, and in the future. In New York Committee for Occupational Safety and Health (Ed.), *Don't mourn, organize: Lessons from the Triangle Shirtwaist Factory fire*. https://dol.ny.gov/system/files/documents/2021/02/triangle-nycosh-booklet.pdf

Gonzales, E., Shen, H.-W., Perry, T., & Wang, Y. (2019). Intersections of home, health, and social engagement in old age: Formal volunteering as a protective factor to health after relocation. *Research on Aging, 41*(1), 31–53. https://doi.org/10.1177/0164027518773125

Han, S. H., Roberts, J. S., Mutchler, J. E., & Burr, J. A. (2020). Volunteering, polygenic risk for Alzheimer's disease, and cognitive functioning among older adults. *Social Science & Medicine, 253.* https://doi.org/10.1016/j.socscimed.2020.112970

Hannon, K. (2015, August 2). Is it time to abolish mandatory retirement? *Forbes.* https://www.forbes.com/sites/nextavenue/2015/08/02/is-it-time-to-abolish-mandatory-retirement/?sh=5d9fc43e40db

Henning, W. (2011). Triangle's victims left loved ones behind – and quite a legacy. In New York Committee for Occupational Safety and Health (Ed.), *Don't mourn, organize: Lessons from the Triangle Shirtwaist Factory fire*. https://dol.ny.gov/system/files/documents/2021/02/triangle-nycosh-booklet.pdf

Jang, H., Tang, F., Gonzales, E., Lee, Y. S., & Morrow-Howell, N. (2018). Formal volunteering as a protector of health in the context of social losses. *Journal of Gerontological Social Work, 61*(8), 834–848. https://doi.org/10.1080/01634372.2018.1476945

Johnson, K. J., Latham-Mintus, K., & Poey, J. L. (2018). Productive aging via volunteering: Does social cohesion influence level of engagement? *Journal of Gerontological Social Work, 61*(8), 817–833. https://doi.org/10.1080/01634372.2018.1467523

Lazear, E. (1979). Why is there mandatory retirement? *Journal of Political Economy, 87*(6), 1261–1284.

Lewis, K. R. (2020, April 7). Build a career as a consultant in retirement. *Kiplinger.* https://www.kiplinger.com/article/retirement/t049-c000-s004-build-a-career-as-a-consultant-in-retirement.html

Maryland Const. Art. IV § 3 (2015). Retrieved from https://msa.maryland.gov/msa/mdmanual/43const/html/04art4.html

Morrissey, M. (2016, March 3). *The state of American retirement: How 401(k)s have failed most American workers.* Economic Policy Institute. https://files.epi.org/2016/state-of-american-retirement-final.pdf

Morrow-Howell, N. (2010). Volunteering in later life: Research frontiers. *The Journals of Gerontology: Series B, 65B*(4), 461–469. https://doi.org/10.1093/geronb/gbq024

New York State Office for the Aging. (n.d.-a). *Foster Grandparents program.* Retrieved March 4, 2021 from https://aging.ny.gov/foster-grandparents-program-fgp

New York State Office for the Aging. (n.d.-b). *Retired Senior Volunteer Program (RSVP).* Retrieved March 4, 2021 from https://aging.ny.gov/retired-senior-volunteer-program-rsvp

Olson, E. (2017, August 7). Shown the door, older workers find bias hard to prove. *The New York Times.* https://www.nytimes.com/2017/08/07/business/dealbook/shown-the-door-older-workers-find-bias-hard-to-prove.html

Pension Benefit Guaranty Corporation. (2000). *A predictable, secure pension for life: Defined benefit plans.* https://www.pbgc.gov/documents/A_Predictable_Secure_Pension_for_Life.pdf

Part 121 Pilot Age Limit, 14 CFR 121 (2009). Federal Register. https://www.federalregister.gov/documents/2009/07/15/E9-16777/part-121-pilot-age-limit

Schanzenbach, D. W., Nunn, R., & Bauer, L. (2016, June 29). *The changing landscape of American life expectancy* [Framing paper]. The Hamilton Project. https://www.hamiltonproject.org/papers/the_changing_landscape_of_american_life_expectancy

Seminario, P. (2011). Even after tragedy, it takes organized action to bring change. In New York Committee for Occupational Safety and Health (Ed.), *Don't mourn, organize: Lessons from the Triangle Shirtwaist Factory fire.* https://dol.ny.gov/system/files/documents/2021/02/triangle-nycosh-booklet.pdf

Smith, P. (2011). The best way to remember Triangle victims is to improve the health and safety of today's workers. In New York Committee for Occupational Safety and Health (Ed.), *Don't mourn, organize: Lessons from the Triangle Shirtwaist Factory fire.* https://dol.ny.gov/system/files/documents/2021/02/triangle-nycosh-booklet.pdf

Social Security Administration. (n.d.). *Receiving benefits while working.* Retrieved December 28, 2020 from https://www.ssa.gov/benefits/retirement/planner/whileworking.html

Social Security Administration. (2020). *You may be able to get Supplemental Security Income (SSI)* [Publication No. 05-11069]. https://www.ssa.gov/pubs/EN-05-11069.pdf

Social Security Online. (2013). *Benefits for spouses.* https://www.ssa.gov/oact/quickcalc/spouse.html

Squillace, M. R., Remsburg, R. E., Harris-Kojetin, L. D., Bercovitz, A., Rosenoff, E., & Han, B. (2009). The National Nursing Assistant Survey: Improving the evidence base for policy initiatives to strengthen the certified nursing assistant workforce. *The Gerontologist, 49*(2), 185–197. https://doi.org/10.1093/geront/gnp024

U.S. Equal Employment Opportunity Commission. (n.d.). *Age discrimination.* Retrieved December 29, 2020 from https://www.eeoc.gov/age-discrimination

Workplace Flexibility 2010, Georgetown University Law Center. (2010). A timeline of the evolution of retirement in the United States. *Memos and Fact Sheets*, 50. http://scholarship.law.georgetown.edu/legal/50

Yang, J. (2020). Formal volunteering buffers the negative impact of unemployment among older workers: A longitudinal analysis. *Journal of Gerontological Social Work, 63*(3), 189–208. https://doi.org/10.1080/01634372.2020.1744057

Credit

11

Health Policies

INTRODUCTION

To preface this chapter it is important to acknowledge that the reason we need a chapter on health policies is that the United States does not have universal basic health insurance. In general, access to health insurance is linked to employment or purchased through a state or federal exchange established by the **Patient Protection and Affordable Care Act** (**ACA**) (2010). Not only that, but since the passage of the ACA, there have been multiple attempts by Congress to repeal it, and it has been

challenged in the Supreme Court on several occasions. At the time of this writing, we are awaiting a Supreme Court decision that could impact the future of the ACA; by the time you read this, those parts may look different. What that says is that the underlying assumption about health care in the United States is that it is a privilege, not a right. Further, that privilege must be earned, such as through gainful employment. You will see that healthcare coverage for those who do not earn it through employment (Medicaid) is only available to those with low incomes and few assets.

MEDICARE

Medicare is the primary source of health insurance for people over the age of 65 in the United States. Created as Title XVIII of the Social Security Amendments of 1965, it added a health care benefit for those who received retirement benefits through Title II of the Social Security Act of 1935 (Klees et al., 2009). Eligibility for retirement benefits (Chapter 10) is based on employment history and lifetime earnings, thus Medicare eligibility is based on work history too. Medicare is divided into four parts: A, B, C, and D.

Medicare Part A is provided to all people over the age 65 who are eligible for retirement benefits, generally free of charge, even if they choose to delay collection of the retirement benefits (Klees et al., 2009). Most people over the age of 65 qualify for retirement benefits through their own work history or that of a spouse, so Medicare is often considered to be the closest thing the United States has to universal healthcare. Many 2020 presidential candidates dubbed their health plans "Medicare for all," acknowledging this reference, despite policy differences that would need to occur to provide everyone with healthcare coverage. Medicare Part A (Hospitalization Insurance) covers inpatient hospital care, home health, hospice, and "skilled nursing." (Skilled nursing refers to short-term stays in a nursing home, following a hospital stay, when the patient requires the skilled care of a nurse or therapist. This does NOT include coverage for long-term care, which will be discussed later in this chapter. There are restrictions based on benefit periods and lengths of stay, which are beyond the scope of this book.) The latest Medicare coverage guidelines can always be found at medicare.gov.

Medicare Part A, like Social Security, is financed by payroll taxes. Those taxes are collected from all workers and are placed in the Medicare trust fund. As will be discussed later in this chapter in the section entitled Cost, healthcare spending by individuals and insurers has been growing. For Medicare, not only has the absolute value of the spending been growing, but Medicare has also been rising as a proportion of federal spending, meaning a greater percentage of the federal budget has gone towards Medicare each year and continues to rise (Cubanski et al., 2019). At some point the system will not be able to sustain these rising costs. Without policy intervention, the Medicare trust fund is predicted to be depleted in the next 10 years (Cubanski et al., 2019). Possible interventions include collecting more taxes, restructuring payments, and/or restricting payments, none of which are politically popular.

Medicare Part B (Supplemental Medical Insurance) is an optional benefit available to people age 65 and over and disabled people who are entitled to Medicare Part A (Klees et al., 2009). Beneficiaries who choose Part B pay a monthly premium, determined on an annual basis. The premium is based on a beneficiary's adjusted gross income from 2 years prior. For people who receive Social Security or some other types of federal retirement benefit, the Part B premium is deducted from their monthly checks. Medicare Part B covers outpatient medical services and supplies such as physician visits (including those provided by psychologists, social workers, physician assistants, and nurse practitioners), urgent care, home health care, lab tests and imaging, screening, physical/occupational/speech therapy, radiation therapy, dialysis, durable medical equipment, diabetes care, and ambulance services under certain conditions. All of these services come with out-of-pocket costs.

People who choose Medicare A and B coverage have out-of-pocket deductibles and co-insurance for which they are responsible. For example, in Part A, every hospital stay has a new **deductible** that must be met. A deductible is an amount of money the subscriber pays themselves, out of pocket, after which insurance starts paying based on coverage parameters. In Part B, Medicare generally pays 80% of covered services, leaving the patient to pay out of pocket the remaining 20% (**co-insurance**), which can add up to thousands of dollars, depending on the service. Medicare participants can opt to purchase "**Medigap**" plans from private insurers, designed to fill the gaps in Medicare coverage. These plans supplement Medicare A and B benefits by covering charges such as coinsurance and deductibles (Medicare.gov, n.d.-b).

Medicare Part A and B together make up *traditional fee-for-service Medicare*. **Medicare Part C** is an alternative to traditional fee-for-service Medicare. Beneficiaries can opt to receive their Medicare benefits through a **Medicare Advantage** (Part C) plan instead of Medicare Parts A and B. Medicare Advantage plans are provided by *private insurance companies* (not the federal government) and must cover at least what Part A and B cover, except for hospice, though many do include hospice in their benefits packages. The advantage (no pun intended) to Medicare Advantage plans is that they provide more services, and/or lower out-of-pocket costs for services, than traditional Medicare. These additional services may include vision and dental care or international coverage. The drawback, of course, is that they come at a cost, in the form of a premium.

Medicare Part D, which passed into law in 2004 as part of the Medicare Modernization Act and went into effect in 2006, provides optional prescription drug coverage. Medicare beneficiaries who access their benefits through Part A and/or Part B can purchase a standalone prescription drug plan that reduces or eliminates out-of-pocket costs for prescription drugs. Medicare Part D prescription coverage can be integrated into Medicare Part C/Medicare Advantage plans. Subscribers just need to ensure that the plan they choose has a prescription drug benefit. Medicare Part D plans are provided by private insurance companies, and each has a different **formulary**, the set of drugs they cover at preferred rates. So older adults who rely on multiple medications must do research to choose the plan with the formulary that most closely matches the medications they take.

Confusing, right? In addition, all parts of Medicare only cover certain services. Prior to the ACA, nearly all coverage focused on acute, curative treatment, with the exception of hospice services. The ACA added a Medicare benefit for an annual wellness visit and removed co-insurance and deductibles on certain screening tests. Medicare does not cover any chronic, custodial care that someone might need daily for maintenance of life and health. People who cannot afford to pay for care in the home, who have some money, must spend that money until they qualify for **Medicaid**.

MEDICAID

Medicaid was also created in 1965, as Title XIX of the Social Security Amendments, in the same legislation that created Medicare. Medicaid is health insurance for "eligible low-income adults, children, pregnant women, elderly adults and people with disabilities" (Medicaid.gov, n.d.-a). Medicaid is different from Medicare in several important ways. First, while Medicare is a fully federal program, Medicaid is funded through state/federal partnerships. There are federal mandates as to what Medicaid programs must cover, but states have a fair amount of leeway as to how to implement those programs. Second, Medicaid is not tied to employment.

TABLE 11.1 Mandatory and Optional Medicaid Benefits for Older Adults

Mandatory Benefits	Inpatient hospital services Outpatient hospital services EPSDT: Early & Periodic Screening, Diagnostic, and Treatment services Nursing Facility services Home health services Physician services Rural health clinic services Federally qualified health center services Laboratory and x-ray services Nurse Midwife services Certified Pediatric and Family Nurse Practitioner services Transportation to medical care

Optional Benefits	Prescription Drugs
	Clinic services
	Physical, occupational, and speech therapy
	Respiratory care services
	Podiatry
	Optometry
	Dental services/dentures
	Prosthetics
	Eyeglasses
	Chiropractic services
	Private duty nursing
	Personal Care
	Hospice
	Case management
	Services for Individuals Age 65 + in an Institution for Mental Disease (IMD)
	Services in an intermediate care facility for Individuals with Intellectual Disability
	State Plan Home and Community Based Services - 1915(i)
	Self-Directed Personal Assistance Services - 1915(j)
	Community First Choice Option - 1915(k)
	TB related services
	Inpatient psychiatric services for individuals under age 21
	Health Homes for Enrollees with Chronic Conditions – Section 1945

Adapted from https://www.medicaid.gov/medicaid/benefits/mandatory-optional-medicaid-benefits/index.html

Table 11.1 shows the services Medicaid programs are required to provide, and those that are optional, specifically as they relate to older adults. There are additional mandates for pediatric and maternity coverage that are not relevant to this book. As it sounds, states must include all of the mandatory services in their state Medicaid plan. States may provide any or all of the optional services, and there is significant variability between state plans. The ACA attempted to use Medicaid to provide expanded healthcare coverage to individuals who were previously ineligible and often uninsured.

Medicaid costs are rising, which is challenging to states and the federal government. As will be discussed further in the long-term care financing section, the largest single Medicaid expense is nursing home care. This means that while older adults represent a small portion of states' Medicaid enrollees, they represent an outsized portion of the costs.

MEDICAID EXPANSION

When the ACA passed in 2010, it contained a provision requiring states to expand their Medicaid health insurance programs to individuals whose income was up to 138% of the federal poverty line or risk losing the federal payments portion of the state/federal partnership (Liptak, 2012). Many states objected to this provision, stating that it put the state's entire Medicaid funding at risk (Kaiser Family Foundation, 2012). Several states sued, and in *National Federation of Independent Business v. Sebelius* (2012), the Supreme Court of the United States issued

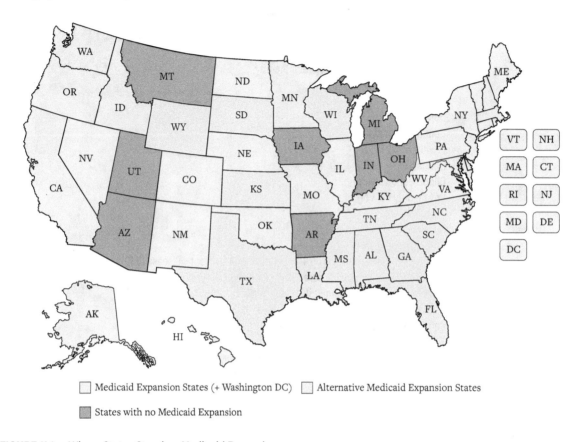

FIGURE 11.1   Where States Stand on Medicaid Expansion

a complicated, two-part decision related to Medicaid expansion. In the first part, they ruled in favor of the states, finding that the federal government's requirement for states to expand Medicaid was unconstitutionally coercive. However, in a separate decision, they allowed Medicaid expansion to remain in the law. The result changed Medicaid expansion from a requirement to an option, and those states that opted to expand Medicaid received enhanced federal funding for a period of time.

COSTS

Medicare and Medicaid represent a substantial part of the federal budget and a substantial part of the total number of healthcare dollars spent each year in the United States. In 2018, all healthcare spending amounted to $3.6 trillion, almost 18% of the Gross Domestic Product for the United States. The two largest sources of that money were the federal government (28.3%) and private citizens (28.4%) (Centers for Medicare and Medicaid Services [CMS], 2020). This means two things. First, many Americans who oppose universal healthcare say it's because they don't want the government in their health care, but they are missing that the federal government is already there, in a substantial way. A systematic approach to universal healthcare could potentially make this spending more efficient. Second, despite the patchwork of health insurance that people have through employers and the ACA in the United States, households are responsible for a large portion of health care expenses, and those expenses disproportionately burden lower-income households. Medical debt is a primary cause of bankruptcy for two thirds of all people who file (Konish, 2019). The ACA increased the number of people with health insurance, but not enough to make a difference in bankruptcy, because health insurance is often not enough to prevent it (Konish, 2019).

Out-of-pocket medical expenses, medical debt, and bankruptcy impact people of all ages, yet those impacts have important ramifications for older adults. In 2014, older adults were the smallest population group (15%), yet they accounted for 34% of all health care spending. Per capita, older adults spent more than five times the amount per year as children, and three times as much as younger adults, to the tune of $19,000 per year (CMS, 2020). Additionally, debt accrued in younger years affects people's ability to save for retirement. Serious illness also influences earning potential, and thus lifelong income and assets.

LONG-TERM CARE FINANCING

One of the largest late-life medical expenses for which people find themselves unprepared is **long-term services and supports** (**LTSS**). LTSS help those unable to perform their own **Instrumental Activities of Daily Living** (**IADLs**) and **Activities of Daily Living** (**ADLs**) across a range of settings. IADLs are independent living tasks such as medication management, finances, grocery shopping, chores, laundry, meal preparation, and transportation. ADLs are personal care tasks such as bathing, grooming, dressing, toileting, and feeding. As physical needs change (see Chapter 5), older adults may need assistance in one or more of these areas. In the United States, in part because of a lack of a social safety net, the majority of this care is provided by family and friends (see Chapters 7 and 8), who also lack a safety net in the form of paid leave. People who need to hire non-family members to assist with this care very often need to pay out of pocket, as almost no insurance covers long-term custodial care. Medicare covers skilled care needed after the recuperation from a hospitalization or illness at home or in a skilled nursing facility, on a short-term basis.

LTSS exist along a continuum. The lowest levels of assistance are services that may or may not be aging specific, such as home-delivered meals, transportation services, and chore services. During the COVID-19 pandemic, many people became used to getting meals through GrubHub or UberEats, which remain available to older adults who can afford them, in communities where those services are available. Meals on Wheels is a national program that exists in nearly every community in the United States (Meals on Wheels America, 2020a). They deliver nutritionally balanced meals to homebound seniors, and in some communities they manage congregate meal sites such as those at senior centers as well (Meals on Wheels America, 2020a). These meals are provided at a nominal cost and on a sliding-scale basis, meaning that those who cannot afford them pay reduced rates. Nearly 40% of Meals on Wheels funding comes from federal dollars through the **Older Americans Act**. First passed in 1965, the Older Americans Act was most recently reauthorized in 2020, for 5 years. Other funding varies by location and may include state, local, and private dollars, depending on the needs of the community (Meals on Wheels America, 2020b). Meals on Wheels also provides socialization by way of the daily visits of the volunteer who delivers the meals.

The Older Americans Act funds a number of community-based services to support older adults remaining in the community, such as senior centers, health promotion, benefits enrollment, caregiver support, and transportation (National Council on Aging, 2020). Older adults with IADL challenges may access these at different points in times to help maintain independent living.

As older adults require additional care, the options become more diverse and more complicated. Individuals who rely on their families may use **adult day care** or adult day services. Similar to child day care services, adult day services provide a place for an adult in need of care to go during the day. Social adult day programs provide supervision, meals, and activities. Family caregivers often access these programs to provide supervision and social interaction for their care recipient while they work. Social programs are not covered by insurance and are typically paid for by the older adult or their family. Medical adult day programs provide additional hand-on services such as assistance with bathing, transferring, and toileting. More expensive than social programs, medical programs may be covered by long-term care insurance or other programs. The national average daily cost of medical adult day care in 2016 was $68 (U.S. Department of Health and Human Services, 2020).

The **Program of All-Inclusive Care for the Elderly** (**PACE**) is a capitated Medicare/Medicaid program for people who would otherwise qualify for nursing home care but wish to remain in the community. PACE is also sometimes called a nursing home without walls, because its participants are eligible for a nursing home level of care but receive services in the community. All participants have Medicare, and most also have Medicaid (Herr & Berman, n.d.). Capitated means that Medicare and Medicaid each pay the program a fixed amount per month, per participant, and the program is responsible for meeting their medical needs within that budget. Much of this is achieved through the use of their own adult day services. Similar to adult day care, above, PACE adult day services also provide primary care, medication management, transportation, and other services not typically covered under Medicare and Medicaid in one location, which allows them to help someone stay at home as long as possible. People without Medicaid can enter PACE programs—they must pay the Medicaid portion out of pocket, but it is important to note that there are policy barriers that make this impractical in nearly all cases. Advocates are designing policy proposals to address these barriers, but to date, none have passed in Congress.

THE ROLE OF MEDICAID IN LONG-TERM CARE FINANCING

Medicaid provides essential services for lower-income people of all ages, including older adults, but the greatest source of spending for Medicaid is the financing of long-term care. Medicaid finances much long-term nursing home care, but it also funds some home-based LTSS. Home-based LTSS are extremely expensive and beyond the means of many older adults and their families. Medicaid covers home-based services on a limited basis, through waiver programs and programs like PACE, to participants who are both financially eligible for Medicaid and physically in need of the services.

Money Follows the Person is a federal demonstration project that aims to transition eligible participants from nursing homes to community-based settings by paying for community services that are not otherwise covered by Medicaid through enhanced federal matching funds (Musumeci et al., 2019). An additional goal is to reduce state-level barriers to covering home- and community-based services (Medicaid.gov, n.d.-b), which are preferred to nursing homes for financial and quality-of-life reasons (Musumeci et al., 2019). This program, which exists in 44 states, has for the most part been successful at moving people out of nursing homes. However, its success, particularly in terms of participant quality of care and quality of life, is contingent upon the availability of community-based services, which is uneven throughout the country (Musumeci et al., 2019).

According to the U.S. Department of Health and Human Services (2020), the national average for an hour of home health aide service or homemaker service is around $20. This does not consider the variation that occurs based on time of day, with evenings/weekends often being more expensive, or the fact that there are sometimes minimums of 2–4 hours to access services. Custodial nursing home care, care that provides for daily ADLs and IADLs on a long-term basis, averages $82,000/year in the United States (U.S. Department of Health and Human

Services, 2020) and can be more than $150,000/year in some large, high-cost metropolitan areas (Genworth, 2020). Few older adults can afford to pay for long-term nursing home care. As a program for the poor, Medicaid will cover long-term care once a person exhausts their ability to pay for long-term care.

Medicaid's coverage of nursing home care is necessary, but it creates problems at many levels. First, it represents a significant expense for states and the federal government. Taking federal and state dollars combined, Medicaid spent $180.5 billion on LTSS—which accounts for about a third of all Medicaid spending—on only 5.9% of the Medicaid population (Colello, 2018). Individually, a person must impoverish themselves through paying for their care in order to access this option. This precludes them from being able to leave assets for their children or any kind of financial legacy. While some people try to give money in advance to their children, or to charities, etc., to allow them to give these gifts and still qualify for care, many states have look-back periods within which any transfers will result in disqualification from Medicaid for those months. **Spousal impoverishment** laws allow community-dwelling spouses to maintain some joint assets to support the person remaining in the community (Medicaid.gov, n.d.-c), which is a lifesaver for those families but favors legally married couples; therefore, not long ago, this was not an option for same-sex couples. Medicaid pays for nearly two thirds (62%) of all nursing home residents (Kaiser Family Foundation, 2017). Reimbursements from Medicaid have failed to keep pace with the costs of care, and nursing homes with higher percentages of residents relying on Medicaid may be of poorer quality.

END-OF-LIFE POLICIES

How someone dies is sometimes considered to be beyond their own control. And in some ways, that is true. But as technology has increased our ability to prolong life, many more people are dying in later life. Yet those treatments are not miracles, and everyone may reach a point where the treatments may be as difficult to handle as the disease and may not ultimately lead to longer life. There are two assumptions that underlie end-of-life policies. First, the assumption of individualism—that individuals should be able to make decisions regarding their end-of-life care preferences. Second, the assumption that quantity of life is the most desirable outcome, and that in the absence of prior directives, all means of extending life should be pursued.

Decision-making was addressed in the **Patient Self-Determination Act**. The Patient Self-Determination Act was part of the Omnibus Budget Reconciliation Act of 1990 and gave patients greater control over end-of-life decision-making (Galambos, 1998). This was part of a budget reconciliation act because medical advances that allow us to postpone death have also greatly increased medical costs, especially costs to Medicare and Medicaid. Under the Patient Self-Determination Act, medical facilities who receive Medicare and Medicaid funds must provide patients with information to make decisions about treatment options, the right to refuse treatments, and any relevant policies about advance directives. Providers must keep a record of the patient's existing advance directives and establish policies about how they obtain and track those directives (Galambos, 1998).

STATE-LEVEL POLICIES RELATED TO SURROGATE DECISION-MAKING

The Patient Self Determination Act created the legal mechanism for advance care planning and advance directive documents. Advance care planning is the process in which people decide what treatments they want or do not want at some future time, in case they cannot make those decisions for themselves, and also decide who they

ADVANCE HEALTH CARE DIRECTIVE FORM

PART 1
POWER OF ATTORNEY FOR HEALTH CARE

(1.1)   DESIGNATION OF AGENT: I designate the following individual as my agent to make health care decisions for me:

_____

(name of individual you choose as agent)

_____   _____   _____   _____

(address)   (city)   (state)   (ZIP Code)

_____   _____

(home phone)   (work phone)

OPTIONAL: If I revoke my agent's authority or if my agent is not willing, able, or reasonably available to make a health care decision for me, I designate as my first alternate agent:

_____

(name of individual you choose as first alternate agent)

_____   _____   _____   _____

(address)   (city)   (state)   (ZIP Code)

_____   _____

(home phone)   (work phone)

OPTIONAL: If I revoke the authority of my agent and first alternate agent or if neither is willing, able, or reasonably available to make a health care decision for me, I designate as my second alternate agent:

_____

(name of individual you choose as second alternate agent)

_____   _____   _____   _____

(address)   (city)   (state)   (ZIP Code)

_____   _____

(home phone)   (work phone)

(1.2)   AGENT'S AUTHORITY: My agent is authorized to make all health care decisions for me, including decisions to provide, withhold, or withdraw artificial nutrition and hydration and all other forms of health care to keep me alive, except as I state here:

_____

_____

(Add additional sheets if needed.)

(1.3)   WHEN AGENT'S AUTHORITY BECOMES EFFECTIVE: My agent's authority becomes effective when my primary physician determines that I am unable to make my own health care decisions unless I mark the following box.
If I mark this box ☐, my agent's authority to make health care decisions for me takes effect immediately.

FIGURE 11.2   California State Health Care Proxy Form

ADVANCE HEALTH CARE DIRECTIVE FORM

(1.4.)   AGENT'S OBLIGATION: My agent shall make health care decisions for me in accordance with this power of attorney for health care, any instructions I give in Part 2 of this form, and my other wishes to the extent known to my agent. To the extent my wishes are unknown, my agent shall make health care decisions for me in accordance with what my agent determines to be in my best interest. In determining my best interest, my agent shall consider my personal values to the extent known to my agent.

(1.5)   AGENT'S POSTDEATH AUTHORITY: My agent is authorized to donate my organs, tissues, and parts, authorize an autopsy, and direct disposition of my remains, except as I state here or in Part 3 of this form:
:
_____

_____

_____

(Add additional sheets if needed.)

(1.6)   NOMINATION OF CONSERVATOR: If a conservator of my person needs to be appointed for me by a court, I nominate the agent designated in this form. If that agent is not wiling, able, or reasonably available to act as conservator, I nominate the alternate agents whom I have named, in the order designated.

PART 2
INSTRUCTIONS FOR HEALTH CARE

If you fill out this part of the form, you may strike any wording you do not want.

(2.1)   END-OF-LIFE DECISIONS: I direct that my health care providers and others involved in my care provide, withhold, or withdraw treatment in accordance with the choice I have marked below:

☐   (a) Choice Not to Prolong Life

I do not want my life to be prolonged if (1) I have an incurable and irreversible condition that will result in my death within a relatively short time, (2) I become unconscious and, to a reasonable degree of medical certainty, I will not regain consciousness, or (3) the likely risks and burdens of treatment would outweigh the expected benefits, OR

☐   (b) Choice to Prolong Life

I want my life to be prolonged as long as possible within the limits of generally accepted health care standards.

(2.2)   RELIEF FROM PAIN: Except as I state in the following space, I direct that treatment for alleviation of pain or discomfort be provided at all times, even if it hastens my death:

_____

_____

(Add additional sheets if needed.)

(2.3)   OTHER WISHES: (If you do not agree with any of the optional choices above and wish to write your own, or if you wish to add to the instructions you have given above, you may do so here.) I direct that:

_____

_____

(Add additional sheets if needed.)

FIGURE 11.2   California State Health Care Proxy Form (continued)

ADVANCE HEALTH CARE DIRECTIVE FORM

PART 3
DONATION OF ORGANS, TISSUES, AND PARTS AT DEATH
(OPTIONAL)

(3.1)   ☐ Upon my death, I give my organs, tissues, and parts (mark box to indicate yes).
By checking the box above, and notwithstanding my choice in Part 2 of this form, I authorize my agent to consent to any temporary medical procedure necessary solely to evaluate and/or maintain my organs, tissues, and/or parts for purposes of donation.

My donation is for the following purposes (strike any of the following you do not want):

      (a) Transplant

      (b) Therapy

      (c) Research

      (d) Education

If you want to restrict your donation of an organ, tissue, or part in some way, please state your restriction on the following lines:

_____

If I leave this part blank, it is not a refusal to make a donation. My state-authorized donor registration should be followed, or, if none, my agent may make a donation upon my death. If no agent is named above, I acknowledge that California law permits an authorized individual to make such a decision on my behalf. (To state any limitation, preference, or instruction regarding donation, please use the lines above or in Section 1.5 of this form).

PART 4
PRIMARY PHYSICIAN
(OPTIONAL)

(4.1)   I designate the following physician as my primary physician:

_____
(name of physician)

_____
(address)   (city)   (state)   (ZIP Code)

_____
(phone)

OPTIONAL: If the physician I have designated above is not willing, able, or reasonably available to act as my primary physician, I designate the following physician as my primary physician:

_____
(name of physician)

_____
(address)   (city)   (state)   (ZIP Code)

_____
(phone)

FIGURE 11.2   California State Health Care Proxy Form (continued)

ADVANCE HEALTH CARE DIRECTIVE FORM

PART 5

(5.1)   EFFECT OF COPY: A copy of this form has the same effect as the original.

(5.2)   SIGNATURE: Sign and date the form here:

_____   _____
(date)   (sign your name)

_____   _____
(address)   (print your name)

_____
(city) (state)

(5.3)   STATEMENT OF WITNESSES: I declare under penalty of perjury under the laws of California (1) that the individual who signed or acknowledged this advance health care directive is personally known to me, or that the individual's identity was proven to me by convincing evidence (2) that the individual signed or acknowledged this advance directive in my presence, (3) that the individual appears to be of sound mind and under no duress, fraud, or undue influence, (4) that I am not a person appointed as agent by this advance directive, and (5) that I am not the individual's health care provider, an employee of the individual's health care provider, the operator of a community care facility, an employee of an operator of a community care facility, the operator of a residential care facility for the elderly, nor an employee of an operator of a residential care facility for the elderly.

First witness	Second witness
_____	_____
(print name)	(print name)
_____	_____
(address)	(address)
_____ _____	_____ _____
(city) (state)	(city) (state)

_____   _____
(signature of witness)   (signature of witness)

_____   _____
(date)   (date)

(5.4)   ADDITIONAL STATEMENT OF WITNESSES: At least one of the above witnesses must also sign the following declaration:

I further declare under penalty of perjury under the laws of California that I am not related to the individual executing this advance health care directive by blood, marriage, or adoption, and to the best of my knowledge, I am not entitled to any part of the individual's estate upon his or her death under a will now existing or by operation of law.

_____   _____
(signature of witness)   (signature of witness)

FIGURE 11.2   California State Health Care Proxy Form (continued)

would want to speak for them. Advance directives are where they write them down. Each state has its own laws as to what is required for legal documentation. The forms typically allow people to name their representative and outline their wishes and/or their values.

The representative document is called a health care proxy or durable power of attorney for health care. The appointee is supposed to make decisions in the context of what the person would have wanted if they could tell the doctors themselves. A living will is how someone can write down what they would want for their health care proxy or for their doctors. In the absence of such directives, health care providers are expected to choose interventions that prolong life whenever possible.

POLST

In the early days of advance directives, not long after the Patient Self Determination Act was passed, it became clear that without standardization of forms, sometimes patients' wishes were not being met. Oregon convened a task force to discuss the issue in 1993, and they discovered that the greatest challenges were with long-term care and emergency services, when events might occur without the proper documents in place and other institutions' documents could not be accepted. They created a medical cover sheet, which became the first **Portable Orders for Life Sustaining Treatment** or **POLST form** (OHSU Center for Ethics & Oregon POLST Coalition, 2020). This brightly colored form summarized a person's medical treatment wishes, was portable between settings, and was signed by a physician, making it actionable. Now there are similar programs in nearly every state and Washington DC, in various stages of development, many guided by the National POLST organization. Each state has chosen its own name to capture best what they think the form represents, so the acronym sometimes refers to physician's orders, and in other cases removes the term "life-sustaining" because some programs feel that is value-laden (National POLST, 2020). After many years, Oregon disaffiliated from the national organization due to disagreements, but continues to maintain its own form and program (OHSU Center for Ethics & Oregon POLST Coalition, 2020). Many states have their own form, but there is a national form recognized in many states that captures the essence of what the program tries to accomplish (see Figure 11.3).

HOSPICE

Hospice is a comprehensive, interdisciplinary set of services available to improve symptom management and quality of life for people nearing the end of life. The idea of hospice started in the 1960s. Dame Cicely Saunders established the first modern hospice at St. Christopher's in London in 1967 (National Hospice and Palliative Care Organization [NHPCO], n.d.). Much of how hospice is practiced in the United States, such as the requirement that someone be in the last 6 months of life, is a result of Medicare policy.

In 1979, the Health Care Financing Administration (HCFA), the precursor to the Centers for Medicare and Medicaid Services (CMS), created a demonstration project to define what hospice should entail and to determine cost effectiveness (NHPCO, n.d.). Hospice ultimately became a Medicare benefit in 1983, under Medicare Part A. For people who have traditional fee-for-service Medicare, hospice care is completely covered. However, people who choose hospice care forfeit coverage for curative treatments for the terminal illness and related illnesses (Medicare.gov, n.d.-a). Hospice is customized to the needs of each patient. It may include any or all of the following: physician services; a nurse; equipment such as wheelchairs, walkers, shower chairs, etc.; supplies; medications related to the terminal illness for symptom control; limited aide and/or homemaker services; physical/occupational/speech therapy for comfort; social work services and grief counseling for family;

HIPAA PERMITS DISCLOSURE OF POLST ORDERS TO HEALTH CARE PROVIDERS AS NECESSARY FOR TREATMENT
SEND FORM WITH PATIENT WHENEVER TRANSFERRED OR DISCHARGED

Medical Record # (Optional)

National POLST Form: A Portable Medical Order

Health care providers should complete this form only after a conversation with their patient or the patient's representative. The POLST decision-making process is for patients who are at risk for a life-threatening clinical event because they have a serious life-limiting medical condition, which may include advanced frailty (www.polst.org/guidance-appropriate-patients-pdf).

Patient Information.	**Having a POLST form is always voluntary.**
This is a medical order, not an advance directive. For information about POLST and to understand this document, visit: www.polst.org/form	Patient First Name: _____ Middle Name/Initial: _____ Preferred name: _____ Last Name: _____ Suffix (Jr, Sr, etc): _____ DOB (mm/dd/yyyy): ___/___/___ State where form was completed:_____ Gender: ☐ M ☐ F ☐ X Social Security Number's last 4 digits (optional): xxx-xx-___ ___ ___ ___

A. Cardiopulmonary Resuscitation Orders. Follow these orders if patient has no pulse and is not breathing.

Pick 1

☐ YES CPR: Attempt Resuscitation, including mechanical ventilation, defibrillation and cardioversion. (Requires choosing Full Treatments in Section B)

☐ NO CPR: Do Not Attempt Resuscitation. (May choose any option in Section B)

B. Initial Treatment Orders. Follow these orders if patient has a pulse and/or is breathing.

Reassess and discuss interventions with patient or patient representative regularly to ensure treatments are meeting patient's care goals. Consider a time-trial of interventions based on goals and specific outcomes.

Pick 1

☐ Full Treatments (required if choose CPR in Section A). Goal: Attempt to sustain life by all medically effective means. Provide appropriate medical and surgical treatments as indicated to attempt to prolong life, including intensive care.

☐ Selective Treatments. Goal: Attempt to restore function while avoiding intensive care and resuscitation efforts (ventilator, defibrillation and cardioversion). May use non-invasive positive airway pressure, antibiotics and IV fluids as indicated. Avoid intensive care. Transfer to hospital if treatment needs cannot be met in current location.

☐ Comfort-focused Treatments. Goal: Maximize comfort through symptom management; allow natural death. Use oxygen, suction and manual treatment of airway obstruction as needed for comfort. Avoid treatments listed in full or select treatments unless consistent with comfort goal. Transfer to hospital **only** if comfort cannot be achieved in current setting.

C. Additional Orders or Instructions. These orders are in addition to those above (e.g., blood products, dialysis).
[EMS protocols may limit emergency responder ability to act on orders in this section.]

D. Medically Assisted Nutrition (Offer food by mouth if desired by patient, safe and tolerated)

Pick 1

☐ Provide feeding through new or existing surgically-placed tubes   ☐ No artificial means of nutrition desired
☐ Trial period for artificial nutrition but no surgically-placed tubes   ☐ Not discussed or no decision made (provide standard of care)

E. SIGNATURE: Patient or Patient Representative (eSigned documents are valid)

I understand this form is voluntary. I have discussed my treatment options and goals of care with my provider. If signing as the patient's representative, the treatments are consistent with the patient's known wishes and in their best interest.

✗ (required)

If other than patient, print full name:

Authority:

The most recently completed valid POLST form supersedes all previously completed POLST forms.

F. SIGNATURE: Health Care Provider (eSigned documents are valid)   Verbal orders are acceptable with follow up signature.

I have discussed this order with the patient or his/her representative. The orders reflect the patient's known wishes, to the best of my knowledge. [Note: Only licensed health care providers authorized by law to sign POLST form in state where completed may sign this order]

✗ (required)

Date (mm/dd/yyyy): Required
___/___/___

Phone # :
( )

Printed Full Name:

License/Cert. #:

Supervising physician signature: ☐ N/A

License #:

A copied, faxed or electronic version of this form is a legal and valid medical order. This form does not expire.   2019

FIGURE 11.3 National POLST Form

National POLST Form – Page 2 *****ATTACH TO PAGE 1*******

Patient Full Name:

Contact Information (Optional but helpful)

Patient's Emergency Contact. (Note: Listing a person here does **not** grant them authority to be a legal representative. Only an advance directive or state law can grant that authority.)

Full Name:		Phone #:
	☐ Legal Representative ☐ Other emergency contact	Day: ( ) Night: ( )

Primary Care Provider Name:	Phone: ( )

☐ Patient is enrolled in hospice

Name of Agency:

Agency Phone: (   )

Form Completion Information (Optional but helpful)

Reviewed patient's advance directive to confirm no conflict with POLST orders: (A POLST form does not replace an advance directive or living will)	☐ Yes; date of the document reviewed:_____ ☐ Conflict exists, notified patient (if patient lacks capacity, noted in chart) ☐ Advance directive not available ☐ No advance directive exists

Check everyone who participated in discussion: ☐ Patient with decision-making capacity   ☐ Court Appointed Guardian   ☐ Parent of Minor   ☐ Legal Surrogate / Health Care Agent   ☐ Other: _____

Professional Assisting Health Care Provider w/ Form Completion (if applicable): Full Name:	Date (mm/dd/yyyy): / /	Phone #: ( )

This individual is the patient's: ☐ Social Worker ☐ Nurse ☐ Clergy ☐ Other:

Form Information & Instructions

- **Completing a POLST form:**
    - Provider should document basis for this form in the patient's medical record notes.
    - Patient representative is determined by applicable state law and, in accordance with state law, may be able execute or void this POLST form only if the patient lacks decision-making capacity.
    - Only licensed health care providers authorized to sign POLST forms in their state or D.C. can sign this form. See www.polst.org/state-signature-requirements-pdf for who is authorized in each state and D.C.
    - Original (if available) is given to patient; provider keeps a copy in medical record.
    - Last 4 digits of SSN are optional but can help identify / match a patient to their form.
    - If a translated POLST form is used during conversation, attach the translation to the signed English form.
- **Using a POLST form:**
    - Any incomplete section of POLST creates no presumption about patient's preferences for treatment. Provide standard of care.
    - No defibrillator (including automated external defibrillators) or chest compressions should be used if "No CPR" is chosen.
    - For all options, use medication by any appropriate route, positioning, wound care and other measures to relieve pain and suffering.
- **Reviewing a POLST form:** This form does not expire but should be reviewed whenever the patient:
    - (1) is transferred from one care setting or level to another;
    - (2) has a substantial change in health status;
    - (3) changes primary provider; or
    - (4) changes his/her treatment preferences or goals of care.
- **Modifying a POLST form:** This form cannot be modified. If changes are needed, void form and complete a new POLST form.
- **Voiding a POLST form:**
    - **If a patient or patient representative (for patients lacking capacity) wants to void the form:** destroy paper form and contact patient's health care provider to void orders in patient's medical record (and POLST registry, if applicable). State law may limit patient representative authority to void.
    - **For health care providers:** destroy patient copy (if possible), note in patient record form is voided and notify registries (if applicable).
- **Additional Forms.** Can be obtained by going to www.polst.org/form
- As permitted by law, this form may be added to a secure electronic registry so health care providers can find it.

State Specific Info	For Barcodes / ID Sticker

For more information, visit www.polst.org or email info@polst.org   Copied, faxed or electronic versions of this form are legal and valid.   2019

FIGURE 11.3   National POLST Form (continued)

short-term inpatient care as needed to bring pain or other symptoms under control; and respite care if your informal caregiver needs relief or support (Medicare.gov, n.d.-a). Many of these items are things that are not usually covered under Medicare but are covered for people eligible for hospice.

To be eligible for hospice under Medicare, a patient needs to be certified by two physicians to have an expected prognosis of 6 months or less (Medicare.gov, n.d.-a). This reflects how people lived and died in 1983, when cancer was the most common reason someone sought hospice services. Cancer has a fairly predictable trajectory in the absence of lifesaving treatments, and 6 months was a reasonable time frame for most types of cancer. The options to treat cancer were much more limited then, so outcomes overall were more predictable. Now, with advances in cancer care, more older adults are dying from **chronic conditions**, conditions that last more than a year, require ongoing medical attention and/or cause limitations in daily activities (Centers for Disease Control and Prevention, n.d.), such as congestive heart failure and chronic obstructive pulmonary disease, which are marked by episodic acute exacerbations but not continuous decline. More adults are also dying from dementia, which has a much less predictable course than cancer although it is progressive. In these ways, it is harder for physicians to certify a prognosis of 6 months or less, making it more difficult for patients to access hospice. Once someone is on hospice, they may continue to receive services beyond 6 months as long as they continue to show decline at the re-assessment periods. However, this may be difficult to show for the more episodic diseases, as patients may improve or plateau. So-called "live discharge" from hospice can be disruptive to older adults and their caregivers alike, removing established services, causing grief, and pushing people back into situations where their Medicare covers fewer home-based services (Wladkowski, 2016, 2017).

Case Study: Hospice, Hospitalization, & Nursing Home Care

People with serious illnesses and those approaching end of life may need different types of care to meet different goals. Specialists such as oncologists, pulmonologists, and cardiologists might address the life-threatening conditions, while palliative care specialists may address symptom management. Hospitalization and sub-acute skilled nursing care, which might be needed to manage symptoms and treatments, are covered under Medicare Part A. Hospice also falls under Medicare Part A. However, Medicare Part A will not cover hospitalization, hospice, and sub-acute skilled nursing care at the same time.

Jean was diagnosed with Stage IV cancer. Her cancer was fairly advanced, and her hopes for cure were few. Her treatment options were limited to two different potent cocktails of chemotherapy. The outcomes from both were similar, so she opted for the one that was rumored to have the fewest side effects. Jean lived a full life and loved her children and grandchildren. She did not want to miss out on any time with them, but she also did not want to spend the remaining time she had left feeling ill and miserable. If she couldn't go and do the things she wanted to do, she did not want to prolong her life.

Her array of specialists included her oncologist, her pulmonologist, and a palliative care team. Her treatments were managed on an outpatient basis for the most part, but she needed to be admitted to the hospital a couple of times, for procedures or when her breathing got too bad to be managed at home. Those admissions were covered under Medicare Part A. Were she to have needed skilled nursing to manage her various ports and drains short term at a skilled nursing facility, that would have been covered under Medicare Part A too. That the policy will not cover hospitalization and skilled nursing care at the same time is sensible, as a person is not typically in a nursing home and the hospital at the same time.

As long as Jean was receiving curative treatments, she was not able to access hospice services, even though hospice focuses on quality of life. Medicare Part A will not cover hospice as long as a patient is using hospitalization and/or skilled nursing services. After several months of treatment, the chemotherapy stopped working. Jean tried a different chemotherapy option, but it made her so sick she decided to stop curative treatments. At that time, Jean ceded her hospitalization and skilled nursing coverage to sign on to hospice. In order to gain care that focused solely on quality of life, she needed to give up her curative treatments. In opting for hospice, she gained in-home nursing, social work, aide service, and some medications. The lone notable exception would have been that hospice patients may be hospitalized under circumstances such as a condition unrelated to the terminal illness—like if someone dying of cancer fractured their hip—or under hospice for acute symptom management, like pain that is not being controlled at home.

The way Medicare Part A policy is written, people only get access to whole-person, quality-of-life care when they have given up other types of treatments. They are not able to access the home care or supportive aspects of hospice care that could benefit them, during other parts of serious illness treatment. Other hospice requirements, such as the prognosis of 6 months or less, make hospice a difficult benefit to access. What policy interventions could increase access to hospice?

DEATH WITH DIGNITY

The final end-of-life policy area this chapter will cover goes by many names in policy and in the popular media. **Death with dignity**, assisted suicide, medical aid in dying, and medically assisted suicide all appear in the literature and the policy space. They refer, generally, to policies that permit individuals with life-limiting conditions to obtain medications from a physician to hasten their death. In the United States, in all cases, the patient must self-administer the medication, which makes these policies different from euthanasia, in which someone else can administer the life-ending drugs.

From a policy perspective, in the United States, there are no national policies permitting or creating parameters for death with dignity. However, death with dignity is legal in several states. Oregon legalized death with dignity by ballot initiative in 1994. A court challenge prevented the implementation of this law, and it was finally legalized after the resolution of the challenge and another ballot initiative in 1997. Oregon's policy established criteria for eligibility for accessing death with dignity and procedures for assessing decision-making capacity. It is up to two physicians (attending and consulting) to determine whether a patient has met these criteria (Oregon Health Authority, n.d.).

After Oregon legalized death with dignity, the U.S. Congress passed the **Assisted Suicide Funding Restriction Act** (1997). This act established that federal healthcare funds (those appropriated by Congress) could not be used for any service related to assisted suicide (Assisted Suicide Funding Restriction Act, 1997). This includes the physician and consultant visits, medications, and any other medical expense associated with death with dignity. Oregon keeps detailed annual records on those who access death with dignity. In 2019, the most recent year for which there is publicly available data, the median age of those who accessed death with dignity was 74, and 75% of those who accessed it were over the age of 65. Federally funded insurance, including Medicare and Medicaid, was the primary insurance of 69% of people who used death with dignity (Oregon Health Authority, Public Health Division, 2020). The inability to use these federally funded programs to pay for costs limits access to this option; it is only available to those who are able to afford it.

After the Oregon law was passed, eight other states and the District of Columbia passed laws permitting death with dignity. They are Washington (2008), Colorado (2016), Hawaii (passed 2018, in effect 2019), New Jersey (2019), Vermont (2013), the District of Columbia (passed 2016, in effect 2017), Maine (2019), California (passed 2015, in effect 2016), and New Mexico (2021). Montana is a special case. Montana has no law permitting death with dignity; however, a Montana state Supreme Court case ruled that there was nothing in the state law that prohibited physicians from participating in death with dignity practices, so it is allowed (Death with Dignity, n.d.). North Carolina similarly has a permissive policy, where medical aid in dying is not explicitly banned, so it is permitted (Pope, 2020). These laws continue to change at a rapid pace, so by the time you read this, other states may have added legislation.

SUMMARY

In the United States, the federal government provides healthcare coverage for older adults through Medicare, and for low-income older adults through both Medicare and Medicaid. Medicare is connected to work history, based on the U.S. ideal that health care should be provided to those who work for it, but it is also the closest thing to universal health insurance that exists, as it is near universal for people over age 65. Neither of these programs provides the ongoing, day-to-day support that some older adults need for ADLs and/or IADLs to be able to continue to live in the community, except through specific programs like PACE, or the Money Follows the Person demonstration.

As policy shapes how people live in the United States, it also shapes how they die. Laws like the Patient Self-Determination Act encompass the U.S. value of independence and self-determination by allowing people to have choice and control over the medical care they receive. This law enables people to plan in advance for care that they may or may not want when they are unable to make their own decisions, and to document these plans in a living will. It also allows them to appoint someone to make their decisions for them when they are unable to, through a health care proxy or a durable power of attorney for health care.

The approach of end of life also brings the potential opportunity to access two types of services. Hospice is a comprehensive, interdisciplinary program that is available to people with expected prognoses, as determined by a physician, of 6 months or less. Patients with Medicare have no costs associated with hospice, and hospice provides services not normally covered under Medicare. Medicare recipients do give up the other parts of their Part A benefits—hospitalization and curative treatments—in order to access hospice. The other type of service is death with dignity, the process by which people with life-limiting illnesses can access a physician's assistance to hasten death. This is not legal across the United States, and some states carry criminal penalties for those who assist with death in this way. But support is growing: from one state, Oregon, in the 1990s, to the eight states and the District of Columbia that permit these practices at the time of this writing. In all but two of these states, there is a permissive law in place, not only allowing the practice but also laying out procedures for how it should take place. In Montana, it is permitted by way of a court decision. Legislation has been introduced in several other states, including New York, Maryland, North Carolina, and Connecticut, but thus far has failed to pass.

As policy shapes practice, it is important to understand how these policies shape the way people live and die in the United States. It is also important to understand the reasons for and the implications of policy decisions, such as covering older adults nearly universally but not covering people of other age groups. Finally, it is important to understand how, in a country without universal health insurance, the federal government, through Medicare and Medicaid, finances and regulates nearly all the health care that is provided.

KEY TERMS

Activities of Daily Living (ADLs)

Adult Day Care

Assisted Suicide Funding Restriction Act

Chronic conditions

Co-insurance

Death with dignity

Deductible

Formulary

Hospice

Instrumental Activities of Daily Living (IADLs)

Long-term services and supports (LTSS)

Medicaid

Medicare

Medicare Advantage

Medicare Part A

Medicare Part B

Medicare Part C

Medicare Part D

Medigap

Money Follows the Person

Older Americans Act

Patient Protection and Affordable Care Act (ACA)

Patient Self-Determination Act

Physician Orders for Life-Sustaining Treatment (POLST)

Program of All-Inclusive Care for the Elderly (PACE)

Spousal impoverishment

DISCUSSION QUESTIONS

1. Medicare is provided to older adults who are eligible through their own work history or that of a spouse. Discuss the benefits and drawbacks of tying health insurance to work history.

2. ADLs and IADLs are those activities people need to be able to do to live independently. Choose two ADLs and two IADLs and give examples of what types of assistance people might receive with them.

3. Think about your own advance directives. Who would you ask to make decisions for you if you were unable? Why? Discuss your choice and your reasons with a classmate.

Ancillary materials for student practice can be found within Active Learning

REFERENCES

Assisted Suicide Funding Restriction Act of 1997, 42 U.S.C. 138 § 14401 *et seq.* (1997). https://uscode.house.gov/view.xhtml?path=/prelim@title42/chapter138&edition=prelim

Centers for Disease Control and Prevention. (n.d.) *About chronic diseases.* https://www.cdc.gov/chronicdisease/about/index.htm

Centers for Medicare and Medicaid Services. (2020). *National Health Expenditure (NHE) fact sheet.* https://www.cms.gov/Research-Statistics-Data-and-Systems/Statistics-Trends-and-Reports/NationalHealthExpendData/NHE-Fact-Sheet

Colello, K. J. (2020). *Who pays for long-term services and supports?* Congressional Research Service. https://crsreports.congress.gov/product/pdf/IF/IF10343

Cubanski, J., Neuman, T., & Freed, M. (2019, August 20). *The facts on Medicare spending and financing* [Issue brief]. Kaiser Family Foundation. https://www.kff.org/medicare/issue-brief/the-facts-on-medicare-spending-and-financing/

Death with Dignity. (n.d.). *Death with dignity acts.* https://www.deathwithdignity.org/learn/death-with-dignity-acts/

Galambos, C. (1998). Preserving end of life autonomy: The Patient Self-Determination Act and the Uniform Health Care Decisions Act. *Health & Social Work, 23*(4), 275–281.

Genworth. (2020). *Cost of care survey.* https://www.genworth.com/aging-and-you/finances/cost-of-care.html

Herr, A., & Berman, A. (n.d.). *ASA: Let's pick up the PACE: Expanding the reach of the gold standard Program of All-Inclusive Care for the Elderly.* West Health. https://www.westhealth.org/lets-pick-up-the-pace-expanding-the-reach-of-the-gold-standard-program-of-all-inclusive-care-for-the-elderly/

Kaiser Family Foundation. (2012). *A guide to the Supreme Court's decision on the ACA's Medicaid Expansion.* [Policy Brief]. https://www.kff.org/wp-content/uploads/2013/01/8347.pdf

Kaiser Family Foundation. (2017). *Medicaid's role in nursing home care.* https://www.kff.org/infographic/medicaids-role-in-nursing-home-care/

Konish, L. (2019, February 11). This is the real reason most Americans file for bankruptcy. *CNBC.* https://www.cnbc.com/2019/02/11/this-is-the-real-reason-most-americans-file-for-bankruptcy.html

Meals on Wheels America. (2020a). *What we deliver.* https://www.mealsonwheelsamerica.org/learn-more/what-we-deliver

Meals on Wheels America. (2020b). *How Meals on Wheels is funded.* https://www.mealsonwheelsamerica.org/docs/default-source/fact-sheets/2020/2020-national/mowa_2020factsheet_funding.pdf?sfvrsn=25a8b53b_2

Medicaid.gov. (n.d.-a). *Medicaid.* https://www.medicaid.gov/medicaid/index.html

Medicaid.gov. (n.d.-b). *Money Follows the Person.* https://www.medicaid.gov/medicaid/long-term-services-supports/money-follows-person/index.html

Medicaid.gov. (n.d.-c) *Spousal impoverishment.* https://www.medicaid.gov/medicaid/eligibility/spousal-impoverishment/index.html

Medicare.gov. (n.d.-a). *Hospice care.* https://www.medicare.gov/coverage/hospice-care

Medicare.gov. (n.d.-b). *What's Medicare Supplement Insurance (Medigap)?* https://www.medicare.gov/supplements-other-insurance/whats-medicare-supplement-insurance-medigap

Musumeci, M. B., Chidambaram, P., & O'Malley Watts, M. (2019, November 25). *Medicaid's Money Follows the Person program: State progress and uncertainty pending federal funding reauthorization* [Issue brief]. Kaiser Family Foundation. https://www.kff.org/medicaid/issue-brief/medicaids-money-follows-the-person-program-state-progress-and-uncertainty-pending-federal-funding-reauthorization/

National Council on Aging. (2020). *Older Americans Act for advocates.* https://www.ncoa.org/public-policy-action/older-americans-act/

National Federation of Independent Businesses v. Sebelius, 567 U.S. 519 (2012). https://www.supremecourt.gov/opinions/11pdf/11-393c3a2.pdf

National Hospice and Palliative Care Organization. (n.d.). *History of hospice.* https://www.nhpco.org/hospice-care-overview/history-of-hospice/

National POLST. (2020). *National POLST program designations.* https://polst.org/programs-in-your-state/?pro=1

OHSU Center for Ethics & Oregon POLST Coalition. (2020). *Oregon POLST® History.* https://oregonpolst.org/history

Oregon Health Authority. (n.d.). *Public Health's role: Oregon's Death with Dignity Act.* https://www.oregon.gov/oha/PH/PROVIDERPARTNERRESOURCES/EVALUATIONRESEARCH/DEATHWITHDIGNITYACT/Pages/ohdrole.aspx

Oregon Health Authority, Public Health Division. (2020). *Oregon Death with Dignity Act: 2019 data summary.* https://www.oregon.gov/oha/PH/PROVIDERPARTNERRESOURCES/EVALUATIONRESEARCH/DEATHWITHDIGNITYACT/Documents/year22.pdf

Pope, T. M. (2020, October). Medical aid in dying: Key variations among U.S. state laws. *Journal of Health and Life Sciences Law, 14*(1), 25–59.

U.S. Department of Health and Human Services. (2020). *Costs of care.* https://longtermcare.acl.gov/costs-how-to-pay/costs-of-care.html

Wladkowski, S. P. (2016). Live discharge from hospice and the grief experiences of dementia caregivers. *Journal of Social Work in End-of-Life & Palliative Care, 12*(1–2), 47–62. https://doi.org/10.1080/15524256.2016.1156600

Wladkowski, S. P. (2017). Dementia caregivers and live discharge from hospice: What happens when hospice leaves? *Journal of Gerontological Social Work, 60*(2), 138–154. https://doi.org/10.1080/01634372.2016.1272075

Credits

CHAPTER

12

Life Policies

INTRODUCTION

Policy affects how we live life every day, in ways that we probably don't even think about. Policies determine where roads go, how often they are repaved, where the traffic lights are, and what the speed limits are. Policies determine where the transit routes are, how often they run, what type they are (buses, trains, light rail), and how much it costs to ride. Policies determine types of housing (Chapter 7) allowed in a community, such as apartments, single-family houses, row homes, and so on. Policies determine where schools are located, how large classes are, and what curriculum is taught. Policies dictate acceptable levels of noise at different times of the day. Policies like these affect quality of life in visible and invisible ways. They also shape the decisions we make about what we do and how we spend our time. Noise is one factor that can affect the quality of someone's sleep, which in turn impacts mood, behavior, and cognitive performance. People are more likely to walk for exercise or pleasure if there are paths or sidewalks available that are safe from cars and crime. People are more likely to walk for errands or socialization if there are stores and gathering places to which they can walk. Incorporating walking and other movement into a person's day improves health and mood. This chapter will discuss both aging-specific policies and policies that are not aging-specific but have a significant impact on how older people live in community.

CHAPTER-LEVEL LEARNING OBJECTIVES

By the end of this chapter, students will be able to

1. Describe how policy impacts the way people live day to day.

2. Understand the Older Americans Act and name three services that help older people remain in the community.

3. Discuss the benefits and drawbacks of age-segregated and age-integrated housing models.

OLDER AMERICANS ACT SERVICES

The **Older Americans Act (OAA)** is the largest single aging-specific policy that impacts day-to-day life. The OAA was passed in 1965 on the federal level. Within what was then the Department of Health, Education and Welfare, the OAA created the Administration on Aging (now the **Administration for Community Living**) to provide oversight of OAA programs. The OAA encompasses a vast array of services and supports that help older Americans to age in community (Administration for Community Living [ACL], 2020). According to the ACL (2020), the OAA was created in response to a lack of community-based services to meet the needs of older adults. The OAA further called on states to create their own specific units to address the needs of their aging citizens. The programs covered under the OAA have expanded over time, and the OAA must be reauthorized by Congress periodically (the most recent reauthorization was in 2020).

The largest group of underserved older adults that the OAA sought to address were low-income older adults. In late life, as in many other areas of life, people with financial resources are typically able to access goods and services to address their needs. There are several ways the OAA addresses the needs of low-income seniors. The first set of programs provides opportunities for seniors to remain engaged with their communities while receiving financial compensation: the **Foster Grandparent program**, the **Retired Senior Volunteer Program** (**RSVP**), and the **Senior Companion program**. You may remember the financial benefits of these programs from Chapter 10. Foster grandparents are paired with children to provide support, attention, and mentoring through the development of an interpersonal, intergenerational relationship (Xu et al., 2020). RSVP volunteers work in an array of human service settings across the community (Americorps, n.d.). Senior Companions provide social support to homebound older adults through one-on-one visits (Carr et al., 2015). These programs are quite innovative. They take older adults whose time and talent might otherwise be wasted and use them to meet the unmet needs of other vulnerable groups, and they provide low-income older adults with financial assistance to help with their own situations. These programs are criticized for failing to reach all of the low-income older adults who would potentially qualify, but at the same time, they have extensive waiting lists, suggesting that the demand for them is there. Carr et al. (2015) posited that the stipend provides value to many older adults on a fixed income who might want to volunteer anyway, but for whom the small monetary compensation covers the costs of volunteering that they might not be able to afford on a fixed income. With additional funding, these programs would be able to reach more older adults, and more community members.

Case Study: Adeline's Story

By Marie Gualtieri

When I met Adeline at her home, she sat at her kitchen table sipping hot tea as she recalled the time she went grocery shopping and could not remember where she was. A task she had done for decades had now become a source of anxiety, and not easily accessible for her own safety. At 93 years old, she explained that many things that were once easy to her, she could no longer do, like cooking. Forever seared in my mind was when she rolled up the sleeve of her pink floral bathrobe to show me the burn marks she sustained from trying to boil water.

Because Adeline could no longer cook meals for herself, she relied on microwavable meals for herself, which were often high in sodium and were not recommended by her doctor given Adeline's high blood pressure. For a better alternative, Adeline contacted the local Meals on Wheels provider to sign up for the program. Meals on Wheels America supports more than 5,000 community-based programs across the nation that are dedicated to addressing senior hunger and isolation. Unfortunately, because of demand, Adeline was placed on the waiting list.

Adeline was not alone on the waiting list. While programs such as Meals on Wheels are dedicated to serving older adults, a report by the Government Accountability Office (2019) found that prior to the pandemic, some communities had at least 12,000 names on their meal delivery waiting lists due to funding constraints—and the situation now is even worse. Community partnerships that rely on volunteers and donations can help close the gap, but more funding is needed to meet all of the need.

Meals on Wheels programs are vital. They allow older adults to engage in social interaction, as well as allow for volunteers to conduct safety checks of clients. During the pandemic, federal and private funds were crucial in delivering these services to older adults, especially as more older adults stayed home to reduce their risk of contracting COVID-19. This meant that congregate meal programs had to shift their services to home-delivered meals, and the demand for programs like Meals on Wheels skyrocketed.

Meals on Wheels America (2020b) compared their operations in April 2020 to the week before March 1. In that short amount of time, 89% of programs saw an increase in meal requests; of those, 79% reported the number of new requests for meals had at least doubled, and waiting lists for home-delivered meals grew by 26%.

I think of Adeline often, even though she is no longer with us. When she passed, Adeline was still on the waiting list for home-delivered meals.

NUTRITION PROGRAMS

Adequate and nutritious food is essential for people of all ages, including older adults, some of whom are managing health conditions or taking medications that require access to consistent meals. According to Meals on Wheels America (2020b), even before COVID-19, nearly 10 million (9.7 million) older adults were "marginally food insecure," meaning they were unable to access food on a consistent basis. **Malnutrition** is a disorder resulting from not taking in enough nutrients, not being able to metabolize those nutrients appropriately, or overnutrition or undernutrition (Hamirudin et al., 2016) and is sometimes associated with food insecurity. In older adults, undernutrition is the greatest concern because, unfortunately, many seniors are not able to access nutritious food due to food deserts (Chapter 9) or income (Chapter 10), or due to physical (Chapter 5) or cognitive (Chapter 6) challenges that make it difficult to obtain groceries or prepare meals. Malnutrition among older adults is associated with a variety of poor outcomes including increased mortality, worse quality of life, more difficulty performing activities of daily living, and longer recovery times when ill (Hamirudin et al., 2016). Older adults who are food insecure eat fewer overall calories than those who are food secure and are more likely to experience vitamin and mineral deficiencies (Lloyd & Wellman, 2015). Routine nutrition screening for community-dwelling older adults can help identify older adults who are at risk for or experiencing malnutrition and get them connected with programs to meet their nutritional needs (Hamirudin et al., 2016). The OAA funds two programs that address food security and malnutrition and also provide important socialization: **Meals on Wheels** and **congregate meals.**

Meals on Wheels are home-delivered meals provided to homebound seniors who live in their own homes in the community. Typically Meals on Wheels provides a hot meal at the lunch hour; some programs will also provide breakfast and/or dinner (Meals on Wheels America, 2019). In most communities, meals are delivered by regular volunteers who get to know the recipients and provide a daily check-in for safety and socialization (Meals on Wheels America, 2019; Morris et al., 2019). Some people live in communities where daily meals are unavailable, but 97% of all local Meals on Wheels programs offer home-delivered meals, and 80% offer those meals 5 days a week (Meals on Wheels America, 2019). One older woman lived in a community without daily meal delivery and could only receive a week's worth of frozen meals once a week. Meals on Wheels meals are provided to those who qualify on a sliding-scale cost, meaning you only pay what you can afford (Meals on Wheels America, 2020a). Meals on Wheels provides over 144 million meals to 3.9 million clients each year (Meals on Wheels America, 2019).

Home-delivered meals are also associated with other improved outcomes and are considered a gateway for accessing other services. Participants in Meals on Wheels programs often receive ongoing formal screening and/ or monitoring for nutritional status (Hamirudin et al., 2016) and other service needs. This proactive screening can help address unmet needs and prevent adverse effects. Informally, recipients receive a daily check-in by the delivery driver. In urgent situations, 9-1-1 or other emergency services is able to be notified to respond to acute changes such as a fall or a medical condition. Some programs are pilot testing the use of technology to help drivers report non-urgent changes in condition of meal recipients. Non-urgent changes might be a deterioration in the condition of the house, or a meal recipient who appears more disheveled over time, experiences changes in mood or behavior, or shows a decline in mobility status such as no longer being able to walk with a cane (Morris et al., 2019). In the Morris et al. (2019) study, these referrals were routed to a case manager, who connected the meal recipient with other needed services. Similar referral services exist in other communities too.

Meals on Wheels programs report that many recipients need home modifications to be able to remain safely in their homes (Meals on Wheels America, 2019). Some local Meals on Wheels programs provide these home modifications, while others refer to community services. Thomas and colleagues (2018) explored whether home-delivered meals prevented falls, for example. They theorized that the increase in nutritional status provided by the meals, and having to get up every day to greet the delivery person, would increase activity such that together, falls risk would be decreased. While overall they found that the study group who received daily home-delivered meals was no different than other groups in regards to falls, they did find that participants who were previously at high risk for falls had fewer falls while receiving the home-delivered meals.

It is important to note that Meals on Wheels programs have limited capacity and limited budgets. In areas where the demand for subsidized or sliding-scale meals exceeds capacity, there may be waiting lists, or clients who need food may be turned away (Meals on Wheels America, 2020a). Adeline's story in the case study describes such a situation. While the average wait for home-delivered meals is 4 months, 13% of Meals on Wheels providers report wait times of more than 1 year (Meals on Wheels America, 2019).

Congregate meals programs serve a similar population to those who receive Meals on Wheels. Congregate meals are meals served to older adults in a group setting. The most substantive difference between Meals on Wheels participants and congregate meal participants is that congregate meal recipients are more mobile, and thus are able to travel to settings such as senior centers (Meals on Wheels America, 2019). Eligibility for congregate meal programs through the OAA at the federal level is being 60 or more years of age. States and municipalities may have additional criteria (ACL, 2021b). The goals of the congregate meal programs are the same as for home-delivered meals: reducing hunger, food insecurity, and malnutrition; promoting socialization/ reducing social isolation; and improving health (ACL, 2021b; Lloyd & Wellman, 2015).

Participants in congregate meals tend to be older than the U.S. aging population as a whole, and are more likely to live alone (ACL, 2021b). OAA nutrition programs are required to provide the meals, nutrition education and/or counseling, and, where appropriate, screening and assessment (Lloyd & Wellman, 2015). Meals must comply with current federal dietary requirements, meaning they must be nutritional and provide at least one third of a person's daily nutrient intake (Lloyd & Wellman, 2015). Local jurisdictions have flexibility within the requirements to be able to adjust meals to accommodate locally relevant religious and cultural groups, as well as to adjust meals to meet individual health needs such as diabetes (Lloyd & Wellman, 2015).

OAA congregate meals make a big difference in reducing hunger. While the meals are intended to provide one of a day's meals, or one third of total daily calories, more than half of participants in congregate meal settings say the meals provide half or more of the total food they eat in a day (ACL, 2021b). Typically OAA congregate meal programs provide full hot meals at the lunch hour on weekdays. Many lunchtime meal programs also provide the option to take home a cold meal for the evening. These programs are offered at a nominal cost, which may be waived if someone is unable to afford it (Erie County, NY, n.d.). In 2021, for example, one senior center's suggested contribution was $3.00 per meal. By providing these meals at senior centers, congregate meals programs are able to work in conjunction with other local and OAA programs. For example, senior centers may provide their own transportation, or work with senior transportation in the community, to help older adults get to meals and other services. The senior center may provide activities, or social work services, to link meal recipients with additional community resources.

Not only do OAA nutrition programs make significant strides towards meeting their goals of reducing hunger and food insecurity, but they are also effective at promoting socialization, health, and well-being (Lloyd & Wellman, 2015). Despite their demonstrated effectiveness, they are chronically underfunded. Additionally, their funding is not permanent, so they must rely on the periodic reauthorizations of the OAA to ensure the continuation of what funding they do have. In the 40 years that the OAA nutrition programs have existed, their funding has increased six-fold. Compare this to federal funding for the Women, Infants, and Children (WIC) program, which has grown 332-fold in the same time frame (Campbell et al., 2015).

AREA AGENCIES ON AGING

State Units on Aging are broken into Area Agencies on Aging (AAAs or Triple-As). AAAs are often on the county or regional level, though there is significant variability. Nevada and Delaware, for example, have a single agency that serves as both a state and area agency on aging. The national average is 12 AAAs per state (Kunkel et al., 2014). AAAs are central hubs for coordinating health and social services for older adults within a region. In this capacity, they were addressing **social determinants of health** (**SDOH**) in the aging population long before the wider discussion on SDOH was happening. As discussed elsewhere in this book, SDOH are those social, economic, and behavioral factors generally considered to be outside of health care that have significant impacts on individual and population health (Brewster et al., 2018).

AAAs may provide services themselves, or they may contract with local providers to provide services (Lloyd & Wellman, 2015). They provide and/or coordinate services for the region including case management and information and referral. They do this through the construction of regional aging services networks. Network structures vary across AAAs, and the structure matters, both in types of organizations and in breadth of connections. Evidence suggests that older adults in communities whose AAAs have extensive informal networks with a broader range of organizations have lower levels of hospital readmission than those with fewer connections (Brewster et al., 2018). Therefore, the existence of robust social services can impact the use of physical health care services. Types of connections in networks include healthcare organizations such as hospitals, providers, and insurance companies, and long-term care providers and non-healthcare organizations such as adult protective services, public housing, education, transportation, and disability and developmental disability service organizations (Brewster et al., 2018). AAAs may both refer people to these organizations and receive referrals from them. Congregate meals and Meals on Wheels are both considered to be gateway services, meaning they may be the first door that an older adult enters, but through them, those older adults are connected with other services that they need. Communities that have more open dialogue between service providers may be able to be more responsive to emerging needs, thus creating a more robust safety net.

Even though AAAs were created by the OAA, they were part of a directive that states provide for the needs of their aging citizens, and many have been designed to meet a variety of needs. Thus, most modern AAAs generally receive only a portion of their budget from OAA funds. In fact, the national average is around 40%. The second largest source of funds is from Medicaid—a proportion that has been increasing over time and hovers just under 30%. The Medicaid proportion represents a shift in the focus of AAAs from completely social services to a health and social services model. It also represents a shift to combining aging and disability services through one central office (Kunkel et al., 2014). Some opponents to this model are concerned that this combination takes the focus away from older adults. However, from a resources standpoint, this combination makes sense. There is overlap in the types of services both groups need to be able to remain in the community with appropriate supports.

When AAAs form partnerships with other service providers, significant cost savings can be achieved across the community, and health and social outcomes for older adults can be improved. Brewster et al. (2020) found that the largest improvements occur when AAAs formally partner with mental health organizations and hospitals. This may make sense when you consider that these areas are complementary to the services traditionally provided by AAAs through the OAA. These relationships create a coordinated network between social service needs, mental health needs, and physical health needs, and coordinated care is associated with better outcomes.

Creating a coordinated network makes more sense from the perspective of the client and their caregiver too, because it means there is no wrong door, and any provider can help connect them to services they need. Given the improved outcomes and the ease of use for clients, from a policy perspective, it is important to figure out how to incentivize these partnerships. Often it is Medicare that saves the most money in this scenario—not the AAAs, the hospitals, the mental health agencies, or the clients—so policy makers need to figure out which benefits these institutions experience from such partnerships. The Centers for Medicare and Medicaid Services (CMS) has begun to invest in community organizations to help with care transitions; this is one way policy makers are supporting these partnerships (Blumberg et al., 2012/2013).

From a community-facing perspective, one of the key services of an AAA is **information and referral** (**I & R**). Information and referral is literally just that. Older adults or their caregivers can contact the AAA to receive information about a wide range of services including but not limited to adult day care, caregiver support, case management, elder abuse resources, financial assistance programs, home health, home repair or modification services or assistance, nutrition, personal care, socialization, and transportation (Eldercare Locator, n.d.). The benefit to receiving information on these services from an AAA, and not from the internet or phone book, is that the AAA has I & R specialists who can assess for other unmet or unstated needs and be familiar with community programs. I & R may be provided via telephone hotline, website, or web form. The variety of media provides access to a greater number of older adults and their caregivers and addresses inequities in technology access or literacy.

CASE MANAGEMENT

Title III of the OAA covers several essential supportive services through grants for states and community programs on aging, including **case management**, discussed in this section, and **transportation** (below) (National Committee to Preserve Social Security and Medicare, 2021). Case management is "a comprehensive service provided to individuals age 60 and over who may be experiencing complex or multiple problems that affect the individual's ability to remain independent" (Multnomah County, 2017, p. 8). Case managers serve as problem solvers and point people for older adults who need services and are at risk of injury, harm, or nursing home placement without them. Case management services are provided on an ongoing basis to connect these individuals to the other services they need, ensure they remain connected to those services, and provide ongoing assessment for additional service needs. Some states, such as Oregon, supplement OAA case management services with state-funded in-home services, and/or case management services for family caregivers (Multnomah County, 2017). In this way, case management is like ongoing, individualized I & R.

Transportation (Title III)

Transportation for older adults has been called "the silent need," because it often goes unmentioned and restricts access to other necessary services (National Center on Senior Transportation, 2010). This is why it is discussed so many times in this book. Senior transportation is also a patchwork of services. In Chapter 9 we discussed neighborhood walkability and public transportation, including paratransit services for people with disabilities. Factors that promote walkability, such as safety and road design, and public transportation services, are publicly funded and are available to everyone in a community. Later in this chapter we will discuss the emergence of rideshare services and their impact on transportation for older adults. Here we will discuss transportation through the OAA.

In 2010, the National Center for Senior Transportation (2010) found that nearly half of older adults who use aging-specific transportation rely on services funded by the OAA for nearly all their rides. What that means is that those individuals would be essentially homebound were it not for OAA services. AAAs play a variety of roles in the provision of transportation, from advocating for transportation services in the community, to providing information and referral to existing transportation infrastructure, to identifying existing gaps and working to fill them. AAAs "provide" transportation, but only deliver about a quarter to a third of those services themselves. This means that they contract with existing transportation providers for the remaining services and only provide the services when there is no other option (National Center for Senior Transportation, 2010).

When the OAA, through AAAs, assesses a community for transportation, they consider a "family of transportation services" (National Center for Senior Transportation, 2010, p. 7). Included in this family are the types of transportation we have discussed so far—paratransit and fixed-route public transportation, and door-to-door or **door through door** transportation services. **Door through door** refers to services where the driver goes into the building when picking someone up, helps them get to/into the vehicle, and helps them get out of the vehicle and into the building at the destination. Other types of services AAAs consider are the availability of driver transition services when someone has to stop driving, older driver safety courses and services, travel training such as orientation to use public transportation, voucher programs for low-income travelers, and escorted transportation services (National Center for Senior Transportation, 2010). It is important to note that just because the service exists in a community that does not mean that there is sufficient capacity to meet needs. Each AAA may handle access to the services differently. Approaches include providing vouchers for reduced fares, providing van rides to congregate meals—sometimes provided under the umbrella of senior centers and sometimes not—and providing rides for medical appointments (California Department of Aging, 2021). In many states, Medicaid pays for medical transportation. Title III of the OAA helps those who make too much for Medicaid but not enough to afford their own transportation.

CAREGIVERS

Chapter 8 extensively discusses the role of informal or family caregivers in the United States. This section discusses policies and services that support caregivers, particularly those funded through the OAA. According to the ACL (2021a), as of the 2016 reauthorization of the OAA, the following groups of caregivers are now eligible for services: (1) adult family members or other informal caregivers age 18 and older providing care to individuals 60 years of age and older; (2) adult family members or other informal caregivers age 18 and older providing care to individuals of any age with Alzheimer's disease and related disorders; (3) older relatives over age 55 who are providing care to children under the age of 18 to whom they are not the parents; and (4) older relatives, including parents, age 55 and older, providing care to adults ages 18–59 with disabilities (paraphrased from paragraph 4).

Caregivers have always been able to access OAA services for care recipients who were over age 60, and for themselves if they are over age 60. What this program does is that it provides additional services designed to address some unique needs of caregivers. Specifically, the National Family Caregiver Support Program provides access to resources that help address and relieve the stresses of caregiving—**respite** services and **counseling/support services**.

Respite provides temporary relief from caregiving by providing supportive services for the person in need of care, either at the person's home or in a setting like an **adult day care** or an institution like a **nursing home** or **assisted living**. An **adult day care** is so called because it functions much like child day care. Programs generally operate Monday through Friday during the day. Programs typically provide lunch and snacks, activities, and supervision. These programs are ideal for people with early- to mid-stage dementia who would be unsafe if left alone at home. They also increase socialization, and allow the caregiver much-needed time to address their own health, needs, or responsibilities. Respite in an adult day care may be provided on an ongoing basis to allow a caregiver to work. **Assisted living** facilities are residential care settings where people who require some assistance can go. A **nursing home** provides a higher level of support and care than an assisted living facility does. Nursing homes include round-the-clock nursing care, medication management, meals, and hands-on assistance with activities of daily living. Many older adults and their caregivers would prefer to avoid nursing homes and assisted living facilities on a permanent basis. Through the National Family Caregiver Support Program, a person may be able to stay in an assisted living facility or nursing home temporarily, to give their usual caregiver a break.

Counseling and **support services** for caregivers can range from individual counseling focused on the stresses of caregiving to peer support groups to training. The training teaches caregivers about caregiving and provides them with skills to cope with the stresses that result from caregiving, such as role conflict and how to manage the needs of their family member. **Role conflict** in caregiving is when the different roles someone plays—such as caregiver, spouse, employee, grandparent, and so on—conflict, placing untenable demands on the caregiver. An example would be when workplace policies prevent a caregiver from being able to take time off to take the person they care for to a doctor's appointment. They may feel conflicted between the need to keep their job and the importance of their care recipient receiving appropriate medical care. **Peer support** groups can help caregivers cope by allowing them to hear about others' shared experiences or by sharing actual coping tips that others used to address caregiving problems. Since the OAA started covering caregiver support, other legislation has passed addressing these issues, like the **RAISE Family Caregivers Act** in 2018 (ACL, 2021c). More on the RAISE Family Caregivers Act can be found in Chapter 8.

ELDER JUSTICE

Elder justice is a catchall term that encompasses efforts to prevent and detect **elder abuse**, treat victims, and punish perpetrators (Colello, 2020). **Elder abuse** encompasses a wide range of intentional acts that cause harm or the risk of harm to someone, generally aged 60 or older, perpetrated by a caregiver or someone in a trusted relationship with the elder. Elder abuse includes active harm through **physical abuse**, **emotional or psychological abuse**, **sexual abuse**, and **financial exploitation**. It also includes passive threats such as **neglect**, when the caregiver refuses or fails to meet the needs of an older adult in their care, or **abandonment**, when the caregiver entirely deserts an individual for whom they have agreed to care. **Self-neglect** is often included in discussions of elder abuse. Self-neglect is when an individual's own actions threaten their health or safety, such as refusal to eat or drink enough, take medication, or engage in personal hygiene. Self-neglect requires a different set of interventions than other types of elder abuse but may come under the same policy umbrella (Colello, 2020).

The OAA has addressed elder justice in different ways, at varying points, through reauthorization statutes. For example, the Nursing Home Reform Act of 1987 provided for **Long-Term Care Ombudsman** programs, which fell under the OAA. Ombudsmen are paid or volunteer advocates for nursing home residents who can intervene when "protection and advocacy services become necessary" (ACL, 2020). The 1992 reauthorization expanded the focus on elder rights, adding a new Title VII which encompassed four programs: the Long-Term Care Ombudsman; elder abuse prevention; the development of legal assistance programs for older adults; and benefits outreach, counseling and assistance programs (ACL, 2020).

INNOVATION

Since 1969 the OAA has included funds for demonstration programs. Demonstration programs are small model programs that allow states and municipalities to try out interventions to see if they work. Successful demonstration programs can be expanded to meet previously unmet needs. Demonstration programs also help governments to address unique needs that exist in their communities.

While OAA programs meet needs in many communities, with the growing numbers of older adults, there have been calls for innovative programs to address many of the similar needs addressed by OAA programs. Diallo and colleagues (2020) implemented a university-community partnership program in a Southern city that combined some of the best aspects of home-delivered and congregate meals to reduce food insecurity and social isolation. They recruited older adults in four subsidized senior apartment buildings, three of which were located in areas classified as food deserts. These apartment buildings also had transportation barriers that limited their residents' access to grocery stores, due to changes in the bus routes. The program provided weekly home-delivered hot meals, a weekly 8-week-long cooking class, and a mobile market. The cooking class provided socialization and lessons on preparing healthier meals. Participants in the class received a meal to eat at the end of class and the ingredients to make the recipe themselves another day. A local non-profit farm also brought a mobile farmers market to each of the buildings to increase access to fresh fruits and vegetables. This program was successful in that it brought together disparate entities such as the university, community-based service providers, the senior apartment buildings, and the non-profit farm, and it appeared to be effective at reducing food insecurity and social isolation. However, innovative programs like this one are hampered by having to find ongoing financial support. OAA programs receive ongoing financial support through their renewals by the federal government; however, their funding may be inadequate to meet community needs.

ADMINISTRATION FOR COMMUNITY LIVING ORGANIZATIONAL CHART

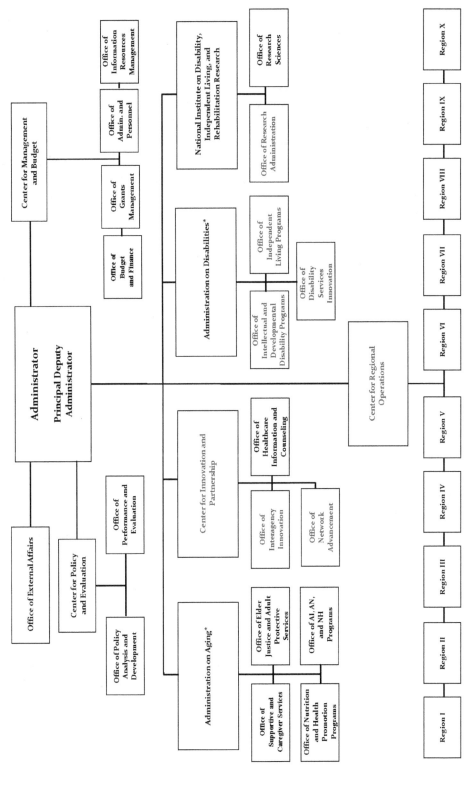

* The Administration on Aging is headed by the Assistant Secretary for Aging, who is also the ACL Administrator. The Deputy Assistant Secretary for Aging supports the Assistant Secretary in overseeing the Administration on Aging. The Deputy Assistant Secretary for Aging also serves as the Director of the Office of Long-Term Care Ombudsman Programs consistent with Section 201 of the Older Americans Act.

** The Administration on Disabilities is headed by a Commissioner who also serves as: the Commissioner of the Administration on Developmental Disabilities as described by the Developmental Disabilities Act; and the Director of the Independent Living Administration, reporting directly to the ACL Administrator in carrying out those functions, consistent with Section 701 A of the Rehabilitation Act.

FIGURE 12.1   Administration for Community Living Organizational Chart

Special Transportation Needs and Services

OAA programs are aging-specific services that impact how people live every day. There are many other policies that impact all people in a community, including older adults. Chapter 9 discussed transportation infrastructure and the way that it impacts older adults, including the types (rail, bus, and car, for example), frequency, location, and accessibility. Chapter 9 also discussed policies that impact services such as paratransit. Earlier in this chapter we discussed OAA transportation. Now we will discuss rideshare transportation services such as Uber and Lyft, aging-specific rideshare services, and what happens when there is no transportation at all.

Habib (2019) used statistical modeling to explore types of transportation used by people of different ages and genders. Habib's (2019) modeling suggested that when a car and a driver's license is available, most people prefer to travel by car on their own to the destination of their choice. In fact, that study found that parking cost is the most common deterrent to that choice, which makes sense since the study took place in a large urban area (Toronto, Canada). However, according to the modeling, older females are the least likely to choose this option. Older adults may choose to stop driving due to the physical and cognitive changes outlined in Chapters 5 and 6. Changes in vision and hearing can make driving less safe, as can changes in reaction time. Some vision changes can make it harder for older adults to adjust to changes in light. As a result, older adults may stop driving at night. Given the preferences for car travel and the barriers to driving that may occur in later life, it makes sense to consider car-based transportation options for older adults.

Transportation is an area in which informal caregivers such as family and friends provide significant support, such as rides to doctor's appointments, social engagements, errands, and religious services. Informal caregivers spend up to 13 days per month performing instrumental activities of daily living tasks, including transportation (Family Caregiver Alliance, 2019).

Uber and **Lyft** are rideshare services accessed using a web-based app and staffed by individuals who provide rides in their private cars. Rideshare services are a new and burgeoning industry that seeks to fill gaps in transportation, and are also part of a new trend toward gig work for individuals who are trying to supplement their income. Rideshare services have the potential to transform transportation options that were previously limited for older adults (Freund et al., 2020). Some modelling has suggested that older adults prefer more traditional means of transportation, such as taxis, to rideshares (Habib, 2019), but other research concludes that Uber and Lyft have the potential to dramatically alter this market. There is not yet enough information to understand how this market impacts older adults, but future transportation interventions need to consider their presence.

Rural areas have always needed to be treated differently when it comes to transportation because the distances that need to be traversed are so much greater, and because there is a general lack of public transportation (Payyanadan et al., 2017). Additionally, a larger challenge is that the density of rural areas varies. There are rural areas within an hour by car of many major metropolises and rural areas that are multiple hours from medical services, stores, and population centers. Transportation is an issue that impacts people of all ages who reside in rural areas. People who are young must rely on parents and friends for rides. Adults need to ensure a working vehicle for access to work, supplies, and recreation. Older adults often find themselves back in the same situation they were in when they were young—relying on family and friends for rides—as their finances make it difficult to afford a car or their senses make driving a challenge (Payyanadan et al., 2017). All in all, rural older adults are more disadvantaged when it comes to transportation than their urban counterparts (Shirgaokar et al., 2020).

Housing Policies: Age-Segregated Versus Age-Integrated Communities

In recent years there has been a proliferation of independent living communities targeted at people, most often aged 55 or 60 and older. Many offer apartments, townhomes, and other types of dwellings, around a central community gathering place. Some include meals, activities, transportation, and other amenities. They advertise services such as lawn care, snow removal, and so on. This is an example of an age-segregated community. Other types of **age-segregated** communities include college dorms, graduate student housing, and student apartments, which gather people together (based on certain characteristics) who are most often of similar ages.

Age-segregated communities have benefits. Services can be tailored to needs that are shared by members of a demographic, such as age-appropriate medical care or shared recreation activities. People who choose to live in age-segregated communities often do so because they are seeking to be around people with whom they identify, and they want to pursue common interests. Some providers feel that it is more cost efficient, as services can be provided to more people at the same time. Chapter 8 discussed the **Program of All-Inclusive Care for the Elderly** (**PACE**), which provides services for individuals dwelling in the community at a centralized day center. One model of PACE includes a **shared aide** component. Participants in shared aide PACE receive all of the traditional PACE services according to the traditional model, and they live in the community. However, the community dwelling in which they live is a senior apartment building, and the PACE program enrolls many residents of the same building. Then, to maximize efficiency in staffing, they hire aides full time to work in the building, where they are able to see many PACE clients in the same shift, and are available to return to the apartment of a PACE client who finds themselves in need of additional help.

Another type of age-segregated housing and service model is a **Naturally Occurring Retirement Community** (**NORC**). A NORC is a geographic area that contains a significant proportion of older adults who are aging in place, in housing that was not specifically designed for older adults (Ormond et al., 2004). NORCs are diverse in housing type and in defining criteria. That means that NORCs can be neighborhoods, apartment buildings, townhomes, and any combination therein (Ormond et al., 2004). The research literature disagrees about what proportion of the population constitutes a "significant proportion," and at what age a community member is considered an older adult. We discuss NORCs in this chapter because some states and municipalities elect to embed supportive service programs into NORCs, thereby addressing unmet needs where they exist, in these naturally occurring age-segregated communities (Ormond et al., 2004).

Age-integrated communities are those where people of all different ages and abilities can live together. Theoretically, any community that does not have age-specific restrictions is age-integrated. However, there are policy factors that may make communities more or less age-integrated. One example is the style of housing. Chapter 9 discussed how zoning laws influence multigenerational households because of the availability of in-law and other types of apartments. Housing stock influences the overall age integration of a neighborhood too. Neighborhoods that offer a variety of housing styles and sizes are more likely to be age integrated than those that are not. If all of the houses are of one size, they may be too small to be desirable for families raising children or too large to be desirable for couples or individuals, which would influence age integration. Of course, any person of any age can live in any sized house, but housing stock does influence the likelihood of different populations.

Age-integrated communities offer benefits to older and younger people. There was a story that circulated on the internet several years ago about a 3-year-old who became friends with his 80-year-old neighbor. It became a human interest story when the 80-year-old moved out because he needed additional help, and their families tried to help the two stay connected. Both older and younger people can learn from each other. Living in the same community provides opportunities for them to interact. While there are more likely to be policies that directly create age-segregated communities, age-integrated communities tend to occur due the absence of exclusionary policies. Housing policies, zoning laws, school board policies, and so on tend to influence the existence of age-integrated housing. They also influence the level of interaction between generations in communities.

Aging in Place and Policy Influence

Aging in place refers to the ability for someone to grow older and have their changing needs met in the environment in which they were living prior to their needs changing. The choice to age in place successfully—that is, to be able to remain in your home because you want to, rather than be stuck there because of a lack of other options—is significantly related to income and assets. Services to address many of the problems discussed in this chapter are available in the private sector: meal preparation and meal delivery and transportation, to name a few. Policies are needed for when people need these services and are unable to afford them. And as a society, it is less expensive to provide these community-based services than to finance a person's stay in a long-term care facility through Medicaid.

Aging-specific services are targeted to address specific gaps. Policies that create community-wide services are also targeted, but they address gaps across the life course, which may include older adults. Both types of policies are essential for aging in place. Looking back to Chapter 9, the WHO factors of livability make a community more inclusive and more accessible for everyone. Using universal design and ensuring that public buildings are compliant with the **Americans with Disabilities Act** ensures that everyone who uses an assistive device can access them—from the football player with a sprained ankle who is on crutches, to the person who uses a powered wheelchair due to multiple sclerosis, to an older adult who needs a cane or walker due to age-related changes discussed in Chapter 5. One type of policy may not be better than the other at specifically addressing the needs of older adults. A policy analysis will be able to reveal the effects to you. However, considering universal policies does have the impact of not leaving anyone out.

Case Study: Home-Based Primary Care

Everything old is new again. Home-based primary care is not a new concept. A hundred years ago, nearly half of all health care was delivered at home (Cornwell, 2019). It makes sense if you think about it. With the barriers some older adults experience in getting to appointments, it may be easier to bring the medical services to them. Technology has also expanded to allow access to medical records via mobile devices, mobile lab draws, and mobile imaging such as x-ray or ultrasound (Cornwell, 2019). As much, if not more, can be done in the home than could be done in an office.

When Mark joined the home-based primary care program operated out of a local hospital, he had not been to the doctor in several years. Leaving his house meant climbing down three steep stairs with no railing. Mark is a big man, and it is difficult for family members to assist him in getting out of the house. He also has congestive heart failure, and the periodic swelling of his legs makes it even harder for him to walk. His diabetes was poorly controlled, and he had no idea what was happening with his blood pressure.

Home-based primary care changed everything for him. He began receiving regular visits from a primary care physician (PCP) who got to know him. Being in the home, the PCP was able to see that Mark really did not have anywhere to sit to elevate his legs when they began to swell, and to see the large box of sugar-sweetened cereal that Mark ate throughout the day because he did not have to cook anything. The PCP was able to connect Mark with the practice's social worker, who also visited him in the home. They were able to make referrals to Meals on Wheels and to work with a community program for durable medical equipment to get him a recliner to sit in.

During the regular physician visits, the PCP could teach Mark how to use his glucose monitor to check his blood sugar, and knew when new test strips needed to be ordered from the local pharmacy that provided delivery. The PCP was able to counsel Mark on better choices to tell his daughter, who picked up any extra groceries he needed on her day off. It wasn't a miracle cure—he still had trouble getting around outside of his house—but his quality of life inside his house improved significantly. He had more energy and less pain, ate better, and controlled his blood sugar and his blood pressure.

SUMMARY

This chapter has demonstrated how aging-specific and more general policies come together to shape the day-to-day lives of older adults. These policies ensure nutrition, safety, transportation, and other services to help people live in communities, independently, for as long as possible. It is important for policy advocates to consider the unique needs of older adults in the context of existing policy when looking for solutions for unmet needs, and to consider the unintended consequences of policy changes on older adults in the community.

KEY TERMS

Abandonment

Administration for Community Living (ACL)

Adult day care

Age-integrated

Age-segregated

Aging in place

Americans with Disabilities Act

Area Agency on Aging (AAA)

Assisted Living

Case management

Congregate meals

Counseling/support

Door through door

Elder abuse

Elder justice

Emotional or psychological abuse

Financial exploitation

Foster Grandparent program

Information and referral (I & R)

Long-Term Care Ombudsman

Lyft

Malnutrition

Meals on Wheels

Naturally occurring retirement community (NORC)

Neglect

Nursing home

Older Americans Act

Peer support

Physical abuse

Program of All-Inclusive Care for the Elderly (PACE)

RAISE Family Caregivers Act

Respite

Retired Senior Volunteer Program (RSVP)

Rideshare

Role conflict

Self-neglect

Senior Companion program

Sexual abuse

Shared aide

Social determinants of health (SDOH)

Transportation

Uber

DISCUSSION QUESTIONS

1. This chapter looks at policies that impact how older adults are able to live on a day-to-day basis. Think about something you do every day—maybe how you get to school or work, what type of school you attend, or what your neighborhood looks like. How does policy impact YOUR life?

2. How does the policy you just discussed impact older adults in your community?

3. Do you live in age-integrated or age-segregated housing? What are the benefits and drawbacks to you? Compare and contrast your answers with those of your classmates.

4. Which better addresses the needs of older adults in the community: aging-specific policies that are designed to meet unmet needs, or policies that create universal access for all? Explain to your classmates why you chose the option you chose and provide examples.

Ancillary materials for student practice can be found within Active Learning

REFERENCES

Administration for Community Living. (2020). *Older Americans Act.* https://acl.gov/about-acl/authorizing-statutes/older-americans-act

Administration for Community Living. (2021a). *National Family Caregiver Support Program.* https://acl.gov/programs/support-caregivers/national-family-caregiver-support-program

Administration for Community Living. (2021b). *Nutrition Services.* https://acl.gov/programs/health-wellness/nutrition-services

Administration for Community Living. (2021c). *RAISE Family Caregiving Advisory Council.* https://acl.gov/programs/support-caregivers/raise-family-caregiving-advisory-council

Americorps. (n.d.). *AmeriCorps Seniors RSVP.* Retrieved March 8, 2021 from https://americorps.gov/serve/fit-finder/americorps-seniors-rsvp

Blumberg, M., Berger, C., Cook, G., & Ruby, J. (2012/2013). Integrating care transitions into the aging services network. *Generations: Journal of the American Society on Aging, 36*(4), 28–34.

Brewster, A., Kunkel, S., Straker, J., & Curry, L. (2018). Cross-sectoral partnerships by Area Agencies on Aging: Associations with health care use and spending. *Health Affairs, 37*(1), 15–21. https://doi.org/10.1377/hlthaff.2017.1346

Brewster, A., Wilson, T., Frehn, J., Berish, D., & Kunkel, S. (2020). Linking health and social services through Area Agencies on Aging is associated with lower health care use and spending. *Health Affairs, 39*(4), 587–594. https://doi.org/10.1377/hlthaff.2019.01515

California Department of Aging. (2021). *Supportive services.* https://aging.ca.gov/Providers_and_Partners/Area_Agencies_on_Aging/Supportive_Services/Program_Narrative_and_Fact_Sheets/

Campbell, A. D., Godfryd, A., Buys, D. R., & Locher, J. L. (2015). Does participation in home-delivered meals programs improve outcomes for older adults? Results of a systematic review. *Journal of Nutrition in Gerontology and Geriatrics, 34*(2), 124–167. https://doi.org/10.1080/21551197.2015.1038463

Carr, D. C., Fried, L. P., & Rowe, J. W. (2015). Productivity & engagement in an aging America: The role of volunteerism. *Dædalus, the Journal of the American Academy of Arts & Sciences, 144*(2), 55–67. https://doi.org/10.1162/DAED_a_00330

Colello, K. J. (2020). *The Elder Justice Act: Background and issues for Congress* (Report R43707). Congressional Research Service. https://fas.org/sgp/crs/misc/R43707.pdf

Cornwell, T. (2019, October 8). *Home-based primary care: How the modern day "house call" improves outcomes, reduces costs, and provides care where it's most often needed.* Health Affairs Blog. https://www.healthaffairs.org/do/10.1377/hblog20191003.276602/full/

Diallo, A. F., Falls, K., Hicks, K., McQueen Gibson, E., Obaid, R., Slattum, P., Zanjani, F., Price, E., & Parsons, P. (2020). The Healthy Meal Program: A food insecurity screening and referral program for urban dwelling older adults. *Public Health Nursing, 37*(5), 671–676. https://doi.org/10.1111/phn.12778

Eldercare Locator. (n.d.). *Services available.* Retrieved March 10, 2021 from https://eldercare.acl.gov/Public/About/Aging_Network/Services.aspx

Erie County, NY. (n.d.) *Nutrition.* Senior Services. Retrieved March 4, 2021 from https://www2.erie.gov/seniorservices/index.php?q=nutrition-amp-dining-stay-fit-dining-program

Family Caregiver Alliance. (2019). *Caregiver statistics: Demographics.* https://www.caregiver.org/caregiver-statistics-demographics

Freund, K., Bayne, A., Beck, L., Siegfried, A., Warren, J., Nadel, T., & Natarajan, A. (2020). Characteristics of ride share services for older adults in the United States. *Journal of Safety Research*, *72*, 9–19. https://doi.org/10.1016/j.jsr.2019.12.008

Government Accountability Office. (2019). *Nutrition assistance programs: Agencies could do more to help address the nutritional needs of older adults* (Report GAO-20-18). https://www.gao.gov/products/gao-20-18

Habib, K. N. (2019). Mode choice modelling for hailable rides: An investigation of the competition of Uber with other modes by using an integrated noncompensatory choice model with probabilistic choice set formation. *Transportation Research Part A*, *129*, 205–216. https://doi.org/10.1016/j.tra.2019.08.014

Hamirudin, A. H., Charlton, K., & Walton, K. (2016). Outcomes related to nutrition screening in community living older adults: A systematic literature review. *Archives of Gerontology and Geriatrics*, *62*, 9–25. https://doi.org/10.1016/j.archger.2015.09.007

Kunkel, S., Reece, H., & Straker, J. (2014). The evolution, innovation, and future of Area Agencies on Aging. *Generations: Journal of the American Society on Aging*, *38*(2), 30–39.

Lloyd, J. L., & Wellman, N. S. (2015). Older Americans Act nutrition programs: A community-based nutrition program helping older adults remain at home. *Journal of Nutrition in Gerontology and Geriatrics*, *34*(2), 90–109. https://doi.org/10.1080/21551197.2015.1031592

Meals on Wheels America. (2019). More than a meal comprehensive network study: A story of Meals on Wheels in communities across the country [Study summary]. https://www.mealsonwheelsamerica.org/docs/default-source/research/comprehensive-network-study-public-summary_may-2020.pdf?sfvrsn=66c6b43b_2

Meals on Wheels America. (2020a). *Learn more.* Retrieved March 3, 2021 from https://www.mealsonwheelsamerica.org/

Meals on Wheels America. (2020b). *New survey data: Demand on Meals on Wheels national network swells and wait lists grow due to COVID-19 pandemic* [Press release]. https://www.mealsonwheelsamerica.org/learn-more/national/press-room/news/2020/05/07/new-survey-data-demand-on-meals-on-wheels-national-network-swells-and-wait-lists-grow-due-to-covid-19-pandemic

Morris, A. M., Engelberg, J. K., Schmitthenner, B., Dosa, D., Gadbois, E., Shield, R. R., Akobundu, U., & Thomas, K. S. (2019). Leveraging home-delivered meal programs to address unmet needs for at-risk older adults: Preliminary data. *JAGS: Journal of the American Geriatrics Society*, *67*(9), 1946–1952. https://doi.org/10.1111/jgs.16013

Multnomah County. (2017). *Community services for older adults: 2018–2022 program model* [Report]. https://multco.us/file/67502/download

National Center on Senior Transportation. (2010). *Transportation: The silent need. Results of a national survey of Area Agencies on Aging* [Trends report #1]. https://www.n4a.org/files/Transportation_TheSilentNeed.pdf

National Committee to Preserve Social Security and Medicare. (2021). *Older Americans Act.* https://www.ncpssm.org/documents/older-americans-policy-papers/older-americans-act/

Ormond, B. A., Black, K. J., Tilly, J., & Thomas, S. (2004). *Supportive services programs in naturally occurring retirement communities.* Urban Institute. Office of the Assistant Secretary for Planning and Evaluation. https://aspe.hhs.gov/report/supportive-services-programs-naturally-occurring-retirement-communities/what-norc

Payyanadan, R., Gibson, M., Chiou, E., Ghazizadeh, M., & Lee, J. (2017). Contextual Design for driving: Developing a trip-planning tool for older adults. *Transportation Research Part F: Traffic Psychology and Behaviour*, *46*(B), 462–476. http://dx.doi.org/10.1016/j.trf.2016.08.005

Shirgaokar, M., Dobbs, B., Anderson, L., & Hussey, E. (2020). Do rural older adults take fewer trips than their urban counterparts for lack of a ride? *Journal of Transport Geography*, *87*, 102819. https://doi.org/10.1016/j.jtrangeo.2020.102819

Thomas, K. S., Parikh, R. B., Zullo, A. R., & Dosa, D. (2018). Home-delivered meals and risk of self-reported falls: Results from a randomized trial. *Journal of Applied Gerontology*, *37*(1), 41–57. https://doi.org/10.1177/0733464816675421

Vivoda, J. M., Harmon, A. C., Babulal, G. M., & Zikmund-Fisher, B. J. (2018). E-hail (rideshare) knowledge, use, reliance, and future expectations among older adults. *Transportation Research Part F: Traffic Psychology and Behaviour*, *55*, 426–434. https://doi.org/10.1016/j.trf.2018.03.020

Xu, L., Fields, N. L., Miller, V. J., He, H., & Vasquez-White, T. (2020). The roles of 'grandparents' in the Foster Grandparent program: Perspectives of Chinese immigrant older adults in the United States. *Activities, Adaptation, & Aging.* Advance Online Publication. https://doi.org/10.1080/01924788.2020.1769947

Credit

Fig. 12.1: Source: https://acl.gov/about-acl/organization/organizational-chart.

INTERNATIONAL PERSPECTIVES ON AGING POLICY

13

Canada: A Federal/Provincial Model of Nursing Home Care

INTRODUCTION

This book thus far has focused on U.S. policy approaches to issues related to growing older. However, the United States is not the only country trying to care for its elders, and lessons (positive and negative) can be learned from examining the approaches of other countries. The **Organisation for Economic Co-operation and Development** (**OECD**) is an international organization that establishes best practices and analyzes outcomes on a range of social, economic, and environmental issues,

By the end of this chapter, students will be able to

1. Compare and contrast the U.S. and Canadian systems of long-term care.

2. Identify two societal values reflected in the Canadian approach to care.

3. Discuss provincial differences in Canadian approaches.

4. Name one thing that the United States could incorporate from the Canadian approach.

including health care (OECD, n.d.). When international policy analysis takes place in any of these issue areas, policies are often compared between member nations. The 37 member nations span the globe, but are primarily in the Global North. Twenty-five are nations in Europe, with the remainder in South America (2), North America (3), Asia (4), and Australia/Oceania (2) (OECD, n.d.). Among the **OECD** countries, many studies say that the United States has the least coordinated and most expensive system of healthcare and elder care. That doesn't mean that other systems are perfect, but it does mean that there may be opportunities to learn from other national approaches. One place where discrepancies occur is in long-term care. From a policy perspective, it is not always clear whether long-term care for older adults is health care, aged care, personal care, or a combination therein. This impacts how it is funded and how it is regulated, both of which impact the experiences older adults and their families have in accessing care.

Canada is the United States' neighbor to the north. In fact, the United States is the only country to border Canada. It does so across Canada's entire southern border, and in the portion of northwestern Canada that borders Alaska. The rest of Canada is surrounded by oceans—the Pacific to the west, the Atlantic to the east, and the Arctic to the north. Similar in geographic size to the United States, it has about one tenth of the population (approximately 37 million people as compared to 328 million). Most of Canada's population resides in the southern part of Canada. The region that runs from the Great Lakes to Maine is the most populated.

Canada's capital city is Ottawa, Ontario, which lies directly north of New York State. Similar to the U.S. government, which is covered in Chapter 1, the Canadian government has three branches: executive, legislative, and judicial. Of the three branches, the one most similar to its U.S. counterpart is the judicial branch. Canada's executive and legislative branches are very different because Canada is a **constitutional monarchy**, which recognizes the King or Queen of the United Kingdom as the Head of State. The executive branch in Canada consists of the monarch (Head of State), the Prime Minister (Head of Government), and the cabinet. The king or queen is represented by the **Governor General**. The legislative branch is made up of the **Senate**, which is appointed, and the **House of Commons**, which is elected by the people of Canada (Parliament of Canada, n.d.).

Rather than having 50 states, Canada is divided into 13 **provinces** and **territories**. The 10 provinces are **British Columbia**, **Alberta**, **Saskatchewan**, **Manitoba**, **Ontario**, **Quebec**, **Nova Scotia**, **Newfoundland and Labrador**, **Prince Edward Island**, and **New Brunswick**. Ontario and Quebec are the most populated. The three territories are the **Yukon**, **Nunavit**, and **Northwest** territories. The provinces and territories are the major political subdivisions in Canada. The provinces are more populated, and have more autonomy, than the territories. The territories are mostly in the far north of Canada and represent less than 3% of the total population of the country. The biggest difference between the provinces and the territories is that the provinces have some powers in their own right; any powers the territories have are granted by the federal government (Government of Canada, 2020). Understanding the provinces will be essential to understanding how healthcare and long-term care are structured in Canada. This chapter will describe who is responsible for healthcare and long-term care policy in Canada, how it compares to U.S. policy, and how policy shapes long-term care delivery in Canada.

INTRODUCTION TO THE CANADIAN SYSTEM OF FEDERALISM

This section will offer a brief explanation of the division of power in Canada, and who is responsible for what. **Federalism** is a governmental structure, shared by the United States and Canada, in which power is divided between the central or national government and the state or provincial governments (Stevenson, 2020). In a federalist country, the federal, or national, government has jurisdiction over the entire nation. The states or provinces have jurisdiction over their sub-part of the country. Within a state or province, both federal and state/provincial laws can apply at the same time, but each entity might be responsible for different aspects. While the states or provinces are separate entities, they are not sovereign, meaning they cannot exist without the whole. Canada has had a federalist government from the beginning, but over the years the proportion of power has shifted back and forth between the federal and provincial governments as the political landscape has changed. Generally the federal government controls those things that would be difficult for individual provinces to accomplish on their own (Stevenson, 2020), such as trade, national security, and financial/monetary systems. In healthcare, the federal government establishes standards which the provinces are responsible for implementing.

All Canadians (citizens and permanent residents) are eligible for health care through Canadian **Medicare**, established through legislation at around the same time as U.S. Medicare—the mid-1960s (Tikkanen et al., 2020). Canadian Medicare underwent significant reform in 1984 through the **Canada Health Act**, which standardized the services that are required to be covered across the country. The program covers most hospital and physician services and, for covered services, there are no out-of-pocket costs to patients (Allin et al., 2020). This approach to health care is certainly different than in the United States, where there is no national health insurance and many people remain uninsured despite advances made by the Patient Protection and Affordable Care Act of 2010, which is discussed in Chapter 1, Chapter 11, and several other places in this book. Canada's approach reflects a Canadian belief that health care is a right to which all residents are entitled. While long-term care is not covered under Canadian Medicare, the existence of the national healthcare standards impacts payments for long-term care.

Long-term services and supports (Chapter 11) are a range of services that help people who are unable to perform Instrumental Activities of Daily Living and Activities of Daily Living to function on a daily basis. These services can be provided in someone's home or in a long-term care facility such as a nursing home or care home. Many of these tasks, such as meal preparation, bathing, grooming, dressing, and so on, while being required for daily existence, are not health care and thus fall outside the domain of healthcare policies and services. The line between health care and personal care gets blurred when a person's health status requires 24-hour care such as that provided in residential long-term care. In the United States, certainly, nursing homes are often structured like mini-hospitals, where care is focused around medical needs and operations are structured around the needs of the nursing staff. Similarly, Canadian facilities are also described as medicalized, filled with medication carts, uniformed staff, and a focus on medical staffing (Lloyd, 2016), rather than having homelike features. In both the United States and Canada, there have been attempts to make care more homelike and person-centered, but change has come slowly in both places.

Like in the United States, the Canadian long-term care system struggles with how to strike a balance between homelike features and safety. Many people enter long-term care because they are unsafe at home, due to a risk of falls or an inability to safely manage cooking or medications, so it is tempting to do everything possible to ensure their safety in a nursing home. However, some aspects of safety make it difficult to create a more homelike atmosphere. For example, long hallways and central gathering places make it easier for staff to observe residents who might be at risk for falls or behavioral issues, yet it would be more homelike to break up those hallways with plants and furniture (Armstrong, 2018). Canadian nursing homes tend to be large, averaging more than 100 beds each (Harrington et al., 2017). Despite significant geographic variability in size, 65% of nursing homes in Canada have more than 50 beds, and 35% have more than 100 beds (Lloyd, 2016). Larger nursing homes have more institutional features and are less homelike than smaller nursing homes. A medicalized approach suggests that nursing homes should be covered by healthcare policy, but in both Canada and the United States that is only partially true.

In the United States, Medicare covers short-term skilled care. For people who need long-term care, residents are responsible for the entire out-of-pocket cost, with a national average of $8,800 per month for a private room and $7,700 per month for a semi-private (shared) room (Genworth, 2020). Medicaid is just about the only insurance plan that covers long-term custodial care. More on Medicaid coverage for long-term care can be found in Chapter 11. A few Americans have invested in **long-term care insurance**, which is designed to cover long-term services and supports at home or in nursing homes, but high costs made these plans unpopular and unaffordable for most middle- and working-class people. Additionally, in many long-term care insurance plans, coverage rates have not caught up with nursing home daily costs, such that the plans do not cover all expenses.

Like in the United States, no Canadian insurance program fully covers long-term care, and residents and their families are responsible for significant out-of-pocket costs. One policy feature of the Canadian system, universal healthcare, makes Canadian out-of-pocket costs much lower than in the United States. Canadian nursing homes separate the cost of room and board from the healthcare portion of the cost. Healthcare costs are covered services under the Canada Health Act. Nursing home residents in all provinces are responsible for a share of the room-and-board cost. In Ontario, for example, monthly out-of-pocket costs for a private room were, in Canadian dollars, $2,700 and $2,100 for a semi-private room in 2020. (Note: The exchange rate between U.S. and Canadian dollars changes regularly, as do all currency exchange rates. As of this writing in 2021, one Canadian dollar equals about 78 U.S. cents, making the average costs about $2,100 and $1,600 in U.S. dollars, respectively.) In the past, one province, Nova Scotia, believed that people who could afford to should cover all of their own costs, including medical care, but residents of that province were able to successfully lobby for a change in the law (Stadnyk, 2009). Now, in all provinces, physician care in nursing homes is considered to be primary care within the provincial healthcare system, so physicians bill and are paid for the care they provide to nursing home residents in the same way as they are for community-dwelling residents (Ågotnes et al., 2019).

PROVINCIAL RESPONSIBILITY FOR NURSING HOME CARE

Many Canadians see residential long-term care services much like people in the United States do: as a last resort, when care can no longer be provided safely at home (Lloyd, 2016). In the United States, nursing homes that accept Medicare and Medicaid are regulated by the Centers for Medicare and Medicaid Services (the federal government). States are responsible for enforcing federal regulations and may add their own regulations on top of them. In Canada, there are no national standards for the regulation of nursing homes. In response to the COVID-19 pandemic, Canadian officials announced in September of 2020 that they would be developing federal standards, but gave no indication of when that would happen or what the standards would look like (Armstrong & Cohen, 2020). Without national standards, nursing home care is regulated and financed by the 13 Canadian provinces and territories.

Regulations are rules that are put in place to ensure compliance with minimum standards. When an environment relies on regulations to maintain standards, inspections are the cornerstone of ensuring quality. Since the Canadian system is provincial, each province conducts its own inspections and reports those inspections differently. Public reporting of inspections allows people to make informed decisions about which nursing homes they want to use. Ontario's inspection structure is most similar to the U.S. process, with unannounced inspections occurring approximately once a year. In both the United States and Ontario, the goal of these inspections is to keep nursing homes from breaking regulations by creating fear that they will get caught and be punished. If inspections find non-compliance, nursing homes must create a plan of correction, and may face fines or other punishments. The province of Ontario shares the inspection reports with the public by placing them on a website within 2 months of the inspection. Compare that approach with that of Manitoba, where inspections occur once every 2 years, and in most cases the facilities have advance notice. Manitoba inspectors use one of several sets of standards in conducting the inspection, and often facilities are notified which will be used ahead of time. Homes in Manitoba do need to create correction plans, but inspection reports are not available to the public (Choiniere et al., 2016).

Canadian care homes are owned and operated by a combination of public jurisdictions and private, for-profit entities. Like in the United States, many of the for-profit homes are seen as lower quality and believed to sacrifice quality for greater profits (Lloyd, 2016). Some of that difference in quality can be seen in staffing levels, because state-run and non-profit homes have higher patient/staff ratios than for-profit homes do (Daly,

2015). Additionally, for-profit homes are often parts of large chains that have significant political influence, influencing the policies under which they operate (Harrington et al., 2017). The five largest chains control nearly 1 in 4 nursing home beds in Canada (Harrington et al., 2017); the growth of for-profit homes coincided with a relatively unregulated period for nursing homes, especially in the province of Ontario, that spanned from the end of World War II until the early 2000s. More recently, regulations have been implemented in an attempt to increase quality. Some consequences are that facilities are complaining about the burdens of reporting, and in response to the regulations have had their cultures become more medicalized, focusing more on health care and less on the quality of daily life (Daly, 2015). Often, regulations focus on individual nursing homes and what staff does within those homes, rather than focusing on the structural barriers, such as staffing and training, that create conditions of care (Armstrong & Daly, 2017).

There are other regulations, beyond those regulating long-term care, that influence how care is provided in Canadian nursing homes. Regional Health Authorities and provincial physician professional standards shape how medical care, such as visits by doctors and nurse practitioners, is delivered in long-term care facilities (Ågotnes et al., 2019). These vary across provinces and concern many different areas of care. For example, in British Columbia, all medications residents receive must be prescribed by a physician or nurse practitioner, but there are no standards for how often a physician must see a resident (Ågotnes et al., 2019). On the other hand, in Manitoba, all nursing homes must have a medical director who coordinates physician care for all residents, and staff and residents must have access to a physician 24 hours a day (Ågotnes et al., 2019).

This provincial divide also includes the scope of who works in long-term care homes. In Ontario, for example, the most populated province, the people who provide day-to-day assistance with Activities of Daily Living in nursing homes are called personal support workers (PSWs). Similar to Certified Nursing Assistants (CNAs) in the United States, they are unlicensed, and have no specific practice standards. Regulations governing CNAs in the United States and PSWs in Canada do provide guidelines concerning the number of hours, content, and delivery methods of mandatory training. As of 2010, PSWs in Ontario must complete a 600-hour training course consisting of both classroom and hands-on experience (Laxer et al., 2016). In the United States the national standard for CNA training is a minimum of 75 hours, and while some states require more than that, none comes close to the Ontario standard of 600 hours.

Many of the issues facing PSWs are structural. Like in the United States, PSWs tend to earn low wages and may work less than part-time, which often makes them ineligible for employer-sponsored health insurance and paid sick leave (Laxer et al., 2016). Canadian workers receive publicly funded health insurance, vacation pay, and parental leave through a combination of provincial and national programs (Laxer et al., 2016), but paid sick leave and supplemental health insurance would make the workforce safer and healthier. These care workers face structural barriers that keep them from making the greatest impact in individual nursing homes. Low-wage paid care providers in both the United States and Canada tend to have extensive experience but little training, and have limited decision-making power within long-term care homes (Armstrong & Daly, 2017). Despite differences in provincial and national policies and regulations regarding direct care staff, these problems persist across both Canada and the United States and make it difficult to improve quality of care.

Finally, there are significant provincial differences in requirements for nursing leadership and staffing. As of 2011, six provinces had no requirements at all for the position of director of nursing. Prince Edward Island and Alberta, who had the most stringent director of nursing requirements, only required that each facility have a director of nursing who was an RN (both provinces) or CGN (Alberta only). Ontario pro-rated the number of hours a director of nursing must work based on the number of beds in a nursing home, with only nursing homes with more than 65 beds having a full-time director of nursing (Harrington et al., 2012). Provincial regulations on when and if a registered nurse needs to be in the building varied nearly as much, though six provinces did require a nurse to be in the building 24 hours a day (Harrington et al., 2012). The presence of a full-time RN has been linked to better patient safety and quality, though U.S. policy also does not require nursing homes to have them at all times.

As mentioned earlier in the chapter, one of the challenges of providing and regulating long-term care is the combination of medical care and personal care. This is seen in discussions of whether a nursing home should look more like a home or more like a hospital. Regulations that strengthen the presence of nurses and doctors medicalize the environment, putting greater focus on medications, monitoring, and testing. While this medical focus is sometimes seen as a negative, many people enter long-term care because they need daily care, some of which is medically oriented, such as medications for the management of multiple chronic health conditions, and range of motion and physical rehabilitation. In both countries, daily routine care is provided by unlicensed, low-wage, direct care staff (PSWs and CNAs), and both countries report chronic understaffing of these direct care staff. Situations with not enough staff lend themselves to a greater focus on physical care over quality of life and socialization, in which getting tasks done is emphasized over spending time with people (Lownes & Struthers, 2016). In both the United States and Canada, policy approaches to improving care have meant strengthening regulations, making them more prescriptive and restrictive, and increasing the presence of medical staff, rather than addressing the underlying direct care workforce issues. These approaches further deemphasize quality of life, resident choice, and homelike atmosphere. Policies that address the structural barriers facing direct care workers are needed to improve staffing, jobs, and care.

HOW LONG-TERM CARE WORKS

In Ontario, long-term care homes are regulated and funded by the provincial government. Government agencies determine who is eligible to be admitted to long-term care, and manage the wait lists.

Each home owner/operator is granted a license to operate by the provincial government. Homes are required to follow the requirements of the **Long-Term Care Homes Act**, one of the most stringent pieces of nursing home legislation in the world.

Long-Term Care Funding
The provincial government provides funding for all the staff and supplies related to nursing and personal care, resident social and recreational programs and support services, and raw food (used to make meals). In addition, long-term care homes receive other government funding for specific needs, such as falls prevention equipment.

Residents pay an accommodation fee to the long-term care home that is used to pay for expenses such as non-care staff, utilities, and mortgages, as well as building maintenance and major capital repairs (like a new roof). The government sets the rate for resident fees and provides subsidies for residents as needed.

Long-Term Care Homes Account for Every Dollar
As part of their licensing agreement with the government, homes must rigorously account for all funding provided to them by the province, which can only be used for its specified purpose. Any unspent funds are returned to the government.

Funding from residents' fees is also accounted for, but the home is permitted to keep any surplus funds after expenses are paid.

Every long-term care home produces an audited annual report documenting the home's spending, which is then reviewed and audited again by the government. The final report is presented to each home's Residents' Council and Family Council and posted publicly in the home.

Source: Ontario Long-Term Care Association, 2019.

HOW PROVINCIAL POLICY INFLUENCES INDIVIDUAL COST

Because long-term care in Canada is not covered under the Canada Health Act, residents, mostly older adults, are responsible for a portion of the costs of their care. Canada divides the cost of care into two categories: health and nursing care, and room and board. Health and nursing care are covered under the provincial health insurance, leaving residents with only the room-and-board charges, making out-of-pocket nursing home costs much lower in Canada than in the United States. Out-of-pocket costs are below the U.S. average across Canada, yet these vary from province to province, as do the formulas for determining them. In Ontario, for example, out-of-pocket costs are determined by the Ministry of Long-Term Care, and are the same in every

ONE PROVINCE'S PROCEDURES FOR CALCULATING OUT-OF-POCKET COSTS

Current accommodation costs

Long-term care accommodation costs are set by the Ministry of Long-Term Care and are standard in all long-term care homes across Ontario. The current (maximum) rates [for 2019, in Canadian dollars,] are:

Accommodation Rates (July 1, 2019)

Type of accommodation	Daily rate	Monthly rate
Long-stay Basic[1]	$62.18 [a]	$1,891.31 [b]
Long-stay Semi-private[2]	$74.96 (Basic plus a maximum of $12.78)	$2,280.04
Long-stay Private[2]	$88.82 (Basic plus a maximum of $26.64)	$2,701.61
Short-stay	$40.24	N/A

Government subsidy

If you don't have enough income to pay for the basic room, you may be eligible for a subsidy through the Long-Term Care Home Rate Reduction Program.

What's covered by the subsidy

If you qualify, you could get a subsidy of up to $1,891.31 a month to help you pay for basic long-term care accommodation.

Source: Ontario, 2020.

nursing home in the province (Ontario, 2020). These costs are typically recalculated every year. In Canada, each province subsidizes care for residents unable to afford the costs of care. Even residents who receive subsidies are responsible for some share of the cost, based on their ability to pay (Stadnyk, 2009), but the subsidies are administered differently from province to province. Broadly speaking, some provinces reduce the cost share for eligible residents, while others supplement their income to allow them to afford their care (Stadnyk, 2009).

In the United States, Medicaid is just about the only insurance plan that covers long-term custodial care. More on this can be found in Chapter 11. **Spousal impoverishment** rules create financial allowances for spouses who live in the community, when their spouse who lives in the nursing home must go on Medicaid to cover the cost of care. These rules allow the spouse who lives in the community to keep a portion of the couple's joint income and assets, to allow them to continue to meet their own needs in the community. In Canada, without national policy, the treatment of community spouses varies, causing community spouses in some provinces to struggle with paying for both their own expenses and their spouse's share of the nursing home cost (Stadnyk, 2009).

HOW THE CANADIAN SYSTEM COMPARES TO THE U.S. SYSTEM

Some comparisons of the Canadian system and the U.S. system have been made throughout this chapter. The biggest policy differences are in the regulatory structure. In the United States the federal government, through the Centers for Medicare and Medicaid Services, regulates all of the U.S. nursing homes that accept payments from Medicare and Medicaid. As discussed in Chapter 11, Medicare is a fully federal program that insures people over the age of 65. It pays for nursing home care when someone is receiving skilled services, such as nursing or rehabilitation after a hospitalization. Medicaid, on the other hand, is a joint federal and state policy, and covers the vast majority of long-term nursing home care in the United States. Centers for Medicare and Medicaid Services regulations cover over 15,000 U.S. nursing homes and more than 1 million nursing home residents. Each state is able to add additional regulations to the federal regulations, but any state changes must be more stringent than the federal standards, not less. In Canada, most residents have government-issued health care, but it is provided on the provincial level and varies in cost and coverage. Nursing homes are regulated on the provincial level too, and there are no overarching federal requirements. This regulatory difference leads to many of the other differences that exist between the two countries.

Canadian nursing home residents have lower out-of-pocket costs due to the presence of universal healthcare. In U.S. nursing homes, even though most residents have Medicare, the Medicare coverage does not impact out-of-pocket costs for the nursing home stay at all, other than those first days (up to 100 days) following a hospital stay. While paying for nursing home coverage can be a struggle for middle-income individuals in both countries who do not qualify for subsidies (Canada) or Medicaid (United States), the overall lower out-of-pocket cost for Canadian long-term care makes nursing homes a less dire option than in the United States, where residence in a nursing home can wipe out a person's life savings in short order. The $8,000 monthly average U.S. cost amounts to nearly $100,000 in just 1 year.

Both countries struggle with nursing home quality, the uptake of new innovations, and issues surrounding the provision of direct care by an experienced yet poorly educated and poorly compensated workforce. Based on that observation, perhaps policies are not focusing on the right things. Would different policies have a greater impact on quality? What kinds of policies would improve direct care jobs? Would improving jobs impact quality? These are the types of questions policy makers need to ask, and the types of things that can be learned from looking at the approaches of other countries.

TABLE 13.1   Side-by-Side Comparison of U.S. and Canadian Nursing Homes

	United States	**Canada**
Regulation	Federal and State	Provincial
Payment	Depends on length and type of stay—can be Medicare, Medicaid, out-of-pocket, or combination.	Combines Medicare (Universal Healthcare) and out-of-pocket (room and board). Room and board may be subsidized by provincial government.
Cost	Private pay costs $80,000–$100,000 per year.	Out-of-pocket costs average $24,000–$36,000 per year.
Staffing	Low-wage direct care workers called CNAs provide most hands-on care. Nursing, social work services, physician services, therapy services, and activities are stipulated in the federal guidelines.	Low-wage direct care workers called PSWs provide most hands-on care. Requirements for additional staffing vary by province.
COVID-19	The federal government shut down visitation and group activities, and required personal protective equipment but did not provide it. There were many cases and deaths across the country.	The response varied by province. Many locales shut down visitation and group activities. There were many cases and deaths across the country.

SUMMARY

As with states' rights in the United States, in Canada the rights of provinces are an important part of the governmental structure, which leads to decentralization of many essential human services. In Canada this includes health care and nursing home care. Also like states in the United States, Canadian provinces significantly vary from each other regarding population size and distribution, access to financial and other resources, and political beliefs about the role of government in regulation and redistribution of resources to parts of the population in need. This has led Canada to create a long-term care system operated and regulated by provinces, with significant variation in funding and regulatory structures.

Despite differences between provinces, the funding structure is similar across Canada and is different from that of the United States. The biggest difference is the separation of the health care and room-and-board costs. Since health care is covered across Canada—and that's a separate story—there are national standards for what must be covered, and the health care that people receive in nursing homes is included. Canadians who enter long-term care only need to pay the room-and-board portion of the cost, which makes out-of-pocket costs significantly lower in Canada than in the United States. However, this portion is still a struggle for some people, which is why the provinces help to subsidize these costs for people who need it.

Canada struggles with nursing home quality as much as the United States does. In both countries, pre-existing issues were brought to light during the COVID-19 pandemic in 2020–2021. Both countries struggled to figure out how to control outbreaks. There were shortages of personal protective equipment. Family members were banned from visiting their loved ones in long-term care. Many nursing home residents and staff died. Some policy advocates see the nursing home struggles with COVID-19 as an opportunity to reform long-term care once and for all. Nursing homes have received more public and policy attention during COVID-19 than they have in many years. Attention on a topic can indicate a time for change. This chapter has focused on government structures, and who is in charge of what. But if we were to reform long-term care, what would be the most important issue?

What would different groups say? What would residents value? What is important to family members? What would the priorities of direct care workers be? Policy makers need to consider all of these things in shaping the future of long-term care.

KEY TERMS

Alberta

British Columbia

Canada Health Act

Constitutional monarchy

Federalism

Governor General

House of Commons

Long-Term Care Homes Act

Long-term care insurance

Manitoba

Medicaid

Medicare

New Brunswick

Newfoundland and Labrador

Northwest Territories

Nova Scotia

Nunavut

Ontario

Organisation for Economic Co-operation and
    Development (OECD)

Prince Edward Island

Province

Quebec

Saskatchewan

Senate

Spousal impoverishment

Territory

Yukon

DISCUSSION QUESTIONS

1. Compare and contrast the governmental structures of Canada and the United States.

2. What are the benefits of the Canadian structure in which provinces regulate nursing homes as compared to the federal structure in the United States?

3. Should regulations create staffing minimums or requirements, such as for nurses, physicians, and direct care workers? Why or why not?

4. How should nursing home costs be covered? Should people be responsible for the costs of their care?

Ancillary materials for student practice can be found within Active Learning

REFERENCES

Ågotnes, G., McGregor, M., Lexchin, J., Doupe, M., Müller, D., & Harrington, C. (2019). An international mapping of medical care in nursing homes. *Health Services Insights*, *12*, 1–12. https://doi.org/10.1177/1178632918825083

Allin, S., Marchildon, G., & Peckham, A. (2020). *Health system overview: Canada*. Commonwealth Fund. https://www.commonwealthfund.org/sites/default/files/2020-12/2020_IntlOverview_CAN.pdf

Armstrong, P. (2018). Introduction. In P. Armstrong & R. Lowndes (Eds.), *Negotiating tensions in long-term residential care: Ideas worth sharing* (pp. 11–22). Canadian Centre for Policy Alternatives. https://www.policyalternatives.ca/sites/default/files/uploads/publications/National%20Office/2018/05/Negotiating%20Tensions.pdf

Armstrong, P., & Cohen, M. (2020). *A higher standard: Setting federal standards in long-term care and continuing care*. Canadian Centre for Policy Alternatives. https://www.policyalternatives.ca/publications/reports/higher-standard-0

Armstrong, P., & Daly, T. (2017). Introduction. In P. Armstrong & T. Daly (Eds.), *Exercising choice in long-term residential care* (pp. 11–36). Canadian Centre for Policy Alternatives. https://www.policyalternatives.ca/sites/default/files/uploads/publications/National%20Office/2017/10/Exercising%20Choice%202017_final.pdf

Choiniere, J., Doupe, M., Goldmann, M., Harrington, C., Jacobsen, F. F., Lloyd, L., Rootham, M., & Szebehely, M. (2016). Mapping nursing home inspections & audits in six countries. *Ageing International*, *41*, 40–61. https://doi.org/10.1007/s12126-015-9230-6

Daly, T. (2015). Dancing the two-step in Ontario's long-term care sector: More deterrence-oriented regulation = consolidation. *Studies in Political Economy*, *95*(1), 29–58. https://doi.org/10.1080/19187033.2015.11674945

Genworth. (2020). *Cost of care survey*. https://www.genworth.com/aging-and-you/finances/cost-of-care.html

Government of Canada. (2020). *Provinces and territories*. Retrieved January 25, 2021 from https://www.canada.ca/en/intergovernmental-affairs/services/provinces-territories.html

Harrington, C., Choiniere, J., Goldmann, M., Jacobsen, F. F., Lloyd, L., McGregor, M., Stamatopoulos, V., & Szebehely, M. (2012). Nursing home staffing standards and staffing levels in six countries. *Journal of Nursing Scholarship*, *44*(1), 88–98. https://doi.org/10.1111/j.1547-5069.2011.01430.x

Harrington, C., Jacobsen, F. F., Panos, J., Pollock, A., Sutaria, S., & Szebehely, M. (2017). Marketization in long-term care: A cross-country comparison of large for-profit nursing home chains. *Health Services Insights*, *10*, 1–23. https://doi.org/10.1177/1178632917710533

Laxer, K., Jacobsen, F. F., Lloyd, L., Goldmann, M., Day, S., Chouiniere, J., & Rosenau, P.V. (2016). Comparing nursing home assistive personnel in five countries. *Ageing International*, *41*, 62–78. https://doi.org/10.1007/s12126-015-9226-2

Lloyd, L. (2016). The Canadian long-term residential care system: A British perspective. *Journal of Canadian Studies*, *50*(2), 482–490.

Lownes, R., & Struthers, J. (2016). Changes and continuities in the workplace of long-term residential care in Canada, 1970–2015. *Journal of Canadian Studies*, *50*(2), 368–395.

Ontario. (2020). *Long-term care accommodation costs and subsidy*. Retrieved January 20, 2021 from https://www.ontario.ca/page/get-help-paying-long-term-care

Ontario Long-Term Care Association. (2019). *This is long-term care 2019*. https://www.oltca.com/OLTCA/Documents/Reports/TILTC2019web.pdf

Organisation for Economic Co-operation and Development. (n.d.). *Who we are*. Retrieved January 20, 2021 from https://www.oecd.org/about/

Parliament of Canada. (n.d.). Overview of the Canadian Parliamentary System. Retrieved January 21, 2021 from https://lop.parl.ca/about/parliament/education/ourcountryourparliament/html_booklet/overview-canadian-parliamentary-system-e.html

Stadnyk, R. (2009). Three policy issues in deciding the cost of nursing home care: Provincial differences and how they influence elderly couples' experiences. [Trois enjeux politiques en matière de decisions sur les coûts des services en maison de soins infirmiers: différences entre les provinces et influences sur l'expérience des couples aînés.] *Healthcare Policy*, *5*(1), e132–e144.

Stevenson, G. (2020). *Federalism in Canada*. The Canadian Encyclopedia. https://www.thecanadianencyclopedia.ca/en/article/federalism

Tikkanen, R., Osborn, R., Mossialos, E., Djordjevic, A., & Wharton, G. A. (2020). *Canada*. The Commonwealth Fund, International Health Care System Profiles. https://www.commonwealthfund.org/international-health-policy-center/countries/canada

Finland: Social Safety Net

INTRODUCTION

In 2021, Finland was rated the happiest country in the world by the World Happiness Report (2021) for the fourth year in a row. The World Happiness Report gathers data from the Gallup World Poll and measures things like mutual trust, on which Finland rates very high, in part because it has policies in place that protect the lives and livelihood of its citizens. These policies are the main reason we examine Finland in this chapter. Happiness and well-being are intricately linked. Finland's policies support their citizens throughout the life course. Throughout this book we have explored policies that affect the well-being of older adults, including those policies that are not aging-specific, such as housing, transportation, and zoning. Finland takes a different approach than the United States does in many areas that affect well-being and quality of life, so it is important to include this perspective in this book.

Finland is a small country in Northern Europe, nestled between Sweden and Russia. Geographically, it is about half the size of Texas. It has a population of about 5.5 million (Index Mundi, 2020a), which is smaller than the population of New York City. It has one major metropolitan area, its capital, Helsinki. Some people say that this difference in size makes it impossible to compare Finland with the United States. Yet it is certainly comparable in size and population to a majority of U.S. states; thus, there are lessons to be learned that could be applied to individual states or to the United States as a whole. Given its extreme northern location, much of Finland is sparsely populated and covered with dense forest. Its population density of 18 inhabitants per square kilometer (European Commission, n.d.-a) makes it comparable with states like Oregon and Maine. The northernmost parts of Finland lie above the Arctic Circle. The whole country experiences a long winter season with extremely short winter days. The country, however, does experience all four seasons, and in parts of Finland summer temperatures can be as high as 80 degrees Fahrenheit.

By the end of this chapter, students will be able to

1. Compare and contrast the approaches taken by Finland and the United States to four types of policies that impact people's day-to-day lives.

2. Identify two things about the Finnish approach that could be applied to the United States.

3. Discuss ways in which the United States is different from Finland and the resulting barriers to implementing Finnish-style policies.

4. Identify and describe strategies to overcome those barriers.

Finland has two official languages, Finnish and Swedish, which reflect the ethnic makeup of the country. The **Sami**, a native group, are the largest minority population. Smaller populations of Russians and Estonians are also present (Weibull et al., n.d.). Finland is religiously homogenous, with more than 97% of the country's residents affiliated with a Christian denomination and nearly 70% affiliated with the Lutheran Church. The Lutheran Church is the national church of Finland. However, despite high rates of church membership, attendance rates at churches remain low (Weibull et al., n.d.). Finland has a **Freedom of Religion Act**. As its name implies, this act guarantees residents the right to practice any religion, as long as its practices do not violate any laws. Students receive non-denominational religious instruction in school. This instruction treats religion as a cultural issue, and promotes tolerance towards other religions and ways of thinking (European Commission, n.d.-a).

Like those of Canada and the United States, Finland's federal government has both an executive branch and a legislative branch. As a **parliamentary republic**, it has a parliament as its highest legislative body. The people of Finland directly elect 200 representatives every 4 years. Like the U.S. Congress, the Finnish parliament is responsible for the country's budget. They are also supposed to provide checks and balances to the government by controlling administration and supervising the actions the government takes (European Commission, n.d.-a). The parliament also sets the agenda for the government and elects the **prime minister** from within its ranks.

Unlike in the United States, Finland's **president** is elected directly by the people in the same way they elect legislators. The president serves a 6-year term. As in the United States, the president can introduce bills to the legislative branch, ratifies laws, and is commander-in-chief of the armed forces. The president formally appoints the prime minister and the 18 other ministers that comprise the **Council of State**, commonly called the **cabinet** (President of the Republic of Finland, n.d.). The **cabinet** runs the **government**, which consists of 12 ministries, each with jurisdiction over a particular area of life (European Commission, n.d.-a). The 12 ministries are the Prime Minister's Office, the Ministry for Foreign Affairs, the Ministry of Justice, the Ministry of the Interior, the Ministry of Defense, the Ministry of Finance, the Ministry of Education and Culture, the Ministry of Agriculture and Forestry, the Ministry of Transport and Communications, the Ministry of Economic Affairs and Employment, the Ministry of Social Affairs and Health, and the Ministry of the Environment (Finnish Government, n.d.). The president works with the cabinet and the government to ensure the efficient functioning of national matters (President of the Republic of Finland, n.d.).

Finland is a part of the **European Union**. The European Union is a group of 27 member states across Europe that have decided to come together for the benefit of all members. The European Union is an economic and political union with goals of promoting peace, offering freedom and security, advancing social justice, and combatting social exclusion, all while respecting the cultural and linguistic diversity of member states (European Union, n.d.). One of the most visible signs of the European Union is the use of the **euro** (€), a common currency currently in use by 19 of the 27 member states, including Finland (European Union, n.d.). For purposes of this chapter, the most important thing to know about the European Union is that it is intended to support member nations in achieving common goals in areas such as health, but European Union policies do not replace those of member countries (European Union, n.d.). In Finland, the government is responsible for national preparation of decisions that will be made by the European Union. All other foreign policy matters are the responsibility of the president, in cooperation with the government. Parliament must be involved in any decision to enter or withdraw from international agreements (President of the Republic of Finland, n.d.).

The population of Finland is older than that of the United States, both by median age (42.8 years vs. 38.5 years), and by percentage of the population over age 65 (22.26% vs. 16.85%) (Index Mundi, 2020a, 2020b). In fact, Finland is one of the oldest countries in Europe, aided by longer lifespans and declining birth rates (Finnish Institute for Health and Welfare, n.d.). Like the United States, Finland is also concerned with the rising costs associated with an aging population and the ability to provide adequate staffing for the rising needs of this aging population (Finnish Institute for Health and Welfare, n.d.). However, due to the existence of a robust safety net across the life course, Finnish older adults as a whole are in a different position than U.S. older adults as they approach retirement and other late-life transitions.

THE FINNISH APPROACH TO THE SOCIAL SAFETY NET ACROSS THE LIFE COURSE

Finnish people have high levels of trust for each other, which leads them to be more willing to pay high taxes to support the well-being of others (Thelwell, 2018). Across the board, these taxes support Finnish social welfare policies that are more generous than those in the United States, and Finland is willing to experiment. From 2016 to 2018, a 2-year pilot project experimented with offering **universal basic income (UBI)** to those most in need (Thelwell, 2018). The program intended to investigate whether an unconditional monthly payment would create work incentives and decrease the bureaucracy needed to administer such a benefit (Linnanvirta et al., 2019). The vast majority (69%) of Finnish people supported the idea of such a program, believing it would reduce the need for other forms of charity and improve purchasing power, and that it would reduce stress from uncertainty for individuals used to living at the margins (Linnanvirta et al., 2019). While the results of the UBI experiment are not yet completely clear (Thelwell, 2018), the idea of UBI may be more popular in Finland than in the United States because of the mutual trust held by most Finnish citizens (World Happiness Report, 2021) or the sense that people in Finland are "all in the same boat" (Linnanvirta et al., 2019, p. 275).

U.S. societal assumptions tend to be more suspicious than those held in Finland; there are U.S. societal assumptions that people in need mishandle money when it is provided to them, and that income should be tied to work. While UBI may sound similar to the **Supplemental Security Income (SSI)** offered in the United States, the primary difference is the lack of conditions placed on this income. The amount of UBI provided in the Finland experiment was comparable to an existing form of conditional support, which at that time was €560 (about $670 in 2021). However, recipients did not lose these benefits if they took odd jobs or short-term work for pay to supplement their income, make themselves more self-sufficient, and improve their situation (Linnanvirta et al., 2019).

FAMILY LEAVE

The United States is nearly alone as the only country without national, guaranteed, paid parental leave for new parents, particularly mothers, who are often also recovering from the physical experience of giving birth. The **Family and Medical Leave Act (FMLA)** provides up to 12 weeks of unpaid, job-protected leave to individuals welcoming new children through birth or adoption. Both parents are entitled to take this leave, and parties who take this leave are entitled to keep their employer-provided health insurance during the time they are off (U.S. Department of Labor, n.d.), though they are responsible for any premiums that would normally be deducted from a paycheck.

The barriers to using this leave are extensive. First and foremost, this leave is unpaid. Many families who would benefit most from the ability to take maternity leave are unable to afford to take unpaid time off from their jobs. Parents who birth children are eligible for short-term disability payments for delivery—if they have such coverage, which is optional if it is available at all. Disability payments cover 6 weeks for a vaginal birth and 8 weeks for a caesarean section. These payments also often cover only a portion of the worker's income, not all. In addition, individual companies may allow parents to use vacation or other paid leave, but they are not required to. While both parents are technically eligible to take FMLA leave, the lack of payment often keeps one or both parents from requesting the leave at all.

Secondly, not all employees are covered under FMLA. There are conditions that employers and employees must meet in order to access this coverage. Covered employers include local, state, and federal public agencies, and private agencies employing 50 or more people for 20 or more weeks out of the year. This excludes many small businesses! By the numbers, small businesses make up 99% of all the private companies in the United States, and employ nearly half (47%) of all workers (U.S. Small Business Administration, 2020). Now, to be clear, the U.S. Small Business Administration defines a small business as one with less than 500 employees, and the FMLA excludes businesses with less than 50 employees. However, despite this discrepancy in definitions, this clause excludes many employers from being subject to FMLA laws.

The employee restrictions further exclude many workers. Workers are only covered if they work for a qualifying employer and meet several other criteria including working at a location with 50 or more employees within 75 miles, having worked for that employer for 12 months at the time the leave is required, and having worked at least 1,250 hours for that employer over the previous year (about 25 hours/week) (U.S. Department of Labor, n.d.). This excludes anyone who works part time, or has several part-time jobs to make ends meet. All in total, FMLA excludes about 40% of the workforce (Ludden, 2013).

When it comes to parental leave, Nordic countries, particularly Finland, are at the opposite end of the spectrum. In Finland, mothers are entitled to a **maternity grant** and **maternity leave**. Fathers are entitled to **paternity leave**. In addition to maternity and paternity leave, either parent can take **parental leave**. A maternity grant is financial compensation that a mother receives during pregnancy, either in the form of a tax-free cash payment of €170 or a **maternity package**. The maternity package includes a box which may serve as a crib for a newborn and clothing and supplies for the care of a newborn, including a snowsuit, onesies, pants, coveralls, mittens, socks, towels, bedding, bibs, personal care items, a book, and a toy (Kela, n.d.-a). Maternity leave may begin as early as 50 days before the expected due date and must begin by the latest 30 days before the baby is due. Once a mother goes on maternity leave, the Finnish Social Insurance Program, **Kela**, pays a **maternity allowance** for 105 working days (approximately 21 weeks, or 5 months). In addition to the paid leave given to the mother, fathers are entitled to 54 days of paternity leave, of which 18 days can overlap with the time the mother is at home. When all of the maternity and paternity leave is exhausted, either parent can take parental leave, an additional 158 work days, during which Kela pays a **parental allowance** (European Commission, n.d.-b).

It may seem like parental leave has nothing to do with aging policy, but it does, in several important ways. As discussed in Chapter 8, FMLA in the United States is not only leave for childcare, but also leave for all types of family care. By combining the leaves, the United States: further limits an already restrictive policy; forces some workers, often women in the **sandwich generation**, to choose between their parents and their children; and requires some workers to leave their jobs altogether. The sandwich generation refers to people in middle age who have caregiving responsibilities for both aging parents and young children at the same time. For those workers who have to leave their jobs, this family leave policy has implications for their own ability to be financially secure in their retirement.

Finland's approach to parental leave support is indicative of their societal assumptions about mutual trust and public good. Additionally, the ability to take time off to care for a newborn, and to receive financial assistance at the time of increased expenses in caring for a child, can help Finns be more financially secure as they age into retirement.

Now, Finland is not perfect. For example, despite the availability of paternity leave, many men do not take it. In the Nordic nations, gender equity is an emerging societal assumption and has become embedded in policies such as the presence of leave options for fathers (Hass & Rostgard, 2011). Some researchers suggest that the movement towards equity in policies is a result of grassroots movements led by women, driven by the idea that government should play a role in reducing social inequities and improving the status of women at home and in society (Hass & Rostgard, 2011). Family leave that included fathers first emerged in Finland in the mid-1980s in the form of policies that offered the parental leave entitlement to each child and left it to the family to determine how to use the leave time—for the mother, for the father, or split between the two in some combination. But they noticed a pattern wherein gender norms remained, and most often, the mothers took the majority of the leave. In 2003, Finland began offering bonus weeks to fathers if they took part of the shared leave offered to families, in an attempt to incentivize fathers to share caregiving responsibilities (Haas & Rostgard, 2011). Like elder care (Chapter 8), childcare in heterosexual couples continues to fall disproportionately on the female-identifying parent or mother figure. Some fathers even report that in their male-dominated professions, like law, practically, it remains a career risk to take paternity leave even though the leave itself is guaranteed to them by the government (Choroszewicz & Tremblay, 2018). Some choose to take vacation time as opposed to formal paternity leave, and may choose to remain engaged with the workplace during their time off (Choroszewicz & Tremblay, 2018). From a policy perspective, the trends have been towards creating more of a shared-leave model, with specific time carved out for each parent (Eydal et al., 2015). These policies may be more progressive than the some sectors of the social culture.

A Finnish official, in conversation with an American social worker expressed concern about declining birth rates in Finland that were occurring because young families were choosing not to have children. Coming from the United States, the social worker was perplexed about why this would be the case, when the maternity/paternity benefits were so much greater in Finland than in the United States. The official explained that many fathers were concerned about the professional implications of taking leave. The reason she was concerned about birth rates was because of aging policy and caregiving. Declining birth rates can impact the numbers of people available to care for older generations. This is just one illustration of the fact that no age group is an island, and all social groups need to work together for society to function. The lack of guaranteed, paid parental leave in the United States not only hurts families with children but also impacts the larger society.

EDUCATION/DAY CARE

In addition to having no paid parental leave, the United States also has no system to provide childcare once parents return to work. With the absence of parental leave, some parents return to work as soon as days after giving birth. In most formal day care centers, the youngest age they will accept is 6 weeks. Childcare is a social issue that for generations has impacted primarily working mothers. In the absence of available, affordable childcare, some families choose to have one parent remain at home. This has most often been the mother, which has contributed to greater late-life poverty for women, disrupted career trajectories, and caused greater poverty overall for women and for families with young children.

In the United States, the availability and affordability of childcare has been an issue since the days of industrialization, when mothers began working in factories for pay with little to no available, formal childcare. Prior to industrialization, mothers would take their children with them when they went to work in the fields. Native American mothers are known for using **cradleboards** or slings, to strap their children to their backs or their fronts, respectively, while they worked. There were all manner of wooden contraptions to keep babies and toddlers safe from plows, fires, and other hazards of early American life (Michel, 2011). The **U.S. Children's Bureau**, founded in 1912, sought policy solutions that would allow mothers to stay at home. What they failed to realize was that this was not a realistic option for poor mothers who had no choice but to go out to work. Modern childcare policy can be traced back to 1954 with the introduction of the childcare tax deduction, available to middle- and low-income families (Michel, 2011). Childcare tax deductions and a limited number of childcare subsidies remain the only types of financial assistance for childcare available in the United States (Michel, 2011; Workman & Jessen-Howard, 2018).

Parents in the United States struggle with both the availability of quality childcare and the means to pay for it. While public school is available free of charge for children starting at age 5, there are no public facilities to care for children under the age of 5. Childcare, when available, varies in quality and is nearly always high in cost. The average cost of sending a child to day care for 1 year exceeds the cost of 1 year of in-state college tuition in most states. And, often, that high-cost childcare is not available (Workman & Jessen-Howard, 2018). Parents in many communities put themselves on waiting lists for childcare slots even before they have told family members they are expecting. High-quality preschool is critical for child development and well-being. The first 5 years of life are considered to be the most crucial as far as brain and social development. Interactions with caregivers are opportunities for children to have new experiences, and the more interactions they have with their caregivers, the more they develop. Children who attend day care with adequate, trained staff have more of these interactions than children who do not (Workman & Jessen-Howard, 2018).

Nearly 1 in 5 children in the United States lives in poverty. Poverty in early childhood is a risk factor for many negative outcomes. For example, children in poverty are less likely to get adequate or healthy food to promote body and brain development. In the United States, the **National School Lunch Program** (**NSLP**) provides low-cost or free lunches once students reach school age (U.S. Department of Agriculture, n.d.). For children ages 5 and under, the **Special Supplemental Nutrition Program for Women, Infants, and Children** (**WIC**) provides nutritious foods to supplement a child's diet based on a nutrition education and counseling assessment. There are no requirements for the provision of nutrition through childcare centers.

Children raised in poverty have other developmental risks, as well, that quality childcare may be able to help mitigate. Children in poverty are more likely to have parents who are chronically stressed, and they may live in neighborhoods where exposure to crime is widespread. They are also more likely to be exposed to environmental toxins through pollution, natural disasters, and household substances such as lead paint, due to a variety of policies that put industry and highways near low-income communities, situate low-income communities near areas at risk for flooding and other hazards, and fail to punish landlords whose properties are in poor repair. Quality care can mitigate these hazards by providing consistent, safe places for children to learn, play, and grow. A policy response to this was the development of **Head Start** as part of President Lyndon Johnson's War on Poverty in 1964. Head Start and Early Head Start are a series of programs that include childcare intended to promote school readiness and healthy starts for children from low-income families (Office of Head Start, n.d.). However, these benefits are only provided to families who qualify, leaving children and families at the margins without services, yet still unable to afford quality childcare.

Not so in Finland. In Finland, every child is entitled to full-time early childhood education. This bears repeating. Every *child* is entitled to full-time early childhood education. Think about this fundamental difference in approach. In the United States, we think about early childhood care as a benefit for parents or families. Finland looks at it from the perspective of the child. Every child is legally entitled to full-time early childhood education, which can be provided in a designated center or in a family day care. In addition, municipalities are responsible for ensuring that they provide sufficient early childhood education and care to meet the needs in their community (European Commission, n.d.a.). Children do not typically enter care until the parental leave period is over, when they are 9 or 10 months old. At that point, parents have choices between three different types of care—municipal-provided care centers, municipal-provided home-based centers, and private centers—and they receive financial assistance on a sliding scale. Costs vary, but can be as low as zero euros for families who qualify. The maximum cost is €288 per month (about $344 in 2021) for one child (European Commission, n.d.a.).

Compare the Finnish maximum of €288/month to the average monthly costs of day care in the United States. According to the Center for American Progress, average costs for center-based care are $1,280 per month, and average costs for home-based care are $800 per month (Workman & Jessen-Howard, 2018). In Finland, a child in full-time care must be offered breakfast, lunch, and dinner (Korkalo et al., 2019), as compared to the lack of meal requirements for U.S. care. Children who receive a physically, mentally, and emotionally healthy start to life are better equipped to become productive citizens of a society. Additionally, the financial resources provided to children in Finland stabilize the family situation. Finally, when parents do not need to deplete their funds paying for childcare, they are better able to save for their own retirement, health, and care needs.

Both the parental leave examples and the childcare examples describe ways that policy in Finland cares for its citizens from birth. They are examples of the Finnish societal beliefs in mutual trust, and policies and practices that reflect ideals of the greater good. In the next section we will expand on the discussion of healthcare started in Chapter 11 and conclude with an expansion on the discussion of income from Chapter 10, comparing both to Finnish policies on those topics.

HEALTH CARE

We began Chapter 11 by talking about how the United States does not have universal health insurance. Some groups, like older adults over the age of 65 (for the most part), receive health insurance from the U.S. government in the form of Medicare. Other groups, like low-income children, pregnant women, and older adults, may qualify for Medicaid based on their income. Together, Medicare and Medicaid account for about a third of all health care spending in the United States—21% and 16%, respectively (Centers for Medicare and Medicaid Services, 2020). Despite this large outlay, many people are left out from this equation. Most working-age adults who are insured get their insurance through their employer. Employer-based insurance grew rapidly after World War II. It was relatively inexpensive for employers to provide. Prices were based on community ratings, which meant that plans had a large pool of subscribers that spread out the risk, keeping costs low (Enthoven & Fuchs, 2006). Now, most often, health care benefits are offered by medium to large employers, and even then, only to their full-time employees. As discussed in the FMLA section, nearly half of U.S. employees work in small companies.

Employer-based health benefits are far from perfect. In the years since World War II, a variety of market factors in U.S. business and in U.S. health insurance have combined to make insurance riskier for the companies that provide it because they cover a smaller portion of the population. In order to save money, they must make decisions about what they do and do not cover. They need staff to make those decisions; thus, they have high administrative costs, which lead to high consumer costs (Enthoven & Fuchs, 2006). Employer-based health insurance operates on a cost-share model, where the employer pays a portion of the premium, pre-tax, and the employee contributes a share. The insurance that is offered is through private companies, and the increase in premiums has far outpaced inflation, with double-digit percentage increases being common each and every year. Those who are insured often learn, when they try to seek health care, that there are very specific limits on what is covered, and that nearly all healthcare transactions require a cost share from the insured in the form of a co-pay or deductible.

The **Patient Protection and Affordable Care Act** (ACA) attempted to smooth out some of the most egregious problems with employer-based healthcare. The ACA prevented insurance companies from denying coverage to people with pre-existing conditions, eliminated co-pays on certain preventive visits, called for expanding Medicaid to cover individuals at up to 138% of the poverty line, created healthcare exchanges where people who could not get insurance through their employer could purchase insurance, and created an individual mandate requiring individuals to carry health insurance or pay a tax penalty. The individual mandate was intended to increase the size of the pool of people who had health insurance, reducing overall risk for the insurance companies, which would lower cost. Not all of these components remain intact. As was discussed in Chapter 1, the Supreme Court determined that the federal government could not force states to expand Medicaid. Other sections of the ACA have been brought before the Supreme Court, and under President Trump there were several attempts to "repeal and replace" the ACA in Congress. The individual mandate did not survive, due to Trump-era tax reform. As a result, health coverage in the United States remains patchwork, with the most vulnerable frequently under threat of losing coverage. Access to health care across the life course impacts the health of adults as they age. Having health insurance makes people more likely to get something diagnosed and treated early before it becomes a chronic or serious problem.

The Finnish approach to healthcare is about as close to the opposite of the U.S. approach as you can get. In Finland, everyone living in the country is entitled to healthcare through a public system. According to the Finnish constitution—it's in the constitution!—the public health authorities must provide adequate social, health, and medical services. Private health services are permitted, and in some places the public authorities purchase services from private companies. Municipalities are tasked with organizing and financing health services in their region, and they have options for how to structure them. For example, they may provide health services themselves, purchase health services from private companies, or provide health services in collaboration with other regions or municipalities. As far as the federal government goes, how the services are provided is less important than which services are provided. All treatment must first go through primary health care, provided at municipal health clinics. Patients may then be referred to hospitals for specialized health care. There are five regional centers across the country that provide the highest and most specialized level of care, such as treatment for rare diseases, burns, and childhood cancers (EU-healthcare.fi, n.d.).

Many of the health services are provided directly by the municipalities, though, as stated earlier, some may purchase those services for their residents from private companies or practitioners. Private providers can also sell their services directly to patients. Private healthcare is partially subsidized by public funds. Specifically, they will pay for charges associated with necessary treatments by providers who have a contract with the federal system. A patient who chooses a private provider over the public system is responsible for the difference (EU-healthcare.fi, n.d.; Kela, n.d.-b).

These health services are provided to all individuals across the life course, allowing for a healthy start to life, preventive care in adulthood, and consistent, ongoing care in late adulthood. In the United States, many adults allow conditions to go untreated when they are between the ages of 60–65 if they do not have health insurance, waiting to qualify for Medicare. There are no such gaps in care in Finland, allowing individuals to maintain care and enter retirement age healthier than in the United States.

PENSIONS

Chapter 10 contained an extensive discussion of pensions and retirement funding in the United States. In brief, most Americans with a work history qualify for Social Security payments at the age of 67. Payments are based on previous work history, which disadvantages those who have worked low-wage jobs throughout their life or took substantial time away from the workplace for caregiving or disability. In general, Social Security payments, which were not intended to be the sole source of retirement income, do not provide adequate funds for most people to live on in retirement.

Defined benefit pensions, which provided guaranteed security for earlier generations, do not exist for the majority of the workforce anymore. When workers do have pensions, defined contribution plans are the norm, with employers contributing a fixed amount. Defined contribution plans are tax-deferred savings plans that are invested in the open market, leaving retirees vulnerable to market fluctuations. In the United States this was a major issue during the recession of 2008–2009, when many near-retirees lost a majority of the value of their retirement investments. Many would-be retirees stayed in the workforce, which, along with the economic downturn, stagnated the job market for new graduates and other job seekers.

Finland has a two-tiered pension system, and the two systems are designed to complement each other. The first system is **earnings-related pensions**, which accrue based on work history in Finland. The second system is **national pensions**, which are based on residence in Finland (Nordic Co-operation, n.d.). A person becomes eligible for both pensions at the age of 65 (Organisation for Economic Co-operation and Development [OECD], n.d.), though the age for the earnings-related pension is being increased to age 70 for those born after 1961 (OECD, 2019).

The earnings-related pension system operates similarly to Social Security in the United States in that it is accrued based on previous work. In Finland you can begin to accrue pension eligibility at age 17, age 18 if you are self-employed (Nordic Co-operation, n.d.). Pensionable pay is accrued at a rate of 1.5% for people ages 18–52. Rates go higher as people get closer to retirement age (OECD, n.d.). This system functions by employers taking out a pension insurance policy on their employees and paying the insurance premiums. People who are self-employed are required to purchase their own policy and pay all the premiums (infoFinland.fi, n.d.). Benefits are calculated at retirement by a standard formula. As with Social Security in the United States, there is an option to access your pension early, but also as with Social Security, there is an adjustment in the calculation of the monthly payment for those who choose this option (OECD, n.d.).

National pensions in Finland are intended for persons who have no earnings-related pension, or those for whom the amount of their earnings-related pension is very small (infoFinland.fi, n.d.). As this pension is tied to residence, eligibility and amount are based on how long someone has lived and worked in Finland (infoFinland.

fi, n.d.). A person is eligible for a full national pension after living in Finland for 40 years as an adult (OECD, 2019). Benefits are pro-rated for those who have lived in Finland for shorter periods. In 2018, the full rate of the national pension was €628.85 (approximately $750) per month (OECD, 2019).

Finally, Finland has a **guarantee pension** program. This program functions like SSI in the United States, in that its purpose is to raise all older adults to a minimum standard. As with the national pension, eligibility is based on residence in Finland, and on income level (OECD, n.d., 2019). Since 2011, the minimum pension level guaranteed by the guarantee pension program has been €775.27 (approximately $930) per month. This is approximately $150 more per month than is paid by **SSI** in the United States, which means the minimum **guarantee pension** payment exceeds the federally mandated minimum **SSI** payment by $1,800 per year.

Comparison with U.S. System

As you have seen throughout this chapter, the policies of Finland across the life course embody two principles not seen in U.S. policies: the societal assumption that everyone is in this together, and the assumption that the federal government does bear responsibility for health and social services. As a result of these interventions, the risk of poverty in late life in Finland is nearly zero, as compared to rates in the United States. Finnish older adults do experience income differences, which does impact retirement ages and experiences.

ADEQUACY OF RETIREMENT FUNDING IN FINLAND AND BEYOND

While Finland is significantly smaller than the United States, it is similar in size to several other European countries. The SHARE survey (Survey of Health, Ageing and Retirement in Europe)—a multi-year, multi-national research study—has allowed European nations to compare themselves to each other. Finland recently participated in this survey for the first time, which allowed them to compare older adult well-being in Finland to that of older adults in other European nations.

The availability of adequate finances is tied to both income (Chapter 10) and expenses for health care and other necessities. A shortage of money can impact quality of life because lack of funds can leave needs unmet and force a person to give up recreation and/or hobbies, which contribute to mental and cognitive health. There is significant variability across Europe. In Greece, the nation whose older adults are the financially worst off, nearly 60% of older adults report that a shortage of money often stops them from doing what they want. At the other end of the spectrum, fewer than 5% of older adults in Sweden report that a shortage of money often stops them from doing what they want.

Finland falls somewhere in the middle, closer to the wealthy end. Nordic countries in general have greater social infrastructure and lower levels of poverty than other countries, particularly in Southern and Eastern Europe. Slightly fewer than 10% of Finnish older adults report that a shortage of money keeps them from doing what they want (Palomäki, 2020). In nearly all households, individuals need to prioritize what they do and make decisions based on the availability of funds. What is an acceptable level of unmet desire that still results in a good quality of life?

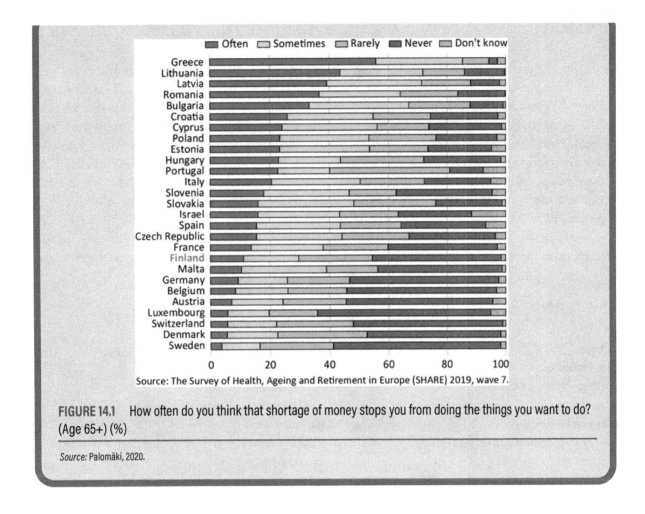

Source: The Survey of Health, Ageing and Retirement in Europe (SHARE) 2019, wave 7.

FIGURE 14.1   How often do you think that shortage of money stops you from doing the things you want to do? (Age 65+) (%)

Source: Palomäki, 2020.

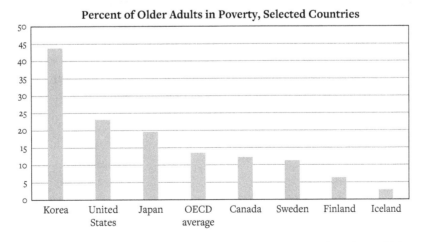

FIGURE 14.2   Percent of Older Adults in Poverty, Selected Countries* *Countries selected were highest and lowest OECD countries, as reference points, and countries mentioned elsewhere in this book.* Source: Compare your country, n.d

SUMMARY

In the United States we often talk about the Nordic countries as being very different than us in the ways they provide social services for their citizens. In this chapter, using Finland as an example, we have demonstrated just how different their approaches are. From months of paid maternity leave to a system that ensures early childhood care to guaranteed healthcare and pensions, the policies of Finland care for its citizens from birth to death. Though this book focuses on policies that impact older adults, you can see from this chapter how the security of having a basic level of care across the life course influences the experience of growing older.

Some people say that comparison with a country like Finland is unfair, given its much smaller size, and that the United States could not possibly provide such services to its citizens. Finland is similar in size to many U.S. states, so perhaps such interventions could be implemented on the state level. States often serve as policy laboratories, trying solutions on a smaller scale before they can be implemented nationally. However, the real difference is in the societal assumption that people are all in it together, and in the resulting policy approaches.

KEY TERMS

Cabinet

Cradleboards

Earnings-related pensions

Euro

European Union

Family and Medical Leave Act (FMLA)

Freedom of Religion Act

Government

Guarantee pensions

Head Start/Early Head Start

Kela

Maternity allowance

Maternity grant

Maternity leave

Maternity package

National pensions

National School Lunch Program (NSLP)

Parental allowance

Parental leave

Parliamentary republic

Paternity leave

Patient Protection and Affordable Care Act (ACA)

President

Prime Minister

Sami

Sandwich generation

Special Supplemental Nutrition Program for Women, Infants, and Children (WIC)

Supplemental Security Income (SSI)

Universal Basic Income (UBI)

U.S. Children's Bureau

DISCUSSION QUESTIONS

1. Finland incorporates significantly different societal assumptions into its social policies than the United States does. Of the four areas discussed in this chapter—parental leave, childcare, health care, and pensions—which do you think the United States would be most likely to be able to implement? Why?

2. How do parental leave and child care relate to well-being in later life? Discuss the ways in which they influence the individual and the family.

3. In Finland, parental leave is its own distinct entitlement and is unrelated to other types of care leave, while in the United States FMLA is used for all types of caregiving. Which approach makes more sense from a business perspective? Is that the same as from the recipient's perspective? Which should the United States adopt and why?

4. Finland, like the United States, ties some of its pension compensation to work history as an earned benefit. What benefits are there to tying pension benefits to years worked and wages earned?

Ancillary materials for student practice can be found within Active Learning

REFERENCES

Centers for Medicare and Medicaid Services. (2020). *NHE fact sheet*. National Health Expenditure Data. https://www.cms.gov/Research-Statistics-Data-and-Systems/Statistics-Trends-and-Reports/NationalHealthExpendData/NHE-Fact-Sheet

Choroszewicz, M., & Tremblay, D.-G. (2018). Parental-leave policy for male lawyers in Helsinki and Montreal: Cultural and professional barriers to male lawyers' use of paternity and parental leaves. *International Journal of the Legal Profession*, *25*(3), 303–316. https://doi.org/10.1080/09695958.2018.1456435

Compare your country. (n.d.). *Pensions at a glance*. OECD. Retrieved from https://www.compareyourcountry.org/pensions/en/1//default/

Enthoven, A., & Fuchs, V. (2006). Employment-based health insurance: Past, present, and future. *Health Affairs*, *25*(6), 1538–1547. https://doi.org/10.1377/hlthaff.25.6.1538

EU-healthcare.fi. (n.d.) *Healthcare system in Finland*. Retrieved April 19, 2021 from https://www.eu-healthcare.fi/healthcare-in-finland/healthcare-system-in-finland/

European Commission. (n.d.-a) *Finland*. Retrieved April 6, 2021 from https://eacea.ec.europa.eu/national-policies/eurydice/content/finland_en

European Commission. (n.d.-b). *Finland - maternity and paternity*. Retrieved April 12, 2021 from https://ec.europa.eu/social/main.jsp?catId=1109&langId=en&intPageId=4514

European Union. (n.d.) *The EU in brief*. Retrieved April 6, 2021 from https://europa.eu/european-union/about-eu/eu-in-brief_en

Eydal, G. B., Gíslason, I. V., Rostgaard, T., Brandth, B., Duvander, A.-Z., & Lammi-Taskula, J. (2015). Trends in parental leave in the Nordic countries: Has the forward march of gender equality halted? *Community, Work & Family*, *18*(2), 167–181. http://doi.org/10.1080/13668803.2014.1002754

Finnish Government. (n.d.). *How does the Government work?* Retrieved April 6, 2021 from https://valtioneuvosto.fi/en/government/how-does-the-government-work-

Finnish Institute for Health and Welfare. (n.d.) *Ageing policy*. Retrieved April 7, 2021 from https://thl.fi/en/web/ageing/ageing-policy

Haas, L., & Rostgaard, T. (2011). Fathers' rights to paid parental leave in the Nordic countries: Consequences for the gendered division of leave. *Community, Work, & Family*, *14*(2), 177–195. https://doi.org/10.1080/13668803.2011.571398

Index Mundi. (2020a). *Finland demographics profile*. Retrieved April 5, 2021 from https://www.indexmundi.com/finland/demographics_profile.html

Index Mundi. (2020b). *United States demographics profile*. Retrieved April 5, 2021 from https://www.indexmundi.com/united_states/demographics_profile.html

infoFinland.fi. (n.d.). *Pension*. Living in Finland. Retrieved April 20, 2021 from https://www.infofinland.fi/en/living-in-finland/work-and-enterprise/pension

Kela. (n.d.-a). *Maternity package 2021.* Retrieved April 12, 2021 from https://www.kela.fi/web/en/maternity-package-2021

Kela. (n.d.-b) *Reimbursements for medical expenses.* Retrieved April 19, 2021 from https://www.kela.fi/web/en/medical-expenses

Korkalo, L., Nissinen, K., Skaffari, E., Vepsäläinen, H., Lehto, R., Kaukonen, R., Koivusilta, L., Sajaniemi, N., Roos, E., & Erkkola, M. (2019). The contribution of preschool meals to the diet of Finnish preschoolers. *Nutrients, 11*(7), 1531. https://doi.org/10.3390/nu11071531

Linnanvirta, S., Kroll, C., & Blomberg, H. (2019). The perceived legitimacy of a basic income among Finnish food aid recipients. *International Journal of Social Welfare, 28*(3), 271–281. https://doi.org/10.1111/ijsw.12362

Lorentzen, T., Bäckman, O., Ilmakunnas, I., & Kauppinen, T. (2019). Pathways to adulthood: Sequences in the school-to-work transition in Finland, Norway, and Sweden. *Social Indicators Research, 141,* 1285–1305. https://doi.org/10.1007/s11205-018-1877-4

Ludden, J. (2013, February 5). FMLA not really working for many employees. *NPR.* Retrieved from https://www.npr.org/2013/02/05/171078451/fmla-not-really-working-for-many-employees

Michel, S. (2011). *The history of child care in the U.S.* VCU Libraries Social Welfare History Project, Virginia Commonwealth University. Retrieved from http://socialwelfare.library.vcu.edu/programs/child-care-the-american-history/

Nordic Co-operation. (n.d.). *The Finnish pension system.* Retrieved April 20, 2021 from https://www.norden.org/en/info-norden/finnish-pension-system

Office of Head Start. (n.d.). *Head Start services.* U.S. Department of Health & Human Services. Retrieved April 16, 2021 from https://www.acf.hhs.gov/ohs/about/head-start

Organisation for Economic Co-operation and Development. (n.d.). *Finland.* https://www.oecd.org/about/publishing/35203549.pdf

Organisation for Economic Co-operation and Development. (2019). *Pensions at a glance 2019: Country profiles – Finland.* Pensions at a Glance 2019: OECD and G20 Indicators. https://www.oecd.org/els/public-pensions/PAG2019-country-profile-Finland.pdf

Palomäki, L.-M. (2020, June 30). *How does the quality of life of older Finnish citizens compare to that of older citizens in Europe?* Finnish Centre for Pensions. https://www.etk.fi/en/blogs/how-does-the-quality-of-life-of-older-finnish-citizens-compare-to-that-of-older-citizens-in-europe/

President of the Republic of Finland. (n.d.) *Presidency.* Retrieved April 7, 2021 from https://www.presidentti.fi/en/presidency/

Thelwell, K. (2018, July 25). *Top 10 facts about poverty in Finland: Issues & solutions.* The Borgen Project. https://borgenproject.org/tag/welfare-system-in-finland/

U.S. Department of Agriculture. (n.d.) *Special Supplemental Nutrition Program for Women, Infants, and Children (WIC).* Food and Nutrition Service. Retrieved April 15, 2021 from https://www.fns.usda.gov/wic

U.S. Department of Labor. (n.d.) *FMLA Frequently Asked Questions.* Wage and Hour Division. Retrieved April 12, 2021from https://www.dol.gov/agencies/whd/fmla/faq

U.S. Small Business Administration. (2020). *Frequently asked questions.* Office of Advocacy. https://cdn.advocacy.sba.gov/wp-content/uploads/2020/11/05122043/Small-Business-FAQ-2020.pdf

Weibull, J., Sandvik, G., Sundblad, I., Sandelin, C. F., Enander, H., Larson, S. R., & Henriksson, M. I. (n.d.). *Finland.* Encyclopaedia Britannica. Retrieved April 5, 2021 from https://www.britannica.com/place/Finland

Workman, S., & Jessen-Howard, S. (2018, November 15). *Understanding the true cost of child care for infants and toddlers.* The Center for American Progress. https://www.americanprogress.org/issues/early-childhood/reports/2018/11/15/460970/understanding-true-cost-child-care-infants-toddlers/

World Happiness Report. (2021, March 19). *In a lamentable year, Finland again is the happiest country in the world.* https://worldhappiness.report/blog/in-a-lamentable-year-finland-again-is-the-happiest-country-in-the-world/

Credits

Japan: Importing Help—The Role of Caregiving Visas

INTRODUCTION

Countries around the world are figuring out how to care for their growing aging populations. In most countries, the majority of direct care is provided by family members or paid direct care workers. These workers are often minimally trained and poorly compensated. A shortage of care providers is particularly acute in higher-income countries, due to a combination of declining birth rates and generally strong economies where other, more desirable jobs are available. As discussed in the chapter on Finland, declining birth rates means there are fewer young people looking for jobs relative to the number of older adults who need care. Care jobs may be less desirable because they pay low wages, often have inconsistent hours, lack benefits, and are physically and emotionally demanding. "[T]he low wages or availability of more attractive jobs mean there is a shortage of workers who have been born in the high-income countries" (Armstrong, 2018, p. 22). Thus, positions often go unfilled. Direct care workers in some settings, such as nursing homes, have untenable patient loads due to worker shortages, adding to stress and burnout. In the community, some older adults and persons with disabilities go without needed care.

CHAPTER-LEVEL LEARNING OBJECTIVES

By the end of this chapter, students will be able to

1. Compare and contrast the approaches taken by Japan and the United States to immigration policies related to the aging care workforce.

2. Identify two things about the Japanese approach that could be applied to the United States.

3. Discuss ways both countries could address caregiving shortages without immigrant workers.

4. Identify and describe strategies to overcome barriers to employing immigrants in the aging care workforce.

PAID CAREGIVERS IN THE UNITED STATES

Direct care workers help with daily tasks such as bathing, grooming, and dressing. In some settings with some certifications, they may also help with blood pressure readings, medication management, and **range-of-motion exercises** (exercises to keep arms and legs mobile). Direct care workers, including **home health aides,**

personal care aides who primarily work in home care, and **Certified Nursing Assistants** who work in nursing homes, are predominantly female (Espinoza, 2017a). Societal assumptions support the idea that caregiving is women's work, much as we saw in Chapter 8, where gender plays into sibling discussions about family caregiving. Women's work is traditionally undervalued, which contributes to the gender pay gap that exists today. While gender wage gaps within occupations persist, nearly half of the pay gap can be attributed to differences between those occupations that are considered to be "male" occupations and those that are considered to be "female" occupations (Schieder & Gould, 2016).

The United States, like other developed countries, is experiencing a shortage of direct care workers. Experts believe this shortage is being caused by a combination of demographic and policy factors. You have a combination of a growing pool of older adults—some of whom will require care, and many of whom would prefer that care be provided in their home—being served by a pool of workers that is not growing nearly as fast (Espinoza, 2017a). Additionally, workers in this field turn over, or leave their jobs, often, due to structural challenges like the low wages, inconsistent hours, lack of benefits, and physical and emotional demands. Shortages of these essential workers leave older adults and persons with disabilities unable to remain in their homes and communities and/or leave them with critical unmet needs, leaving countries to seek new and novel policy solutions.

One way countries fill these gaps is with immigrant workers. Immigrant direct care workers tend to come from countries where economic forces impel workers to relocate for better opportunities (Armstrong, 2018). In the United States, the top five countries of origin for immigrant direct care workers are Mexico, the Philippines, Jamaica, Haiti, and the Dominican Republic (Espinoza, 2017b). One in four direct care workers is an immigrant (Espinoza, 2017b). The status of immigrant workers in the United States varies with administration. For example, during President Trump's administration, the status of immigrants became more uncertain, impacting the workforce in fields ranging from direct care to farm work to the Maryland crab industry (American University Washington College of Law International Human Rights Law Clinic & Centro de los Derechos del Migrante, Inc., 2018). At the time of this writing, it is unclear what the Biden administration will do regarding immigration. Societal assumptions and policies about immigration often change with a change in leadership, and with changes in the economy and global political factors.

THE POPULATION IN JAPAN IS GETTING OLDER—FAST

Many countries across the Northern Hemisphere are experiencing population aging, meaning the average age in the population is increasing. Among the national populations experiencing this, Japan's population is aging so fast that it is being called a **"super-aging"** society. The proportion of people over the age of 65 in Japan is expected to grow from 25% of the country's population in 2020 to 40% by 2060 (Sze-Yunn & Arivalagan, 2020), the largest percentage ever seen in the world. Caused by a combination of declining birth rates and increasing life expectancy, Japan's challenges are actually a result of factors normally considered positive—economic growth and societal improvements (Marlow, 2015; Ogawa & Matsukura, 2007). The negative side of such benefits is that there are not enough workers in the middle ages of the lifespan, and there are increasing numbers of people in need of care. To address this unprecedented growth, the Japanese government is seeking policy and technology solutions that are creative and novel (Sze-Yunn & Arivalagan, 2020).

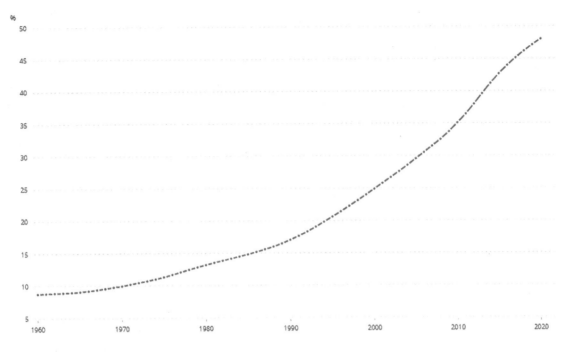

FIGURE 15.1 Age Dependency Ratio, Older Adults, Japan

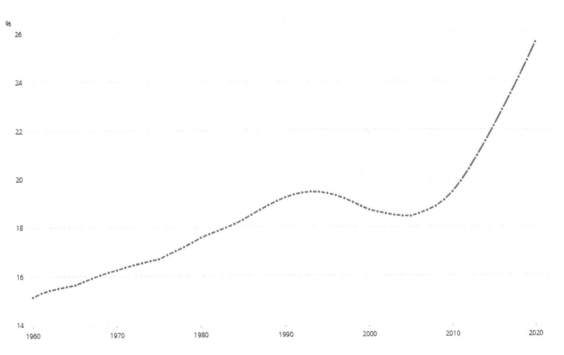

FIGURE 15.2 Age Dependency Ratio, Older Adults, United States

POPULATION DYNAMICS AND THE AVAILABILITY OF CAREGIVERS

Population replacement is the standard by which birth rate is measured. Are enough babies being born to replace the people who are dying every year? Prior to industrialization these numbers were much more fluid, with the dynamics of whole populations being influenced by pandemic outbreaks, famines, crop failures, and droughts. In the modern era, in industrialized countries, as children have become more likely to survive childhood, birth rates are the most accurate measure of population expansion and contraction. Population replacement alone does not ensure the availability of caregivers. In the short term, higher birth rates even lead to fewer caregivers, as children require care. But over the long term, population replacement is required to ensure a supply of caregivers, to sustain a country's economy, and to ensure the sustainability of social insurance programs like Social Security. Even in the United States in the 2020–2021 Covid-19 pandemic, in which more than half a million people died, the population replacement rate was impacted by a combination of births, deaths, and immigration (Friedman & Parker, 2021). The population replacement rate impacts the **dependency ratio**, or the number of people too old or too young to work relative to the number of working age people in a population.

One policy-related way to manipulate the population replacement rate is by attempting to influence the birth rate. There are many reasons for wanting to do this. Italy, for example, has tried to influence its population to have more children—first in the Mussolini era of the 1930s, to encourage more Italian babies and a greater population, and again in the 2010s, this time to balance out distorted population growth curves. Declining birth rates, below the rate of population replacement, have motivated Italian policy makers to offer mother's checks to families that choose to have a third child. Japan, on the other hand, has tried to support the growth of families through policies similar to those described in Chapter 14: child care, parental leave, and per-child allowances (D'Ambrogio, 2020). These policies do not directly influence the birth rate, but they do make it easier for couples when they are considering whether to have a child or to have more children.

Policies can also cause influence the birth rate in ways that cause population decline. These can be direct, such as China's one-child policy, which was enforced for many years. Chinese leaders were concerned that unchecked growth of the population would prevent the country from developing the economy and raising the living standards of the people. Thus, families were not permitted to have more than one child (Potts, 2006). Japan has not tried to decrease the birth rate, but policies can have unintended consequences that indirectly affect population replacement. Some data suggests that birth rates in the United States are lower than some families desire because the United States lacks supportive policies such as parental leave and child care. One reason for Japan's current situation is its advanced family planning policies. The birth rate has been below the rate of population replacement for many years (Muramatsu & Akiyama, 2011). Being below the rate of population replacement causes an increase in the average age of the population, as well as an increase in the median age. As we discussed in the chapter on Finland, population aging has strong implications for the availability of caregivers in a population.

IMPORTING HELP: EXPERIMENTING WITH VISAS FOR PAID CAREGIVERS

Immigration

People choose to relocate for many different reasons. There are always push factors and pull factors that influence the decision-making process (King, 2012; Lee, 1966). A **push factor** is a condition or situation in the location of origin (city, town, country) that makes life there untenable. Push factors include family relationships, economics, and the lack of availability of particular types of opportunities. For example, a person may need to earn more money to support their family than they can earn in their current location. **Pull factors** are conditions in the new location that are not available in the previous location. Similar to push factors, they are most often family relationships, economics, and the availability of particular opportunities. For the person who needs to earn more money, higher-paying jobs in the new location may be a pull factor. Often, the decision-making process is influenced by a combination of push factors and pull factors, which people and policy makers need to weigh in different measure. People who immigrate to a new country often do so for work, sometimes with very limited choices in their home countries and high levels of poverty. Many leave behind their own families who need care, because the financial support they can provide to them is perceived to be more valuable than being there in person (Chuang, 2013; Lutz, 2015). This also makes these workers more "affordable" as well as more vulnerable in many ways. They may be isolated by language, geography, or their own situation, and may either be unaware that employers are taking advantage of them or be powerless to stop it (Lee, 1966; Lutz, 2015).

Throughout the history of the United States, immigrant workers, particularly female immigrant workers, have taken jobs seen as less desirable. In the early days of industrialization they worked in factories and sweatshops, or as domestic help in other people's homes. Immigrant women continue to fulfill domestic and caregiving jobs today. Domestic jobs include housekeeper, nanny, and, yes, caregiver for older adults. There are policies in place that allow the admission to the United States of certain types of workers, such as the special temporary visas offered to au pairs who come to care for children. These policies allow workers to be in the United States with limited benefits on a short-term basis, allow their employers to avoid paying certain benefits such as Social Security, and provide limited oversight once the workers arrive (Chuang, 2013). In recent years, immigrant women have begun to fill more jobs as caregivers in formal settings such as nursing homes and day care centers, without particular visas or immigration mechanisms to support them (Stone, 2016).

Japan

Japan is known for being **insular**—that is, the Japanese government tends toward being uninterested in cultures or ideas from outside of Japan—and this attitude applies to immigrants. Rigid immigration policies have been the norm, permitting entrants only as temporary guest workers who must eventually return home. As of June 2019, less than 2% of the Japanese population was comprised of immigrants (D'Ambrogio, 2020). In the modern era, the largest groups of immigrants who have lived in Japan were Korean and Taiwanese people, during World War II. At that time, Korea and Taiwan were Japanese territories, so these groups were considered Japanese citizens rather than immigrants. However, Korean and Taiwanese people became foreigners at the end of U.S. occupation after the war (Green & Kadoya, 2013). One of the first things the newly independent Japanese government did was pass the **Immigration Control Act**, a restrictive policy that set the tone for Japanese immigration policy for more than half a century.

It is a sign of the scale of Japan's need for caregivers that one of Japan's innovative solutions to its caregiver shortage is immigrant **visas**. A visa is an endorsement on a passport that allows its owner to enter and stay in a country for a defined period of time. Visas are used for many different purposes. Some countries require tourist visas; others are for the purposes of temporary residence or a path to permanent immigration/citizenship. The visas discussed in this chapter are specific types of **work visas**. A work visa allows someone to enter and stay in a country for a defined period of time and legally work for pay during their stay.

Japan opened its doors slowly and cautiously. Starting in 2008, Japan developed two-way **Economic Partnership Agreements**—first with Indonesia, and later with the Philippines and Vietnam. These Economic Partnership Agreements allowed for the temporary immigration of workers from these countries, specifically nurses who were eligible to work in long-term services and supports (D'Ambrogio, 2020; Leading Age, 2019). Workers who came into Japan under these agreements received mandatory language training and job placement in the long-term services sector. In time, the workers provided by these Economic Partnership Agreements were not sufficient to fill all of the available jobs in the long-term services sector (Leading Age, 2019).

In 2018, recognizing the growing need for care workers, Japan amended their **Immigration Control Act**. Originally passed in 1952, the restrictive act limited immigration and prevented Japan from using workers from other countries to address emerging needs in elder care. The 2018 amendments added a new category of resident status for nurses and direct care workers, called caregivers, which reduced the barriers for foreign nurses and caregivers to obtaining jobs and resident status in Japan (Burgess, 2020; D'Ambrogio, 2020). The amendments make it easier for workers to find jobs before they come to Japan and expand the eligible countries of origin. At the same time, the Immigration Control Act amendments tighten Japan's ability to monitor workers perpetuating fraud, such as those who enter the country under work visas but fail to work in the designated field.

Also in 2016, the Japanese government passed the **Technical Training Act.** This act created pathways for the Japanese government to approve and monitor training plans and programs offered to foreigners who want to come to Japan to learn and work in a trade. For example, an organization could develop a training and work placement program for care workers and then advertise in the Philippines for workers to come to Japan. The Technical Training Act certifies the education programs, and ensures those programs adhere to all applicable labor laws. It also provides a way for the foreign-born trainees to lodge complaints against their programs, when needed (D'Ambrogio, 2020).

In addition to nurses, the Technical Training Act created the category of Certified Care Workers. **Certified Care Worker** is a Japanese certification to care for aging adults. This certification includes training in physical care and specialized training in hospice and dementia care. Advertising is targeted at workers from countries like the Philippines. Examples of such advertising can be found at the Japan Association of Training Institutions for Certified Care Workers website (n.d.). Like nurses, care worker trainees must achieve a basic level of language proficiency sufficient for daily interactions (Japan Foundation & Japan Educational Exchanges and Services, 2012; Japan International Trainee & Skilled Worker Cooperation Organization [JITCO], n.d.). Certified Care Workers are required to: have experience working in a foreign country in a related field, such as day-to-day care for older adults and disabled persons in their homes or a care facility; have completed a nursing training course in that country; or have received a nursing certification from another country's government (JITCO, n.d.). The Japan Association of Certified Care Workers (n.d.) is a professional organization that promotes high ethical standards for care workers as well as high levels of competence and professionalism in the performance of care tasks. This demonstrates the importance of this workforce to the elders and people of Japan.

TABLE 15.1 Two Visa Options

Immigration Control Act Amendments	Technical Intern Training Act
Established Specified Skilled Worker I & II for industries with labor shortages	Brings workers in as technical interns for specific roles

Immigration Control Act Amendments	Technical Intern Training Act
Included nurses and direct care workers	Requires Basic Japanese test Requires Basic skills test
Created provisions for acceptance	Work in medical field
Created provisions for hiring organizations	No family members
Temporary stay, extended from three to five years	Temporary stay
Permanent residence not available	Licensing for supervising organizations
	Human rights protections

(Immigration Services Agency, 2019; Ministry of Health, Labour, and Welfare, 2016)

VISA IMPACTS ON AVAILABLE CAREGIVERS

Both domestic and immigrant care workers in Japan are not very well paid. Some scholars attribute the worker shortage and the need for imported labor to those low wages (Lan, 2018). Despite the need for these immigrant workers, they are subject to cultural barriers to integrating into the Japanese culture and are generally treated poorly by others in the workplace (Lan, 2018). Analyses of the policies' impact on immigration suggest that despite the critical need for caregivers, importation of these foreign workers has remained slow due to cultural barriers. Culturally, due to norms about family caregiving, it is difficult for Japanese people to accept any non-family members caring for their elders in the first place, and the idea of having a foreign worker provide such care is, well, foreign (I. Peng, 2016).

At the same time, economic and population factors in the region also influence the availability of care workers to import. Vietnam, long a source of foreign workers, as evidenced by the bilateral agreements, has recently experienced economic growth (S. Peng, 2019). People are less likely to seek job opportunities overseas if there are jobs available in their home countries (fewer push/pull factors). Taiwan is also experiencing caregiver shortages and is experimenting with immigration visas, impacting the overall flow of workers through the region (S. Peng, 2019). Both countries are considering policy solutions with incentives to help them compete for an ever smaller pool of workers (S. Peng, 2019).

DISCUSSION OF FOREIGN-BORN PAID CAREGIVERS IN THE UNITED STATES AND VISA REQUIREMENTS

The United States has not directly sought foreign-born direct care workers and nurses to fulfill caregiving gaps, but as stated in the introduction to this chapter, nearly a quarter of direct care workers are immigrants (Espinoza, 2017b). Immigrant care workers are in the United States under a variety of circumstances and visas. Among nursing home direct care workers, just over half of the immigrant workers are naturalized citizens, while the remainder are not U.S. citizens (Espinoza, 2017b). Most of the foreign-born direct care workers are in the United States legally and have work permits, or "green cards" (Leading Age, 2019). One researcher reported hearing from direct care workers who said they worked as private duty home care aides when they first immigrated because of their legal status and had moved into nursing home work once they established a legal right to work in the United States (Personal communication, N. Kusmaul, 2018). Undocumented workers across professions are at risk for significant workplace abuses and often fail to report those abuses out of fear that their immigration status will be discovered (Peltz, 2021). This combination of naturalized citizens, legal green card holders, and undocumented immigrants makes up a significant portion of the elder care workforce (Stone & Bryant, 2018–2019). The United States has workforce shortages even with its immigrant workers; without them, the need would be dire.

Immigration is a highly charged political issue. Particularly over the past few years, immigrants have been under threat from constantly changing policies in the United States, such as the elimination of DACA, or **Deferred Action for Childhood Arrivals**. This program provided pathways to legal work and education for children brought to the United States undocumented when they were too young to have participated in the decision. As of this writing, it is unclear what action the Biden administration will take regarding immigration. This back-and-forth with regard to immigration policy has existed throughout U.S. history, as periods of economic boom and bust have often been accompanied by opening or restricting immigration policy. Immigrant workers have often filled jobs that U.S. workers were unwilling to fill, often low-paying and dangerous jobs. Both childcare and elder care jobs in the United States are low paying. Elder care comes with significant physical risks—before COVID-19, on-the-job injuries of direct care workers were higher than those in many industries, and in 2020, being a nursing home Certified Nursing Assistant was reported to be the most dangerous job in America (McGarry et al., 2020).

While there are limitations to the comparison of child care to elder care, the idea of importing foreign workers for care jobs is not new. The **Au Pair** program, mentioned above, has provided child care in the United States for many years. An au pair is a foreign-born worker who comes to the United States on a **J-1 cultural exchange visa** to provide paid care to children (Chuang, 2013). An au pair may stay in the United States for up to 2 years (Manko et al., 2020). They are required to have met certain educational requirements in their country of origin and to have experience in providing child care (Chuang, 2013). Au pairs are distinct from direct care workers in several ways. First, they come to the United States for a time-limited period. While there may be some direct care workers who only want time-limited employment or residency, many are looking to immigrate permanently. Second, au pairs are matched with a specific family as opposed to an organization, health care company, or agency; working as an au pair could be similar to home health care, but is very different from nursing home work.

Health care organizations who want to hire direct care workers are at a disadvantage due to the lack of legal options for immigration to the United States. Skilled professional workers such as nurses can immigrate under the **EB-3 visa** program if they are sponsored by an employer. Once approved, an EB-3 worker can bring a spouse and children to the United States who are themselves eligible to live, work, and study. In order to sponsor a worker through the EB-3 program, an employer must demonstrate that they have tried and failed to fill the position with a U.S.-born worker. For nurses, this process is somewhat easier, as there is an established shortage of nurses in the United States (Leading Age, 2019). The EB-3 program, as it is currently designed, would not work for direct care workers because direct care is not considered a professional job under these standards.

The **H-1B visa** is another immigration option available for nurses that would not be available to direct care workers. The H-1B visa requires the employer to demonstrate that the position for which they are recruiting is a specialty occupation that requires at least a bachelor's degree (Leading Age, 2019). Some long-term care employers, have used this option for workers such as care plan coordinators, unit supervisors, and so on (Leading

Age, 2019). Direct care workers such as Certified Nursing Assistants are skilled but not degreed workers, thus excluding them from this option.

SUMMARY

A number of countries across the Global North, including Europe, Asia, and North America, are figuring out ways to address dramatic shortages of direct care workers due to rising numbers of older people and declining birth rates that are reducing available younger workers. One strategy is the use of immigrant workers, many of whom come from nations that are part of the Global South. Currently, about a quarter of the direct care workforce in the United States consists of immigrants, and the United States does not use any particular strategy to recruit immigrant workers.

Japan is experiencing an acute crisis in the supply of care workers due to the "super-aging" of their society, which has resulted in more people needing care and fewer available workers. Traditionally an insular and isolated country, Japan has turned to the import of foreign workers to address their shortage of direct care workers. They have created two work visa programs that have had limited success in recruiting foreign-born care workers. Cultural barriers to the acceptance of care being provided by foreigners and discrimination in the workplace continue to create challenges once the workers are in Japan, and positive economic conditions across the region create recruitment challenges. However, this program is the first sign of the significant actions that may need to be taken to ensure an adequate supply of care workers in countries that are experiencing dramatic population aging. It indicates that countries may be willing to try previously culturally unacceptable policy solutions to resolve these problems.

The United States could learn from Japan, about both the positives and the negatives of their policy approaches. The shortage of care workers may soon mean the United States needs to try innovative policy solutions to meet rising need. Immigration visas could be one option. However, societal assumptions related to immigration, such as anti-immigrant rhetoric that says that all immigrants are illegal or lazy or taking advantage of the United States, may make it difficult to promote immigration reform. If immigration reform were able to occur, precautions would need to be taken to avoid the cultural struggles reported by foreign-born workers in Japan. In addition, the employment of foreign-born, mostly female workers in low-wage jobs, particularly if they leave their families behind in their countries of origin, raises social justice issues that should be considered in any policy discussion.

KEY TERMS

Au pair

Certified Care Worker

Certified Nursing Assistant

Deferred Action for Childhood Arrivals

Dependency ratio

Direct care worker

EB-3 Visa

Economic Partnership Agreements

H-1B Visa

Home health aides

Immigration Control Act

Insular

J-1 Cultural Exchange Visa

Personal care aides

Population replacement

Pull factors

Push factors

Range-of-motion exercises

Super-aging

Technical Training Act

Visa

DISCUSSION QUESTIONS

1. Countries have implemented policies to attempt to influence the birth rate in their population, to either increase it or decrease it. Is this an appropriate use of governmental authority? Why or why not?

2. How do policies that attempt to influence population growth differ from policies on topics such as sex education or abortion? Do they differ?

3. Having immigrant workers serve as caregivers is common in the United States, yet in Japan this was seen as novel due to cultural beliefs and insular government policies. What are the pros and cons of such a solution?

4. Are immigration policies intended to increase the numbers of workers in specific industries exploitive, or are they creative solutions to problems?

Ancillary materials for student practice can be found within Active Learning

REFERENCES

American University Washington College of Law International Human Rights Law Clinic & Centro de los Derechos del Migrante, Inc. (2018). *Picked apart: The hidden struggles of migrant worker women in the Maryland crab industry* [Report]. https://cdmigrante.org/wp-content/uploads/2018/02/PickedApart.pdf

Armstrong, P. (2018). Introduction. In P. Armstrong & R. Lowndes (Eds.), *Negotiating tensions in long-term residential care: Ideas worth sharing* (pp. 11–22). Canadian Centre for Policy Alternatives.

Burgess, C. (2020). Keeping the door closed: The 2018 revisions to the 'Immigration' Control Act as a continuation of Japan's 'No-immigration' principle. *Electronic Journal of Contemporary Japanese Studies, 20*(1). https://www.japanesestudies.org.uk/ejcjs/vol20/iss1/burgess.html

Chuang, J. A. (2013). The U.S. Au Pair Program: Labor exploitation and the myth of cultural exchange. *Harvard Journal of Law & Gender, 36*, 270–343. https://www.researchgate.net/publication/254569151_The_US_Au_Pair_Program_Labor_Exploitation_and_the_Myth_of_Cultural_Exchange

D'Ambrogio, E. (2020, December). *Japan's ageing society* [Research brief]. European Parliament. https://www.europarl.europa.eu/RegData/etudes/BRIE/2020/659419/EPRS_BRI(2020)659419_EN.pdf

Espinoza, R. (2017a). *8 signs the shortage in paid caregivers is getting worse* [Issue brief]. Paraprofessional Healthcare Institute. https://phinational.org/wp-content/uploads/2017/11/workforce-shortages-phi60issues01.pdf

Espinoza, R. (2017b). *Immigrants and the direct care workforce* [Research brief]. Paraprofessional Healthcare Institute. https://phinational.org/wp-content/uploads/2017/06/immigrants_and_the_direct_care_workforce_-_phi_-_june_2017.pdf

Friedman, E. M., & Parker, A. M. (2021, April 12). *An early look at the impact of the COVID-19 pandemic on demographic trends* [Blog post]. The RAND Blog. https://www.rand.org/blog/2021/04/an-early-look-at-the-impact-of-the-covid-19-pandemic.html

Green, D., & Kadoya, Y. (2013). English as a gateway? Immigration and public opinion in Japan [ISER Discussion Paper, No. 883]. Osaka University, Institute of Social and Economic Research (ISER). https://www.econstor.eu/bitstream/10419/92877/1/766845818.pdf

Immigration Services Agency. (2019). *Immigration control and residency management 2019.* http://www.moj.go.jp/isa/content/930004564.pdf

Japan Association of Certified Care Workers. (n.d.). *English: The Japan Association of Certified Care Workers.* Retrieved April 30, 2021 from https://www.jaccw.or.jp/en

Japan Association of Training Institutions for Certified Care Workers. (n.d.). *Asian care industry professionals in Japan.* Retrieved April 30, 2021 from http://kaigoryugaku.kaiyokyo.net/en/

Japan Foundation & Japan Educational Exchanges and Services. (2012). *N1-N5: Summary of linguistic competence required for each level.* Japanese-Language Proficiency Test. https://www.jlpt.jp/e/about/levelsummary.html

Japan International Trainee & Skilled Worker Cooperation Organization. (n.d.). *Technical intern training program.* Retrieved April 30, 2021 from https://www.jitco.or.jp/en/regulation/care.html

King, R. (2012). Theories and typologies of migration: An overview and a primer. *Willy Brandt Series of Working Papers in International Migration and Ethnic Relations, 3/12,* 3–43. https://www.researchgate.net/publication/260096281_Theories_and_Typologies_of_Migration_An_Overview_and_A_Primer

Lan, P.-C. (2018). Bridging ethnic differences for cultural intimacy: Production of migrant care workers in Japan. *Critical Sociology, 44*(7–8), 1029–1043. https://doi.org/10.1177/0896920517751591

Leading Age. (2019, December). *IMAGINE: International migration of aging and geriatric workers in response to the needs of elders* [Report]. https://leadingage.org/sites/default/files/IMAGINE%20International%20Migration%20of%20Aging%20and%20Geriatric%20Workers_Dec2019.pdf

Lee, E. (1966). A theory of migration. *Demography, 3*(1), 47–57.

Lutz, H. (2015). Myra's predicament: Motherhood dilemmas for migrant care workers. *Social Politics: International Studies in Gender, State and Society, 22*(3), 341–359.

Manko, B. A., Rosiński, J., & Johns, T. R. (2020). Improving management & practice in au pair industry: Systems overview from a central Europe–U.S. Perspective. *International Journal of Contemporary Management, 19*(2), 97–124. https://doi.org/10.4467/24498939IJCM.20.007.12672

Marlow, I. (2015, November 13). Japan's bold steps. *The Globe and Mail.* https://www.theglobeandmail.com/globe-investor/retirement/retire-planning/how-japan-is-coping-with-a-rapidly-aging-population/article27259703/

McGarry, B. E., Porter, L., & Grabowski, D. C. (2020, July 28). Opinion: Nursing home workers now have the most dangerous jobs in America. They deserve better. *Washington Post.* https://www.washingtonpost.com/opinions/2020/07/28/nursing-home-workers-now-have-most-dangerous-jobs-america-they-deserve-better/

Ministry of Health, Labour, and Welfare. (2016). Act on Proper Technical Intern Training and Protection of Technical Intern Trainees (Abbr: Technical Intern Training Act). https://www.mhlw.go.jp/english/policy/employ-labour/human-resources/dl/2-00.pdf

Muramatsu, N., & Akiyama, H. (2011). Japan: Super-aging society preparing for the future. *The Gerontologist, 51*(4), 425–432. https://doi.org/10.1093/geront/gnr067

Ogawa, N., & Matsukura, R. (2007). *Ageing in Japan: The health and wealth of older persons* [Report]. United Nations. https://www.un.org/en/development/desa/population/events/pdf/expert/9/ogawa.pdf

Peltz, E. (2021). Giving voice to the silenced: The POWER Act as a legislative remedy to the fears facing undocumented employees exercising their workplace rights. *Columbia Journal of Law and Social Problems*, *54*(3), 503–541. http://blogs2.law.columbia.edu/jlsp/wp-content/uploads/sites/8/2021/07/Vol54-Peltz.pdf

Peng, I. (2016). Testing the limits of welfare state changes: The slow-moving immigration policy reform in Japan. *Social Policy & Administration*, *50*(2), 278–295. https://doi.org/10.1111/spol.12215

Peng, S. (2019, July 14). Japan poaches nursing care personnel abroad with high wages – What does this mean for Taiwan? *Commonwealth Magazine*. https://english.cw.com.tw/article/article.action?id=2477

Potts, M. (2006). China's one child policy: The policy that changed the world. *BMJ*, *333*, 361. https://doi.org/10.1136/bmj.38938.412593.80

Schieder, J., & Gould, E. (2016). *"Women's work" and the gender pay gap: How discrimination, societal norms, and other forces affect women's occupational choices—and their pay* [Report]. Economic Policy Institute. https://www.epi.org/publication/womens-work-and-the-gender-pay-gap-how-discrimination-societal-norms-and-other-forces-affect-womens-occupational-choices-and-their-pay/

Stone, R. I. (2016). The migrant direct care workforce: An international perspective. *Generations: Journal of the American Society on Aging, 40*(1), 99–105. https://www.asaging.org/sites/default/files/files/S16_Gene_40_1_Stone_99-105.pdf

Stone, R. I., & Bryant, N. (2018–2019). The politics of immigration: Who will care for grandma? *Generations: Journal of the American Society on Aging*, *42*(4), 50–56. https://www.jstor.org/stable/26608429

Sze-Yunn, P., & Arivalagan, Y. (2020). *These countries are most ready to deal with ageing populations*. World Economic Forum. https://www.weforum.org/agenda/2020/02/what-are-japan-and-singapore-doing-about-ageing-population/

Credits

Conclusion

This book has provided you with an introduction to what policy is and why it is important in the day-to-day lives of older adults in the United States. You learned about how to figure out the goals of a policy and to evaluate how well it meets those goals. You learned about the relationship between societal assumptions and the policies a society creates. Chapter by chapter, you explored the needs of people as they grow older and the ways U.S. society addresses those needs through policies that are directed at older adults and policies that address social conditions for the whole population. Finally, you learned about how three different countries approach the needs of older adults and families.

Across the globe, countries are trying to figure out how to address the needs of a growing population of people who are growing older. All types of policies shape the day-to-day experiences of those older adults and their families. It is up to all of us, including you—future social workers, sociologists, gerontologists, and many others—to understand how good policy improves quality of life, and to spend public funds in responsible and effective ways. Each of you is growing older and probably has family members who are too. I hope this book allowed you to consider what is important to you and to them in terms of quality of life, and to consider what role you believe government should play in shaping that quality of life. Even if you believe that it is not the role of the government to provide care, it is important to understand how all types of policy shapes day-to-day life.

While some college classes may seem remote from everyday life and everyday experiences, I hope that this book provided you with insights you can apply when you go to the store or drive around your neighborhood. While growing older may seem to you to be a long way away, decisions that both you and policy makers make today will influence what your later life looks like. As you enter your career, you will have the opportunity to influence your own aging and that of future generations.

For many students, policy is abstract, and they have difficulty seeing how it appears in their own lives and the lives of clients. I hope the examples in this book allowed you to see policy at work in the world around you. In future decades, the care of older adults will continue to grow and change, as the population distribution shifts and as the roles of technology and other factors constantly evolve. I hope that this book will make you thoughtful consumers and creators of policy in the years to come.

Index

About the Author

Nancy Kusmaul, PhD, MSW, is an associate professor in the Baccalaureate Social Work program at the University of Maryland, Baltimore County. She received her PhD from the University at Buffalo and her Master's in Social Work from the University of Michigan. She was a nursing home social worker for more than a decade.

Her research focuses on organizational culture, trauma-informed care, and the impact of trauma experiences on workers and care recipients. She is particularly interested in direct care workers, such as Certified Nursing Assistants in nursing homes. She is co-chair of the NASW Maryland Committee on Aging and is a fellow of the Gerontological Society of America. Dr. Kusmaul was a 2019–2020 Health and Aging Policy Fellow. She has done several podcasts on aging, trauma, and nursing homes on various platforms.